ROUTLEDGE LIBRARY EDITIONS: SPECIAL EDUCATIONAL NEEDS

Brian Fleming Research & Learning Li...,
Ministry of Education
Ministry of Training, Colleges & Universities

Volume 20

D1679276

DEAF STUDENTS IN POSTSECONDARY EDUCATION

DEAF STUDENTS IN POSTSECONDARY EDUCATION

Edited by
SUSAN B. FOSTER AND
GERARD G. WALTER

Routledge
Taylor & Francis Group
LONDON AND NEW YORK

First published in 1992 by Routledge

This edition first published in 2019
by Routledge
2 Park Square, Milton Park, Abingdon, Oxon OX14 4RN

and by Routledge
711 Third Avenue, New York, NY 10017

Routledge is an imprint of the Taylor & Francis Group, an informa business

© 1991 Susan B. Foster and Gerard G. Walter

All rights reserved. No part of this book may be reprinted or reproduced or utilised in any form or by any electronic, mechanical, or other means, now known or hereafter invented, including photocopying and recording, or in any information storage or retrieval system, without permission in writing from the publishers.

Trademark notice: Product or corporate names may be trademarks or registered trademarks, and are used only for identification and explanation without intent to infringe.

British Library Cataloguing in Publication Data
A catalogue record for this book is available from the British Library

ISBN: 978-1-138-58532-4 (Set)
ISBN: 978-0-429-46809-4 (Set) (ebk)
ISBN: 978-1-138-59546-0 (Volume 20) (hbk)
ISBN: 978-1-138-59548-4 (Volume 20) (pbk)
ISBN: 978-0-429-48825-2 (Volume 20) (ebk)

Publisher's Note
The publisher has gone to great lengths to ensure the quality of this reprint but points out that some imperfections in the original copies may be apparent.

Disclaimer
The publisher has made every effort to trace copyright holders and would welcome correspondence from those they have been unable to trace.

Additional publisher's Note
These are re-issues of books published some years ago which are inevitably a reflection of the time in which they were published. The language used is indicative of that time and as such no offence is intended by the re-issuing of the books.

Deaf students in postsecondary education

Edited by
Susan B. Foster and
Gerard G. Walter

London and New York

First published 1992
by Routledge
11 New Fetter Lane, London EC4P 4EE

Simultaneously published in the USA and Canada
by Routledge
a division of Routledge, Chapman and Hall, Inc.
29 West 35th Street, New York, NY 10001

© 1991 Susan B. Foster and Gerard G. Walter

Typeset by LaserScript, Mitcham, Surrey
Printed bound in Great Britain by
Mackays of Chatham PLC, Kent

All rights reserved. No part of this book may be reprinted or reproduced or utilized in any form or by any electronic, mechanical, or other means, now known or hereafter invented, including photocopying and recording, or in any information storage or retrieval system, without permission in writing from the publishers.

British Library Cataloguing in Publication Data
A catalogue record for this book is available from the British Library.

Library of Congress Cataloging in Publication Data

Deaf students in postsecondary education / edited by Susan B. Foster and Gerard G. Walter.
   p. cm.
  Includes bibliographical references and index.
  ISBN 0-415-07128-3
1. Deaf—Education (Higher) 2. Deaf—Education (Higher)—United States. I. Foster, Susan Bannerman. II. Walter, Gerard G.
HV2449.D43   1992
371.91'2—dc20   91-30101
                                                                       CIP

Contents

List of tables	vii
List of figures	viii
Contributors	ix
Foreword	xii
Preface	xiv
Introduction	xvi

Part I Demographics of postsecondary educational programs for deaf students in the United States — 1

1 The changing population: a challenge for postsecondary education
   Kenneth R. Nash — 3
   Personal Commentary (*Miguel Sanchez*) — 20

2 Characteristics of programs serving deaf persons
   Gerard G. Walter — 24
   Personal Commentary (*Paul Taylor*) — 39

3 Persistence in college
   Michael S. Stinson and Gerard G. Walter — 43
   Personal Commentary (*Dianne Brooks*) — 60

Part II The environment of postsecondary educational programs for deaf students — 65

4 The deaf learner
   Harry G. Lang and Bonnie Meath-Lang — 67
   Personal Commentary (*Jane Mullins*) — 89

5 Resources for deaf students in the mainstreamed classroom
   Rosemary E. Saur — 96
   Personal Commentary (*Thomas L. Callaghan*) — 114

6 Interaction between deaf and hearing students in postsecondary educational settings
   Patricia Mudgett DeCaro and Susan B. Foster — 118
   Personal Commentary (*Solange C. Sevigny-Skyer*) — 142

7 Student development
   Thomas Holcomb and Judith Coryell — 147
   Personal Commentary (*Willy Conley*) — 163

8 Postsecondary education and political activism
   T. Alan Hurwitz — 168
   Personal Commentary (*Gerald Nelson*) — 178

Part III Outcomes of postsecondary educational programs for deaf students — 183

9 Effect of college on employment and earnings
   William A. Welsh and Janet MacLeod-Gallinger — 185
   Personal Commentary (*Robert Menchel*) — 202

10 Accommodation of deaf college graduates in the work place
   Susan B. Foster — 210
   Personal Commentary (*Jean Cordano*) — 228

   Concluding Remarks
   Robert Panara — 236
   Index — 241

Tables

1.1 Estimates of hearing-impaired students exiting high school without a certificate or diploma — 7
2.1 Size distribution of programs reporting in *College and Career Programs for Deaf Students* — 33
2.2 Support services provided by programs serving deaf students (percentage of programs with services) — 35
9.1 Labor force participation and unemployment rates of deaf and a national population of workers by age level — 190
9.2 Occupational groupings of deaf adults and the national population of workers ages 25–44 — 191
9.3 Median weekly earnings ($) of deaf adults and the national population of full-time workers by age and gender — 192
9.4 Labor force status of deaf high school and college graduates ages 25–44 — 194
9.5 Occupations of deaf high school and college graduates ages 25–44 — 195
9.6 Postsecondary attainment of hearing persons ages 25–44, 1988 — 198

Figures

1.1	Estimate of the number of hearing-impaired students ages 6 to 21 in the US: 1988–9	5
1.2	Comparison of changes in the deaf and hearing population of 18- to 21-year-olds: 1990–5	10
1.3	Pool of white and minority deaf 18- to 21-year-olds: 1982–2000	11
1.4	Comparison of reading comprehension scores on the Stanford Achievement Test for Hispanic, black and white 17-year-olds	14
2.1	College enrollments as a percentage of elementary and secondary enrollments	31
3.1	Effect of persistence rates on total enrollment	45
3.2	Model of factors affecting college persistence with maximum likelihood estimates and standard errors	48
6.1	Models used in deaf education	122
6.2	An ecological framework for analyzing interaction on a postsecondary campus	127
7.1	Chickering's model of the domains of student development	150
9.1	Mean 1985 wages and salaries of deaf and hearing college graduates	196
9.2	Percentage differences in earnings between deaf and hearing workers	197

Contributors

Judith Coryell is an assistant professor in the Department of Human Development at Rochester Institute of Technology's (RIT) National Technical Institute for the Deaf (NTID). Dr. Coryell received her Ph.D. from the University of Rochester. Her research interests include personal/social growth, mainstreaming, and teacher education.

Patricia Mudgett DeCaro is a consultant on deafness in the Rochester, New York, area. Her responsibilities vary from deafness research to interpreting. She is a doctoral student at the University of Rochester and holds a master's degree in counseling from State University of New York College at Brockport, New York.

Susan B. Foster is an assistant professor in the Office of Postsecondary Career Studies and Institutional Research at RIT's NTID. She earned her doctorate from Syracuse University in special education. Her research focuses on the integration of deaf people in the mainstream of college and the world of work.

Thomas Holcomb is an assistant professor in the Department of Human Development at RIT's NTID. Dr. Holcomb received his Ph.D. from the University of Rochester and has conducted research on the impact of mainstreaming on personal/social development.

T. Alan Hurwitz is associate vice president for Outreach and External Affairs, and associate dean and director of the division of Educational Support Service Programs at RIT's NTID. Dr. Hurwitz holds a doctorate in curriculum and teaching from the University of Rochester. He is past president of the National Association of the Deaf.

Contributors

Harry G. Lang is a research associate in the Department of Educational Research and Development and a professor of physics and mathematics at RIT's NTID. His doctorate was earned at the University of Rochester, and he has taught in teacher education programs at the University of Rochester and University of Leeds in the United Kingdom.

Janet MacLeod-Gallinger is a senior research assistant in the Office for Postsecondary Career Studies and Institutional Research, at RIT's NTID. She received her master's degree in career and human resource development from RIT. She manages the Secondary School Graduate Follow-Up Program for the Deaf, which annually collects and reports information to secondary schools for the deaf about the occupational and educational status of their graduates.

Bonnie Meath-Lang is chairperson of the Department of Technical and Integrative Communication Studies and a professor of English at RIT's NTID. Her doctorate was earned at the University of Rochester, and she has taught in teacher education programs at the University of Rochester and University of Leeds in the United Kingdom.

Kenneth R. Nash is associate professor in the Office of Postsecondary Career Studies and Institutional Research at RIT's NTID. He received his doctorate from Columbia University Teachers' College and has been a Visiting Scholar at Cambridge University's Wolfson College. He researches the characteristics of deaf college students and the changing face of postsecondary education for the deaf.

Robert Panara is professor emeritus of Liberal Arts at RIT's NTID. He earned his master's degree from New York University and holds honorary doctorates from Gallaudet University and MacMurray College. He is a nationally renowned teacher of deaf college students and an expert in the area of deaf people in literature.

Rosemary E. Saur is an associate professor at RIT's NTID. Dr. Saur received her Ph.D. from the University of California, Santa Barbara. She has conducted extensive research on mainstreaming and as chairperson for the Department of Science and Engineering Support, directs the provision of resource services for about 200 mainstreamed deaf college students.

S. Richard Silverman was the first chairperson of NTID's National Advisory Group. He is director emeritus of the Central Institute for the Deaf and professor emeritus of audiology at Washington University in St. Louis, Missouri. Dr. Silverman has spent over 50 years working in the field of deaf education. He is an adjunct staff member at the Institute for Advanced Study of Communication Processes at the University of Florida.

Michael S. Stinson is an associate professor in the Department of Educational Research and Development at RIT's NTID. He received a Ph.D. from the University of Michigan and his primary professional responsibility for the past 12 years has been to conduct research on deaf adolescents and youths.

Gerard G. Walter is director of the Office of Postsecondary Career Studies and Institutional Research at RIT's NTID. He earned his doctorate in special education and rehabilitation from the University of Pittsburgh. His main areas of research are student retention and success at the postsecondary level.

William A. Welsh is a research analyst in the Office of Postsecondary Career Studies and Institutional Research at RIT's NTID. He earned a doctorate from the University of Massachusetts in the area of educational research. He researches occupational attainments of deaf adults and follows the job outlook for programs of study offered through NTID.

Foreword

For more than twenty years Rochester Institute of Technology's National Technical Institute for the Deaf (RIT's NTID) has been providing deaf persons the opportunity to acquire competencies to enter the world of work as skilled artists, business people, technologists, and service providers. Since the first 71 students entered in 1968 almost 3000 have graduated and gone on to gainful employment in the mainstream of society. Given the rapid social, economic, and technical changes that will certainly be part of everyday life at the beginning of the next century, the role of higher education in preparing young deaf women and men to enter and successfully compete in the work place will continue to grow. As more deaf students seek a higher education, the need for information about how best to attract, retain, and educate deaf college students will increase.

The National Technical Institute for the Deaf offers a unique environment for the study of issues pertaining to higher education of deaf persons. NTID students develop basic skills in reading, mathematics, and communication in a large variety of developmental and general education offerings, and pursue majors in self-contained classrooms with other deaf students as well as in fully mainstreamed programs offered by eight other colleges of Rochester Institute of Technology. This 'range of options' model enables students to select a course of study, as well as an educational environment, which best meets their learning needs and style. This book is a synthesis of what has been learned about deaf students in college. While it draws heavily on the research and experience acquired at NTID over more than 20 years, it also represents a review of the base of knowledge about educating deaf students at the college level.

A book such as this would lose much of its effectiveness if the information were presented only in the abstract, without any real applications. The incorporation of the comments by deaf persons concerning their experiences while in college, serves to move the reader from the theoretical and data-based discussions of the chapters to the real-life situations in which deaf people find themselves. In a sense the comments serve to provide readers with the reasons for such a book, and the need for special postsecondary educational programming for deaf individuals.

William E. Castle
Vice President for Government Relations, RIT
Director, NTID

Preface

We undertook this project because we believe there is a need in the field of education of deaf students for practical information about the demographics, environment, and outcomes of programs at the postsecondary level. As more deaf students enter college, postsecondary educational institutions will need to adjust to accommodate and support them. The assumption in many colleges is that hiring an interpreter is all that is necessary to place deaf students on a par with their hearing peers. However, experience has shown that this assumption is a gross oversimplification of a complex and challenging situation. For example, the interpreter may provide deaf students access to formal classroom lectures, but not to rapid-fire class discussions or out of class projects requiring team work. Further, integration into the social and extracurricular fabric of the college has been proven integral to student success, yet this is likely to be the area most difficult for deaf students and most resistant to traditional intervention strategies. Planners and developers at postsecondary institutions who want to establish programs for deaf students must consider a multitude of factors if they want their efforts to be fruitful. We hope this book will provide information which they will find useful as they move ahead with these efforts.

We have put together this book with several audiences in mind, including educators of deaf people in countries other than the United States. Much of the information presented here has universal applications, and chapters which at first glance appear specifically 'American' may also be interpreted as examples of methods and strategies which can be applied elsewhere. To this end, we have written a brief introduction to each of the three main parts of the book. In each of these introductions, we describe ways in which the information presented in that part of the book may be useful to any reader providing services to deaf adults in any educational setting. We have no doubt that readers will themselves discover applications for this information which we have not anticipated, and we look forward to learning from – as well as about their perspectives and experiences.

The history of formal provisions for deaf Americans in higher education began in 1864, when the United States government enacted legislation establishing Gallaudet College. Today more than 8,000 deaf students are served by more than 150 programs throughout the United States. Without seeming boastful, this history is certainly unmatched by any other country in the world, and has permitted the development of a significant literature about deaf students in postsecondary education. It is this experience that we hope to share through the medium of this book.

As editors, we have many people to thank for their assistance and support in preparing this manuscript. First, our thanks to the United States government, because much of the material in this document was produced in the course of an agreement between the US Department of Education and the Rochester Institute of Technology. We are grateful to the National Technical Institute for the Deaf, a college of Rochester Institute of Technology, for creating an educational and scholarly environment within which a task such as ours could develop and be brought to maturity. A special thanks to Jack Clarcq for his ongoing support of the project. We want to thank the people who helped prepare the manuscript for publication. Cynthia Wiegand and Rosemarie Seewagen, our secretaries, spent many hours typing and then reading through drafts of the manuscript; we're very grateful for their patience and the wonderful quality of their work. Thanks also to Kathleen Smith and Marcia Dugan for proofreading the final draft, and making many valuable suggestions regarding style and format.

The chapter authors, of course, are the backbone of our enterprise, and we thank them for contributing their expertise and time. The enthusiasm and interest which they demonstrated made this project a 'team effort' in all the best senses of the phrase. Lastly, we are especially grateful to the authors of the personal commentaries which appear at the end of each chapter; their stories brought the chapters to life, and infused the entire book with a reality which is so often missing in works of this sort. We thank them for sharing their lives with us, and for teaching us about the postsecondary educational experiences of deaf people.

Susan B. Foster
Gerard G. Walter

Introduction

S. Richard Silverman

The establishment of the National Technical Institute for the Deaf (NTID) at Rochester Institute of Technology (RIT) underlined the recognition by the United States government that, given the appropriate opportunity, deaf persons could be adequately prepared at a postsecondary level to participate satisfyingly and constructively in the world of work, even against a backdrop of burgeoning technology. Essential among the conditions of establishment was the requirement that NTID conduct an ongoing program of research directed primarily, though not exclusively, on the effectiveness of its admission policies, its administration and organization, its curricula, its academic standards, its outreach influence on the education of deaf people at all levels, and on the communication to potential employers that well-trained deaf persons can contribute productively to their enterprises. The pages that follow document the influence government support can have on the education of deaf persons at the postsecondary level.

The contents and treatment of the book reflect the broad spectrum of experience and professional qualifications of the contributing authors. The methods range from presentation of 'hard core' quantitative data through ingenious 'modeling' to solicited comments of deaf persons, now employed, who are graduates of a variety of educational environments. While the meticulous paradigms of laboratory research are not applicable here, editors Foster and Walter have seen to it that the canons of sociological research and documentation are carefully observed. The interpretations and recommendations are supported by research evidence, informed opinion, and pertinent literature. The reader is immediately struck by this characteristic in the first chapter by Kenneth Nash, which is fundamental to the entire exposition. Nash deals with the changing and declining population to be served at the postsecondary level, including variations in hearing sensitivity, academic skills, ethnic origins, and minority status. Of course, institutional planning needs to take into account these demographic projections.

In his description of existing programs, we are cautioned by Gerard Walter that the term 'postsecondary education' by no means implies universal characteristics. Diversity is more the case than uniformity, especially with regard to size of programs and support services. The crucial issue of social integration of college-level deaf students is addressed thoughtfully by Stinson and Walter, who present an intriguing model of 'college persistence.'

In discussing the 'deaf learner' Harry Lang and Bonnie Meath-Lang make the case for self-directed learning. They recognize realistically that despite technological advances, social change, and increasing acceptance of sign communication alone and in various combinations with oral/aural communication, the isolating effects of deafness remain, particularly for learners in high-pressure mainstream settings. Learning is definitely not to be considered apart from psychosocial and cultural factors.

The underlying concept in the establishment of NTID is that whatever educational opportunities exist for career development at the postsecondary level for hearing students be offered to deaf students. This specific requirement, among others, was the driving force behind the location of NTID as an integral unit of RIT. Its appeal was strengthened by its career-oriented philosophy, its flexibility in accommodating the rapid technological changes in the world of work, its formidable resources for achieving its aims, and, of course, its willingness to put all of this at the disposal of deaf persons. In a sense this was large-scale opportunity for mainstreaming at the postsecondary level. Nevertheless, effective exploitation of mainstreaming possibilities in the other colleges of RIT has been, to put it mildly, fraught with challenge.

Discussion of the successes and disappointments in the mainstreaming programs are beyond the scope of this text, but in her chapter on resources for deaf students Rosemary Saur delineates trenchantly what is necessary by way of resources to accomplish effective mainstreaming. Saur takes issue with the connotation of what are conventionally referred to as *support services*. She maintains that the term 'can easily foster a view of deaf students as passive and dependent, receiving what they need from all-knowing support providers.' She stresses that the purpose of resources is to *empower* deaf students. In this spirit she discusses notetaking, interpreting, counseling, tutoring, technological advancements, contact with instructors, and the importance of advisors-mentors.

The chapter on resources for the mainstreamed classroom is logically followed by the cogent and insightful contribution by Patricia DeCaro and Susan Foster on interaction between deaf and hearing students. They, too, are concerned with *empowering* deaf students. Their point of departure is the assimilation versus pluralism issue – an issue not uncommon in our so-called 'melting pot' culture, particularly with the increased enrollment of *minority* groups in our postsecondary institutions. They raise the question as to whether deafness is a disability or a different ability, which obviously influences the assimilation–pluralism situation. They drive home their points by describing the experiences and feelings of two hypothetical students, Jack and Nancy, at a hypothetical State University (SU) with 35–50 matriculated deaf students and special services designed to facilitate their integration on the campus. Jack is deaf and Nancy arrives at SU with very little experience with deafness. Through the eyes of Nancy and Jack, DeCaro and Foster 'examine the web of interactions between deaf and hearing students in the contexts of the individual, a range of campus settings, and the overall campus culture.' They base their judgments on their research on interaction between deaf and hearing students at RIT and are careful to stress that they have 'included only those findings which can be generalized to other postsecondary settings.' It is not without reason to infer from their modeling and accompanying analysis that the deaf have a 'right' to be 'different.' But ought they have the right to be the same? For all concerned with deaf people, especially deaf people themselves, the paradox persists and requires continuing parsing of its elements of the kind DeCaro and Foster have done.

The thesis of the chapter on student development by Thomas Holcomb and Judith Coryell is that one of the main purposes of colleges and universities should be to encourage and enable intentional development throughout the life cycle through the provision of *purposeful experiences* for students, both inside and outside the classroom. They offer a model from the literature that examines factors for developing skills central to the establishment of identity, which in turn, results in goal orientation, purpose, and personal integrity.

Developmental tasks facing the college are considered. They are: breaking psychological ties and establishing emotional independence, establishing identity and a value system, adjusting to life on one's own, handling peer relationships, choosing and preparing for a career, and preparing for marriage and family life. How these tasks are approached depends, certainly at the outset, on what the student brings to the institution, particularly the kind and context of previous education as well as family attitudes and aspirations. All of this needs to be taken into account in strategies for promoting student development, keeping in mind that the needs of each student are unique. While the constellation of factors that influence personal development varies from student to student, Holcomb and Coryell suggest realistic ways for an institution to help deaf students meet the challenges of attending a mainstream postsecondary program.

The period following World War II was marked by monumental social movements in the United States that recognized the needs and aspirations of minority sectors of our society including, fortunately, the deaf community. Translation of the movement to beneficial action is amply attested to by sustained legislative sanction and generous fiscal support at the national level. Among many prominent enactments is, of course, the establishment of NTID at RIT. These developments did not happen willy-nilly. They grew out of persistent, intelligent, and indefatigable efforts by committed leadership.

The thrust of the chapter on political activism by T. Alan Hurwitz, an outstanding deaf leader and eminently constructive activist, is that, despite heartening developments in the political arena benefiting deaf persons, we need to be sensitive to the need for encouraging continuity in activism. We need to develop an awareness of this need, even at the postsecondary student level, and to foster opportunities for deaf students to acquire the appropriate skills and the motivation to become active as the political and social situation demands.

William Welsh and Janet MacLeod-Gallinger, in their chapter on the effect of college on employment and earnings, document convincingly that 'earnings of deaf people increase dramatically as the degree levels they attain get higher, and . . . the discrepancy between deaf and hearing people decreases steadily at each succeeding higher degree.' However, the nagging problem of poor academic preparedness, especially in linguistic competence, including reading, for postsecondary education persists. We are reminded of this by the forceful statement from the February 1988 publication *A Report to the President and the Congress of the United States by the Commission on Education of the Deaf*:

The present status of education for persons who are deaf in the United States is unsatisfactory. Unacceptably so. This is the primary and inescapable conclusion of the Commission on Education of the Deaf.

(Commission on Education of the Deaf, 1988)

Without improvement in academic preparedness, increasing opportunities for postsecondary education are not likely to achieve the hoped for beneficial results in the work place. Are we dealing with a pleasant atmosphere and a barren soil?

Foster's chapter addresses the crucial problem of accommodation of deaf college graduates in the work place. She makes a convincing case for the *qualitative research* methods on which she bases her judgments and recommendations. The in-depth interview method is rooted in the notion that human behavior is a product of how people interpret their world and gets at people's interpretation of events. In fact, the personal commentaries by deaf persons following each chapter and related to their content are compelling examples of this, and, carefully read and thought through, are as enlightening and informative as a good deal of the *quantitative* data.

Central to accommodation at work is the impact of communication barriers. This issue is highlighted by excerpts from interviews. Poignant comments by interviewees reveal the dilemma faced by the deaf worker – responsibility versus dependency. Should the worker take it upon him- or herself to communicate with the hearing people in the work place or depend on a hearing go-between? What does this do to the deaf person's interpretation of the world of work? And of his or her place in it? And of the inevitable misunderstandings? Foster offers specific suggestions about these matters for curricula and program development. Among them, a rather striking one, is that postsecondary institutions become models for other institutions including employers and service organizations. As Foster notes, 'if they cannot make their environment accessible to deaf students they cannot expect others to do so'.

This text constitutes superb evidence of an institution probing objectively the fundamentals of its mission and what is needed to improve its effectiveness in accomplishing it. The bases for recommendations are a refreshing blend of sober, scholarly analysis and intensely human responses by those for whom NTID – and, indeed, all postsecondary educational programs serving deaf persons – exists.

Part I
Demographics of postsecondary educational programs for deaf students in the United States

Decisions regarding the commitment of resources to postsecondary programs for deaf people must be information-based. A program developed without careful planning runs the risk of being costly to the institution as well as to the students it serves. While the chapters included in Part I reflect a US perspective regarding some of the questions that are fundamental to successful planning, resource allocation and program development, the suggested models can be applied by educational planners in any country, assuming that they adapt specific methods and strategies to fit their social, political, cultural, and economic climate.

The principle underlying Part I is that extensive planning is prerequisite to the development of any postsecondary educational program for deaf students. Furthermore, this planning should include, at minimum, a (1) comprehensive analysis of the population to be served, (2) review of existing services and the need for additional services, and (3) method for evaluating the success of students matriculating in the program. Each of these three areas is described briefly below.

Planners of postsecondary educational programs for deaf students must know the demographics of the population they wish to serve. Components of such an analysis should include information about the numbers of potential students, their level of academic preparation, special support needs they might have, and the types of academic programs they might be expected to pursue. Planners must realistically assess the nature of the program being considered for implementation, the numbers of students who will profit from attending such a program, and the cost effectiveness of the program. Chapter 1 provides an example of how these questions have been answered for one program in the United States.

Before new programs are designed, a thorough description and analysis of historical as well as current postsecondary programs for deaf students should be conducted. This step is necessary to ensure that past programming mistakes are not repeated and that new programs will not duplicate existing services. Analysis of existing programs will also identify gaps in the current service system, and therefore provide clear directions for future development. Chapter 2 provides not only a description of past and present programs for deaf students, but offers some principles to guide the development of new programs to serve deaf students.

As programs are developed, close attention must be paid to the number of students who persist to graduation. If only a relatively small percentage of admitted students graduate, severe pressure will be placed on program administrators to justify continued support for the program. More importantly, there will be losses on the part of students who fail to graduate. Among other things, students have expenses for tuition, room and board, and materials. In addition, failure to obtain a postsecondary degree will almost certainly result in loss of income over a lifetime of employment. It could be argued that, because of these costs, programs enrolling deaf learners assume a responsibility to ensure that these students have a reasonable chance of graduating. For these reasons, it is important that administrators begin thinking early about evaluating the graduation rate for the program, and setting in motion mechanisms for discovering why students withdraw. In Chapter 3, a process for assessing persistence rates is discussed and a model is described for explaining why attrition occurs for students in their first year of study.

In summary, the discussion in Part I is focused on those issues that are important for developing and monitoring a postsecondary program for deaf persons. Without careful planning and documentation of results, administrators will find it difficult to demonstrate that they are meeting their specified goals.

Chapter 1

The changing population: a challenge for postsecondary education

Kenneth R. Nash

INTRODUCTION

The purpose of this chapter is threefold: first, to offer a demographic overview of the population of hearing-impaired[1] school-age persons in the United States; second, to provide projections of the number and type of deaf students postsecondary programs can expect to enroll through the year 2000; and third, to identify some of the major issues that are likely to have an impact on postsecondary education of deaf students over the next several decades. These issues relate to emerging demographic, socioeconomic, and technological trends that will affect all of American postsecondary education and, therefore, programs serving young deaf adults.

Let us begin with a demographic portrait of school-age, hearing-impaired children in the United States. How many are there? Where are they being educated? What is known of their academic performance?

The US Department of Education's *Twelfth Annual Report To Congress on the Implementation of the Handicapped Act* (1990) represents the most comprehensive estimate of the actual number of hearing-impaired students, ages 6 to 21, in the country. It delineates broad national trends and highlights individual differences among states. The *Annual Report* aggregates the child count for hard-of-hearing and deaf students into one broad category entitled 'hard-of-hearing and deaf.' While such an approach is useful from a national accounting perspective, it tends to blur significant differences between the two populations that would be of most interest to those readers concerned with the postsecondary education of persons who are deaf. For this reason, the first part of this chapter is primarily based on 'aggregated data' from the *Annual Report*, while the second section focuses more directly on the population of 18- to 21-year-olds who have a hearing loss of 71 dB or greater.

THE HEARING-IMPAIRED POPULATION: AN OVERVIEW

This section provides an overview of the changing demographic situation of hearing-impaired children, ages 6 to 21, by addressing questions such as: How many hearing-impaired children are there in the United States? How has the population changed? What are the educational placements of the population? How many students earn high school diplomas or certificates? How many drop out? Are there differences in academic performance between deaf and hard-of-hearing students? Answers to these questions are relevant to the subsequent discussion of the changing demographics of the 18- to 21-year-old deaf population, who make up the pool of applicants to postsecondary education.

Estimate of the Population Size

As can be seen from Figure 1.1, the US Department of Education (1990) estimated that, as of 1 October 1989, there were 57,555 hearing-impaired students ages 6 through 21 in the United States and insular territories who were receiving special education. These students were included in the annual count of 4,587,370 children who were receiving federal support for special education. The hearing-impaired children in this count include all those whom the local education agencies deemed to be in need of special education because of a hearing loss, not including those who are judged to be multiply handicapped or deaf-blind.

The Department of Education's estimate of 57,555 hearing-impaired students represents 0.1 per cent of the estimated resident population of all 6- to 21-year-olds in the US and 0.13 per cent of the estimated school enrollment. This population represents the vast majority of hearing-impaired students who may be in need of additional services as they begin postsecondary education.

A Declining Population

The population of hearing-impaired students has been declining for a number of years. This fact has many planning and programming

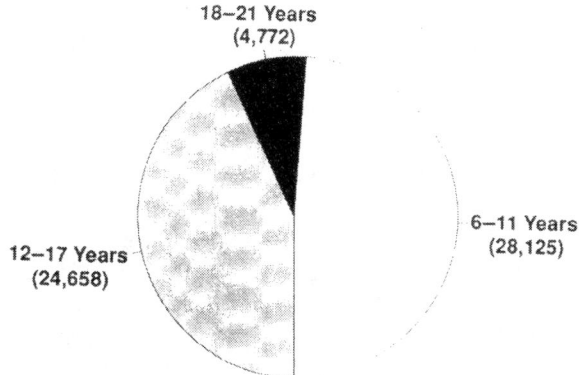

Figure 1.1 Estimate of the number of hearing-impaired students ages 6 to 21 in the US: 1988–9
Source: US Department of Education (1990)

implications for postsecondary programs. For example, since 1976 the total number of hearing-impaired children dropped by 36 per cent (US Department of Education, 1978, 1990). This drop can be attributed to several factors: first, the passage through school of the increased number of children who were born with hearing impairment due to the rubella epidemic of 1962–5; second, the fact that a rubella vaccine was introduced in early 1969 that has reduced the incidence of hearing loss; and third, the fact that the national birth rate has dropped. This general decline will have an impact on the population of 18- to 21-year-olds over the next decade, and, therefore, on postsecondary programs nationally.

Exit Status of Hearing-Impaired Secondary School Leavers

Information on educational outcomes at the secondary level is of great value to the field of postsecondary education. Such data help those responsible for strategic planning and instructional development to understand and assess the nature and scope of their future students. The US Department of Education (1990) found that among the 4,489 hearing-impaired students, age 14 and older, who exited the system in 1987–8, 68 per cent left with either a diploma (56 per cent) or a certificate (11 per cent), and 32 per cent left with nothing.

Among this latter group 6 per cent aged out, 15 per cent dropped out, and 11 per cent were unaccounted for. While caution must be observed when reviewing these findings (states vary in their criteria for graduation), the data do suggest that about 30 per cent of those with hearing impairments appear to be exiting without a high school credential of any kind.

Additional research also supports these findings. Harnisch, Lichtenstein, and Langford (1984), analyzing the drop-out rate among a rather small sample of 371 hearing-impaired students who participated in the *High School and Beyond Study*, report a rate of 28.3 per cent – very similar to that reported by the Department of Education. Butler-Nalin and Padilla (1989), reporting on the first phase of the National Longitudinal Transition Study, found that the graduation rate among 249 hard-of-hearing students was 72.3 per cent, with 15.5 per cent dropping out and another 12.2 per cent aging out. Among the population of 354 deaf students, 71.8 per cent graduated, while 11.8 per cent dropped out and 16.4 per cent aged out.

Perhaps the most comprehensive effort to assess exit status of deaf students was conducted by Allen, Rawlings, and Schildroth (1989) as part of the national study of *Deaf Students and the School-to-Work Transition*. A total of 6,196 students, ages 16 to 22, responded to questionnaires. All students had an unaided hearing threshold of 71 dB or greater. This study confirms the findings reported above: 29 per cent of those who exited school during the study 'dropped out,' while 52 per cent earned a diploma, and 19 per cent received certificates. Further analysis revealed that more females dropped out (33 per cent) as compared to males (25 per cent), more white students received diplomas (59 per cent) as compared to blacks (38 per cent) and Hispanics (36 per cent), and that those 14 states that require some form of competency testing had a much lower rate of diplomas (39 per cent) as compared to those states in which minimum competency testing is not required (57 per cent).

The basic conclusion from these four very different studies is summarized in Table 1.1. Hearing-impaired youth are at great risk of not graduating from high school. From the perspective of postsecondary education this means that the pool of hearing-impaired students with postsecondary potential is reduced by 25 to 30 per cent simply due to the dropout rate. The pool is then reduced another 10 to 20 per cent because many of those earning certificates would not be qualified for postsecondary study. These 'losses' occur before consideration of the academic and communicative barriers that act to deny students access to postsecondary education. Hearing-impaired youth appear to be twice as likely to leave school without graduating, as compared to their hearing peers. It is obvious that the pool of deaf candidates qualified for postsecondary education is surprisingly small.

Postsecondary Education

Wagner (1989) investigated the post-graduation activities of deaf and hard-of-hearing students in the National Longitudinal Transition Study. She found that 38.5 per cent of the deaf students went on to some form of postsecondary education, while only 30.1 per cent of the hard-of-hearing students did so. More deaf students went to two-year colleges (19.0 per cent as compared to 12.7 per cent) and four-year colleges (15.2 per cent as compared to 7.0 per cent), while more hard-of-hearing students attended vocational/trade schools (11.6 per cent as compared to 7.0 per cent). It is likely that these findings, if extrapolated to the nation, would represent an underestimate of the number of hard-of-hearing students attending college, since hard-of-hearing students should have greater access to mainstream college programs and require fewer support services.

Table 1.1 Estimates of hearing-impaired students exiting high school without a certificate or diploma

Study (categories)	Number	Dropped out (%)
Annual Report to Congress		
Hearing impaired	4,489	32.1
High School and Beyond		
Hearing impaired	371	28.3
National Transition Study		
Hard of Hearing	249	27.7
Deaf	354	28.2
Work-to-School Transition		
Deaf	6,196	29.0
Bureau of the Census, (1987)		
All Races (20-24)		15.2
White		14.6
Black		19.0
Hispanic		38.6

Academic Performance

As part of the National Longitudinal Transition Study, Wagner and Shaver (1989) reported on the school achievements of hard-of-hearing and deaf students. Data show some interesting differences between deaf and hard-of-hearing students. Deaf students were two-and-a-half times less likely to have earned a failing grade than their hard-of-hearing peers. One possible explanation for this difference is the connection between degree of hearing loss and type of educational setting. Research has found that the greater the child's hearing loss, the more likely the child is to be in a separate class or special school (Allen and Osborn 1984). Given the differences in educational settings, it is likely that the hard-of-hearing child finds him/herself in the unenviable position of functioning in large classes with limited support services and little appreciation of the impact of hearing loss on the learning process. Such a dilemma can readily result in high levels of failure. Deaf students, by contrast, are more likely to be educated in very small classes using specialized instructional methods, thereby reducing the rate of failure.

Wagner and Shaver (1989) also found that the deaf population in the National Longitudinal Transition Study earned an average Grade Point Average (GPA) of 2.6 (within a 4-point scale) in regular secondary education courses. Since the hard-of-hearing students earned an average GPA of 2.2, on the surface it would appear that the deaf students performed somewhat better than their hard-of-hearing peers. Such average scores must be considered against the fact that only 262 deaf students took regular education courses, while 414 hard-of-hearing students enrolled – almost twice as many hard-of-hearing students took regular classes. Not surprisingly, when special education courses are considered, the reverse situation applies – 543 deaf students enrolled in special education classes as compared to 331 hard-of-hearing students.

Summary

Hearing-impaired students are at great risk: only 50–55 per cent will earn high school diplomas, 10–20 per cent will receive certificates, and 25–30 per cent will drop out. From the perspective of postsecondary education, this means that the pool of hearing-impaired students with postsecondary potential is automatically reduced by at least 50 per cent – before consideration of any of the other factors that prevent hearing-impaired people from entering postsecondary education. From the viewpoint of hearing-impaired students, such a high dropout rate may mean that many students with the potential for advanced study will not gain access to postsecondary education and, as a consequence, may be unable to compete effectively in the work place of the 1990s.

THE COLLEGE-AGE DEAF POPULATION TO THE YEAR 2000

The intent of this section is to consider key national trends that may affect enrollment in postsecondary programs to the year 2000 among students who have a hearing loss of 71 dB or greater. It is these deaf students who require the most intense, sophisticated, and costly support at the postsecondary level. Postsecondary educators who are involved in long-term planning, funding, and programming are concerned with questions such as: What size is the population of deaf 18- to 21-year-olds? Is this population following the declining trend of its hearing peer group? What might be the impact of the growing population of deaf minority students on postsecondary programs through the 1990s?

Size of the Population

The majority of deaf students enter postsecondary programs between the ages of 18 and 21. In 1982 this age group was estimated at 13,186 (Nash and Walter 1990). Given the known rate of decline, by 1990 the population dropped by 31 per cent to 9,119. This decline is due to several factors, including the passing of students who became deaf as a result of the rubella epidemic of 1962–5 through the 18–21 age range, and the fact that the national population of all young people has been declining as a result of the drop in birth rates. Over the next decade, the pool is expected to drop by another 15 per cent to equal 7,762.

It is interesting to note that the declining trend found for the deaf 18 to 21-year-old population (Center for Assessment and Demographic Studies 1989) is very similar to that projected for the general population of 18- to 21-year-olds (Bureau of the Census 1987). Figure 1.2 compares the size and rate of change between the national population of 18- to 21-year-olds and their deaf peers, from 1990 to 1995. If the reduction in the number of children with deafness as a

10 Demographics of educational programs

result of the rubella vaccine is eliminated (Preblud Hinman, and Herrmann 1980), the rates would be almost identical. The entire population of 18- to 21-year-olds is expected to drop 11 per cent between 1990 and 1995 while the deaf group is projected to decline 11.9 per cent.

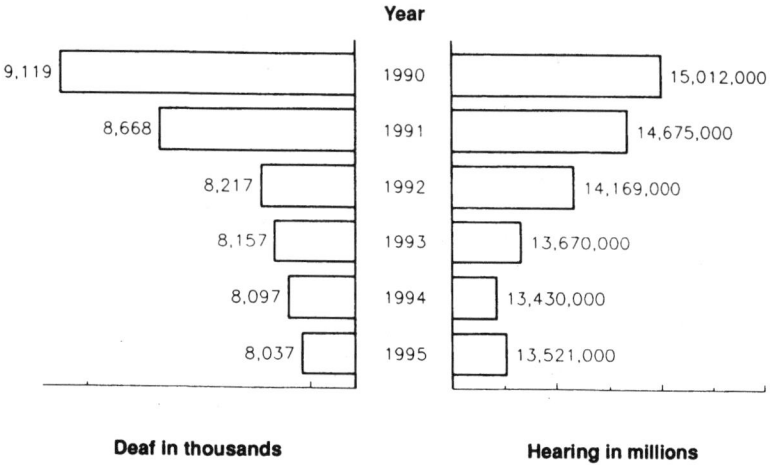

Figure 1.2 Comparison of changes in the deaf and hearing population of 18- to 21-year-olds: 1990–5.

Source: Bureau of the Census (1987); Center for Assessment and Demographic Studies (1989)

Race/Ethnic Character

Not only is the pool of potential students declining, it also is changing in character. The number of minority deaf 18- to 21-year-olds grew from 29 per cent in 1982 to 35 per cent in 1990, and the proportion is expected to grow to 39 per cent by the year 2000. Figure 1.3 shows that, as the size of the white population declines, the number of minority students will remain relatively stable, even though its portion of the total pool will reach almost 40 per cent by the year 2000.

Not only does the deaf population of 18- to 21-year-olds mirror the population curve of its peer group, the deaf school age population also reflects the distribution of race/ethnicity of the overall school age population of the nation. As can be seen from Figure 1.3,

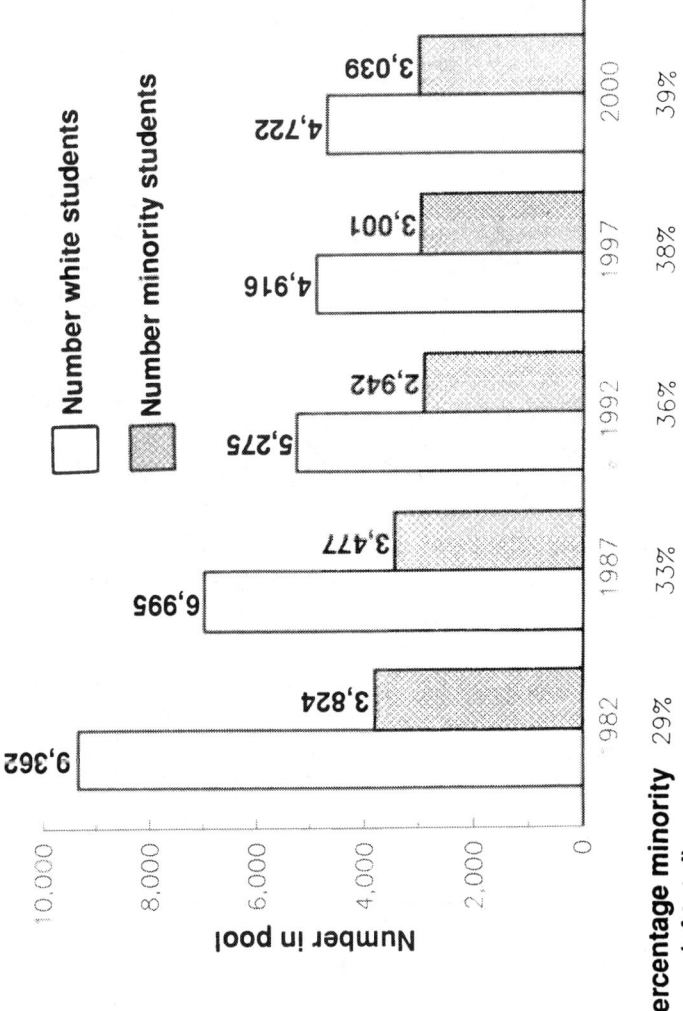

Figure 1.3 Pool of white and minority deaf 18- to 21-year-olds: 1982–2000

Source: Center for Assessment and Demographic Studies (1989)

in 1986 the overall proportion of minority deaf students was estimated at 33.6 per cent (Center for Assessment and Demographic Studies 1989), while the US Department of Education (US Department of Education 1986) estimated that 30 per cent of the general school-age population was minority. The data on deaf students may be a bit over-representative of minority students, most of whom can be found in large urban programs or special schools, since the *Annual Survey* is under-represented among small, hard-to-identify mainstream programs in suburban and rural areas where the number of white students often is higher.

Effect of Growing Minority Population

As noted above, during the 1990s there will be a significant increase in the portion of minority students in the pool at the same time that the size of the pool declines. Consequently, it is important to consider the potential impact of this trend on postsecondary programs. Assuming no major changes in the academic achievements of the minority population and no adjustments in the admission criteria of most postsecondary programs, the brief answer to the question, 'What will be the impact of minority growth on postsecondary programs?' is 'Unfortunately, not much.'

Even though the portion of minorities in the pool has been growing, and will continue to grow, such growth is not likely, by itself, to translate into a major increase in overall minority enrollment. The major barrier to increasing the number of minority students in postsecondary programs is based on the achievement levels and academic skills needed to enter and be successful at the postsecondary level.

The US General Accounting Office (1986), in a study of federally assisted postsecondary programs for deaf students, found that the mean reading level of entering students ranged from a low grade level of 4.0 to a high of 8.0. The mean grade level for mathematics ranged from 5.8 to 11.4. These data illustrate the great variability in the admission requirements for the various federally sponsored programs. The data also suggest that the minimum level for students entering vocationally oriented programs is between fourth and fifth grade.

These admission levels must be discussed within the context of the average achievement level for deaf 17-year-olds who are black, Hispanic, and white. Consider that most basic of all academic skills –

reading. If a reading grade level of 4.0 is the minimum necessary to enter a vocationally oriented program, and a reading level between seventh and eighth grade is the average for new NTID and Gallaudet freshmen (*NTID Annual Report* 1989; *Gallaudet Factbook* 1989), then the percentage of students who will qualify for these programs is clearly limited. Figure 1.4 compares the performance of Hispanic, black, and white deaf 17-year-olds on the Reading Comprehension subtest of the Stanford Achievement Test (Advanced) against the NTID/Gallaudet guidelines for entry. For example, 90 per cent of all Hispanic 17-year-olds are reading at grade level 4.9 or below, and 90 per cent of all black students are reading at 5.3 or below. In contrast, the 90th percentile for the white population is 8.6. These data indicate that over the next decade, only 3–4 per cent of all black and Hispanic students can be expected to have the reading skills required to enter an institution such as NTID or Gallaudet, even though the minority population is expected to reach 40 per cent by 2000. As a result, it is possible that no more than 200 black/Hispanic deaf students will annually enter higher education, out of a pool of more than 3,000. Unfortunately, the graduation rate among those very talented black/Hispanic deaf students who do enter postsecondary programs is known to be less than 45 per cent. In contrast, perhaps 12–15 per cent of white students are likely to have the skills necessary to enter NTID or Gallaudet, and slightly more than 50 per cent are expected to graduate.

The admission requirements for mainstream colleges and universities are much higher. Only a handful of minority deaf students will ever graduate from such institutions. How will they fare in the work place? Where will the minority deaf leaders come from, if not from postsecondary programs? What can postsecondary programs do to facilitate quality education at the elementary and secondary level, thereby helping to increase the number of students qualified for the postsecondary level?

Cohen, Fischgrund, and Redding (1990) note that there are many reasons why minority students do not do well:

> It is likely that culturally biased curricula, inappropriate school placement and/or tracking, and lack of understanding of learning style differences, coupled with lack of awareness about cultural differences, family practices, and value systems have contributed to educational practices that have ill-served minority deaf children and youth. Unfortunately, when children's needs and back-

14 Demographics of educational programs

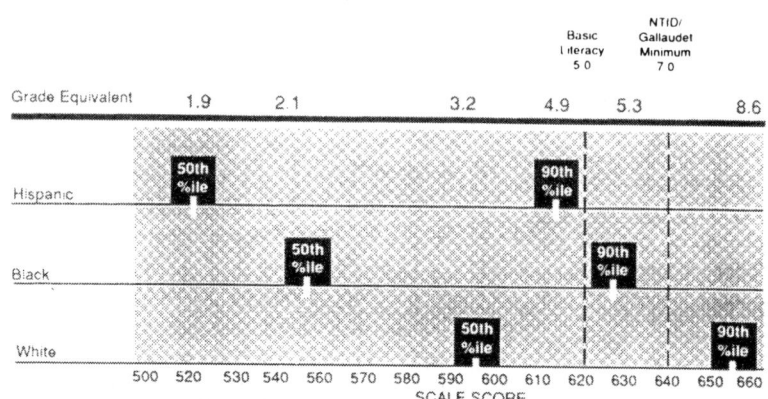

Figure 1.4 Comparison of reading comprehension scores on the Stanford Achievement Test for Hispanic, black and white 17-year-olds
Source: Gallaudet University (1989); NTID (1989)

grounds are poorly understood and when opportunity to learn is limited, depressed achievement is an expected outcome.

Over the next decade, postsecondary education must work closely with elementary and secondary programs if it is to assure a continued flow of qualified students. In addition, if any increase in initial enrollment is to translate into significant numbers of graduates, then the retention rates for minorities and deaf students must be increased significantly. Clearly, reducing attrition and increasing enrollment are the two challenges that every postsecondary program will face in the 1990s.

THE FUTURE: A CHALLENGE AND AN OPPORTUNITY

The demographic trends and issues of postsecondary deaf education largely are a reflection of the broad changes occurring in society. As we move into the 21st century, it is useful to consider the challenges that will be faced and then to reflect on how the challenges could become opportunities for deaf people.

Between 1972 and 1987, the number of students reportedly enrolled in programs designed specifically for deaf students grew by 230 per cent, from 2,271 to 7,490. Much of this growth was due to two factors: the increased number of deaf students reaching the 18–21 age range due to the rubella epidemic of 1962-5, and national education policies, particularly Section 504 and the amendments to the Vocational Education Act of 1968. Section 504 specifically required all higher education programs receiving federal dollars to make their programs accessible to handicapped students. Accessibility for deaf students included the provision of interpreters, notetakers, tutors, and other support service providers as needed. The Vocational Education Act set aside funds to be used exclusively to provide services to handicapped students. During the 1970s and 1980s many junior and community colleges used these monies to establish programs for deaf and other handicapped students. The Office of Vocational Rehabilitation, partly as a result of congressional scrutiny, gave higher priority to students with severe disabilities, including those who were deaf, by adding funding to postsecondary programs, increasing financial support to deaf students, and supporting research on postsecondary education for people with disabilities. As a result of these and other national policy initiatives, the number of programs for deaf students in American colleges and universities increased dramatically from 27 to at least 153 (Stuckless and Delgado 1973; Rawlings, Karchmer, and DeCaro 1988). While the size and quality of these programs varies greatly, such unprecedented growth is the direct result of the fundamental national policy decision made in the 1970s: that all Americans - including those with disabilities - deserve an equal opportunity for a free appropriate public education. By the end of the 1980s the fruits of this new federal policy were evident in the remarkable increase in number of postsecondary programs and in the number of students enrolled.

While the growth rate has been remarkable over the past two decades, the questions remain, 'What will happen to these programs as the population declines through the 1990s?' 'How many programs will emerge strong and vibrant?' 'How many are likely to close their doors?' The combined effects of a declining pool, an increase in minorities, and the general shift of the nation from the Northeast and Central to the South and West could have a major impact on many postsecondary programs, both large and small.

The world is shifting to a transnational economy, an economy built on regional blocks. Traditional political boundaries are being redrawn, based partly on a new but incomplete economic map. The universal 'coinage' of the emerging transnational economy will be information. Information is becoming the organizing force of production and, therefore, the organizing paradigm of the 21st century.

As Drucker (1989) says, 'Information is transnational; like money, information has no fatherland.'

These changes have broad educational implications. Johnston (1987) notes that by the year 2000, more than half the American workforce will require some education beyond high school, and almost a third of all jobs will be taken by individuals with a college degree. In contrast, 22 per cent of all occupations today require a college degree. By the year 2000 the median years of education required by the new jobs will be 13.5, compared to 12.8 for the current workforce. The demand for greater education is driven by the changing job market. White-collar jobs will account for 75 per cent of total job growth, with managerial and professional jobs accounting for 75 per cent of that increase. Administrative support jobs, such as clerical and secretarial, are likely to fall in numbers. Sales jobs will increase rather slowly, while demand for those with precision and craft skills will increase.

The 21st century will be a time of challenge and opportunity for deaf persons. As noted earlier in this chapter, the number of deaf students who now leave high school without a diploma or certificate is estimated at 28–30 per cent. While this rate is lower than the dropout rate for hearing Hispanics (38 per cent), it far exceeds the rate for black (19 per cent) or white (15 per cent) students.

The dropout rate is closely connected to the question of student achievement. Fifty per cent of deaf minority 17-year-olds read at or below the second-grade level, while their white peers perform only slightly better, with 50 per cent reading at or below the third-grade level. If we consider that basic literacy is fifth grade (the level at which most newspapers are written), then the majority of young deaf adults can be considered illiterate. These data suggest that the portion of 'at risk' deaf 17-year-olds is very large: about 90 per cent of black and Hispanic students plus a sizable portion of the white population.

For postsecondary programs the future includes a declining pool of 18- to 21-year-olds, an increase in minority students, and probability of continued high attrition among those deaf students enrolling in postsecondary education. Such circumstances are a marked contrast to the 1970s and 1980s which saw major growth in both students and programs, plus strong local and national support. In the next decade individual programs will wrestle with issues such as: 'How does one maintain a critical mass of students?' 'How does one increase minority participation?' 'How does one reduce attrition?'

And finally, 'How does one maintain national and local financial support?'

The 1990s will also hold opportunities. Deaf people will be in demand *if* they have the appropriate skills. The basis for such optimism is twofold. First, it is expected that slow growth in the labor force, combined with an economy that is producing a large number of jobs, will lead to a labor shortage, especially in the key areas noted above. There will be strong competition among employers to find and keep qualified workers, regardless of whether these workers have a disability. Another force likely to help assure employment opportunities for deaf people is the emergence of a strong coalition of politically active and sophisticated people with disabilities. This group is demanding equal access to the work place. Many members of this group are themselves 'products' of Section 504 and the other federal legislation of the 1970s that provided handicapped people, for the first time, broad though not universal access to postsecondary education. As the United States moves into the 1990s this 'first wave' is coming of age. Among their goals is a bill of rights for all workers with disabilities. The Americans with Disabilities Act (ADA) of 1990 is one reflection of this new activism. As America moves into the 21st century, the national need for skilled new workers and the growing persistence of lobby groups of and for people with disabilities will provide the potential for all qualified deaf people to be employed to the level of their ability.

The corollary to this development is that as long as society judges that postsecondary programs for the deaf are helping to meet the demand for a better educated workforce, financial support will be generous. To the extent, however, that such programs do not demonstrate a responsiveness to the changing job market by graduating well-prepared deaf people of all races and ethnic backgrounds in sufficient numbers to be cost effective, the programs will be in fiscal jeopardy. To assure the continuance of the national network of postsecondary programs that has evolved in the past two decades, the entire field of deaf education, including the postsecondary sector, will have to address the issue of academic achievement among 'at-risk students.' The instructional process itself must be challenged. At times it is a real, though unintentional, barrier to academic development. As Walter (1988) notes, 'Curricula must be devised that provide a balance between language and occupational studies' and postsecondary programs must 'construct and manage an array of approaches to learning that are sensitive to diverse needs of deaf students while taking full advantage of the advancements made by technology' (p. 115). These challenges limit access and encourage attrition. It is in the interest of postsecondary programs to address them.

Adult education and retraining could provide postsecondary programs with a new market. Over the next several decades, deaf workers will need additional education – be it in a traditional postsecondary program or through an 'in-house' program offered by employers, who may even be required to absorb the cost of such training. During the 1990s, corporations are expected to spend up to $25 billion every year just to assure that employees will be productive workers (Amara 1990). This growing trend offers postsecondary programs an opportunity for significant growth, since many employers are ill equipped to provide such training to their deaf workers.

It is likely that two models will emerge. The first is the traditional approach in which students register for a course or program offered by the postsecondary program on a part-time or a short-term intensive basis. The second model involves a somewhat new approach through which postsecondary programs serve as consultants/advisors to corporate trainers who are unfamiliar with the needs of deaf employees/learners.

In conclusion, the next several decades will offer deaf people and postsecondary programs a range of formidable challenges, some new and rather overwhelming, others quite familiar yet unresolved. Opportunities for qualified deaf people will be greater than ever before. To the extent that postsecondary deaf education is perceived to be sensitive to the needs of the deaf student and responsive to the demands of the marketplace, its future is assured.

NOTE

1 The term 'hearing-impaired' refers to all acoustically disabled persons. The term 'deaf' refers to those individuals who have a hearing loss of 71 dB or greater.

REFERENCES

Allen, T.E. (1986) *Special Norms for Subgroups of Hearing-Impaired Norming Population, Understanding the Scores of Hearing-Impaired Students and the Stanford Achievement Test* (7th edn), Washington, DC: Gallaudet Research Institute, Gallaudet University.

Allen, T.E. and Osborn, T.I. (1984) 'Academic Integration of Hearing-

Impaired Students: Demographic, Handicapping, and Achievement Factors', *American Annals of the Deaf* April.

Allen, T.E., Rawlings, B.W., and Schildroth, A.N. (1989) *Deaf Students and the School-to-Work Transition.* Baltimore, MD: Paul H. Brooks.

Amara, R. (1990) 'At work in the US in the 1990s: Some human resource intangibles,' Paper presented at the Fifteenth Annual Corporate Associates Meeting, Institute for the Future, Menlo Park, CA.

American Council on Education (1988) *Minorities in Higher Education.* Washington, DC.

Bureau of the Census (1987) 'School enrollment – social and economic characteristics of students,' *Current Population Reports* (Series P-20). Washington, DC: US Government Printing Office.

Butler-Nalin, P. and Padilla, C. (1989) 'Dropouts: The Relationship of Student Characteristics, Behaviors, and Performance for Special Education Students,' Paper presented to Division G: Social Context of Education at American Education Research Association Meeting, SRI International, Menlo Park, CA.

Center for Assessment and Demographic Studies (1989) *Annual Survey of Hearing-Impaired Children and Youth.* Washington, DC: Gallaudet University.

Cohen, O.P., Fischgrund, J.E., and Redding, R. (1990) 'Deaf chil- dren from ethnic, linguistic and racial minority backgrounds: an overview,' *American Annals of the Deaf.*

Drucker, P. (1989) *The New Realities.* New York: Harper & Row.

Gallaudet University (1989) *Gallaudet University Factbook.* Washington, DC: Gallaudet University.

Harnisch, D.J., Lichtenstein, S.J., and Langford, J.B. (1984) *Digest on Youth in Transition.* Champaign, IL: Champaign Transition Institute.

Johnston, W.B. (1987) *Workforce 2000.* Indianapolis, IN: The Hudson Institute.

Kutscher, R.E. (1989) 'Projections, summary and emerging issues', *Monthly Labor Review.* Washington, DC: US Department of Labor, Bureau of Labor Statistics.

Nash, K., and Walter, G. (1990) 'Estimates of the Deaf 18–21 Year Old Population of the United States,' Technical Report. Rochester, NY: Rochester Institute of Technology.

National Technical Institute for the Deaf (1989) *NTID Annual Report.* Rochester, NY: Rochester Institute of Technology.

Preblud, S.R., Hinman, A.R., and Herrmann, K.L. (1980) 'An evaluation of the United States Rubella Immunization program,' *American Annals of the Deaf,* 968–75.

Rawlings, B.A., Karchmer, M., and DeCaro, J. (1988) *College and Career Programs for Deaf Students.* Washington, DC: Gallaudet University and Rochester, NY: Rochester Institute of Technology.

Spencer, G. (1989) 'Population Estimates and Projections' (Series P-25, No. 1018). Washington, DC: US Government Printing Office.

Stuckless, E.R. and Delgado, G.L. (1973) *A Guide to College/Career Programs for Deaf Students: 1973.* Washington, DC: Gallaudet College and Rochester, NY: Rochester Institute of Technology.

US Department of Education (1986) *Directory of Elementary and Secondary School Districts and Schools and Selected Districts.* Washington, DC: School Civil Rights Survey, unpublished tabulations.

US Department of Education (1990) *Twelfth Annual Report to Congress on the Implementation of the Handicapped Act.* Washington, DC: Division of Innovation and Development, Office of Special Education Programs.

US Department of Health, Education and Welfare (1978) *Progress Toward a Free Appropriate Public Education: An Interim Report to Congress on the Implementation of Public Law 94-142.* Washington DC: Bureau, Education of the Handicapped.

US General Accounting Office (1986) *Deaf Education: Costs and Student Characteristics at Federally Assisted Schools.* Washington, DC: US Government Printing Office.

Wagner, M. (1989) *Youth with Disability During Transition: A Report from the National Longitudinal Transition Study.* Menlo Park, CA: SRI International.

Wagner, M. and Shaver, D. (1989) 'Educational Programs and Achievements of Secondary Special Education Students: Findings from the National Longitudinal Transition Study.' Paper presented to the Special Education Special Interest Group of the American Education Research Association, San Francisco, CA.

Walter, G.G. (1988) 'Megatrends in postsecondary education of the deaf,' *Proceedings of the Third Regional Conference on Postsecondary Education for Hearing-Impaired Persons.* Knoxville, TN: University of Tennessee Press.

Walter, G.G., Foster, S.B., and Elliot, L. (1987) 'Attrition and Accommodation of Hearing-Impaired College Students in the United States,' Paper presented at the Tenth National Conference of the Association of Handicapped Students Service Programs in Postsecondary Education. Washington, DC.

Personal Commentary

Miguel Sanchez

I've been asked to share my experience of deafness and to relate it to the challenge raised in this chapter to describe how, in the early years of the 21st century, educators of deaf children responded to the task of educating an ethnically diverse population, much of it 'at risk,' for the job market of the next century. Well, I suppose I'm a good choice for such a task. I was born in 2000 and lived through many of the changes. And I am, myself, a second-generation Hispanic-American. But I am getting a bit ahead of myself.

Let me begin at the beginning. My deaf *abuela* (grandmother) still loves to tell this story. She and grandfather came from Mexico, actually from Irapuato, a small farm town, deep in the heart of Guanajuato State. There was no work. No future. The day they were married, they promised each other that, for their children, life would be better. So, they turned north, toward the Rio Grande. They hitched rides and walked more than 700 kilometers. I think my old *abuela* was just 19. To stay alive they did odd jobs. On the first moonless night in March, 1980, they slipped across the river avoiding the US Border Patrol and the dogs. They were within yards of the American shore when grandfather slipped into a deep pool. He almost drowned. It took all my grandmother's strength to drag him out. Neither could swim. Soaked to the skin, covered with mud, and scared to death – (just kids really, but they made it). And my *abuela* was three months pregnant. As my old *abuela* likes to say, '*Nosotros somos mojados de verdad, Mi hijito.*' (We are real wetbacks, little one.) When I was growing up the Anglo kids always called us Mexican kids 'wetbacks.' I hated it. We had some big fights over it. Anyway, now it's a name I'm proud of.

My grandparents first picked grapefruit in the Rio Grande Valley. After that they got an old pick-up truck and followed the fruit crop around the Southeast. My mother was born in Georgia. Eventually the family settled in Austin, Texas, where I was born 1 January 2000. My parents were really excited. I was the first child to be born in Austin in the new millennia. Mom and I were interviewed on Spanish TV. Mom says that mostly I cried and needed make-up real bad. How embarrassing! The papers ran a little story. Of course, my *abuela* can't read but she understood the photos. She still has some of the old news clippings. Anyway, Mom had a job as a maid and dad worked two jobs – days as a gardener and nights as a watchman. We lived in the old barrio – the Hispanic ghetto. In those days folks from Mexico and Latin America were still pouring in by the millions. Now we make up 19 per cent of the whole enchilada! We're already the majority in five states.

Most of the time I stayed with my *abuela*. I was about 2 when I came down with a really bad fever. My parents were both working. *Abuela* had no idea what to do. The emergency room doctor said I was lucky to be alive. Afterward I stopped talking, and paid less attention to things. For a long time my parents were really upset. Finally, one of the barrio's Spanish-speaking nurses came to visit. She mentioned a program for 'slow kids.' That's when they found out I was deaf – from meningitis. The irony is that, with treatment just a little earlier, I would have never been deaf, but everyone did the best they could. From then on I was in some kind of a program for deaf kids. My parents came to school, too, for advice on how they could help me at home. Some of the teachers were bilingual, and that helped a lot. I was fitted with a digital hearing aid which made a difference also.

At 16 I was a so-so student, no trouble or anything, but just sort of drifting. Pretty typical. One evening I saw a captioned news program on the life of space construction workers – the men and women who spend their lives in the sky building factories and repairing science platforms. Of course, nowadays those high-tech migrants are like flies; you find them all over the Solar System. The point is, finally, I had a goal. The rest, as they say, is history.

To bring you up to date, I just received my new assignment. Perhaps you've read about that new US/Soviet company, American/Russian Express. That's the one that advertises the Gold Card embossed with the old hammer and sickle. Well, I've just been picked to be senior navigation technician on our first joint venture, the first ever tourist trip to Base Alpha – on Mars.

I know that I've been really fortunate. My parents were very supportive once they knew what to do. My teachers accommodated my needs, but forced me to keep growing. And the special federal program to train deaf Hispanics as teachers of the deaf gave me role models. Even so, I was no Einstein. I was really lucky to get into that special postsecondary program for high risk minority students. I probably owe my new job to the great in-service training I received over the past few years – offered by the Far West Consortium of Postsecondary Programs for the Deaf. There is no other way I could have kept up with all the changes occurring in Imaging Science, and I needed that interpreting support. It was crucial.

Things have changed a lot since my grandparents splashed across the Rio Grande 45 years ago, and not just for deaf people. 'There will never be a Mexican/American president –

not in my lifetime,' my old *abuela* used to swear. Yet, last election who should squeak into the White House, but Eliana Garcia? Surprise! Surprise! The pollsters should learn some Spanish – or get a new job. There's a lesson there someplace.

Last week, my team was completing the final checkout of Heavenly Holiday, our new deluxe space cruiser, with room for 500 tourists. As luck would have it, at dawn we crossed the southwestern tip of the US. Far, far below the new sunlight was a lovely ribbon of blue, wandering slowly across the dry desert. My Soviet teammate nudged me, pointed, and asked 'What's that?'

'Amigo, that's the Rio Grande,' I answered and took a photograph, just for dear, old *abuela*.

Signed,

Miguel Sanchez, Senior Navigation Technician
Heavenly Holidays,
Luxury Class Space Cruiser
American/Russian Express, Ltd.
Base Alpha, Mars
January 1, 2025

P.S. I need to explain some things about America to my Soviet teammates. What's the Russian word for 'wetback?'

Miguel Sanchez was born 1 January 2000. He was educated as an Imaging Technician at NTID and participated in Project Long Shot, the first exploration of Pluto. Much of Mr. Sanchez' additional education came through in-service courses offered by American/Russian Express Ltd., with the assistance of the Far West Consortium of Postsecondary Programs for the Deaf. The Consortium was established to provide educational consultation to high technology companies that have deaf employees.

Chapter 2

Characteristics of programs serving deaf persons

Gerard G. Walter

INTRODUCTION

The era from 1955 to the present has been one of the most active periods in the history of postsecondary education in the United States. During this time, postsecondary education has, without question, been a 'growth industry.' The initial impetus resulted from federal legislation commonly known as the 'GI Bill,' which enabled large numbers of World War II veterans to attend universities and colleges in the postwar period. Subsequently, the sons and daughters of these same veterans ('baby boomers') began entering post-secondary institutions in large numbers during the 1960s and early 1970s prompting massive expansion in staffing, facilities, and curricula. Fueled by demand for higher education, community colleges opened the doors of postsecondary education to large numbers of individuals who would otherwise not have had access to traditional higher education.

Growth during this same period was also fueled by societal changes in attitudes regarding college attendance. Driven by the launching of *Sputnik*, the goal to put a man on the moon, and the civil rights movement, societal goals in education at the collegiate level emerged in the form of concerns regarding *access to* and *training* in the technologies. Technological advancements following World War II, preparedness during the Cold War, and the race to put a man on the moon, resulted in the demand for highly trained specialists in areas such as engineering, mathematics, computer science, and communication technologies. By the year 2000, technicians, professionals in business, industry, health and education, engineers, and supervisory personnel will be needed in even greater numbers than today. Emphasis on more, not less, education by the general population will continue (Johnston 1987).

Access to postsecondary education and choice of school by individuals initially centered on the issue of college opportunities for children from low-income families, but extended to individuals with disabilities with the passage in 1973 of Section 504 of the Vocational Rehabilitation Act.

No otherwise qualified handicapped individual in the United States . . . shall, solely by reason of his handicap, be excluded from the participation in, be denied the benefits of, or be subjected to discrimination under any program or activity receiving federal financial assistance.

(Public Law 93–112: Section 504)

Efforts at the state and federal levels in support of this concept have taken a variety of forms, including financial support for the elaborate network of community colleges and expanded state university systems. In addition, increased direct financial aid to students, either on a loan or on a direct grant basis, has improved access and at the same time contributed to the ability to choose one's school.

These societal efforts to provide access to higher education have also markedly influenced the numbers of deaf persons seeking postsecondary education. The latest edition of *College and Career Programs for Deaf Students – 1986* (Rawlings, Karchmer, and DeCaro 1988), lists 156 postsecondary institutions that provide services specifically for 7,490 deaf students. It is estimated that there are between 30–40 per cent more deaf students enrolled in programs not listed in the *College and Career Programs for Deaf Students – 1986* (Wulfsberg and Peterson 1979; Rawlings and King 1987).

Evidence for these additional numbers comes from the fact that there exists a large number of institutions supporting students through generic special service programs. A 1987 survey of 447 colleges and universities in the United States reports a total of 6,583 deaf students who are supported by special service programs in the responding colleges (Association for Handicapped Student Service Programs in Postsecondary Education [AHSSPPE] 1987). Approximately 3,400 of the deaf students enumerated by this survey were from schools also reporting in the *College and Career Programs for Deaf Students*. If this estimate is taken at face value, it means that there are at least an additional 3,000 deaf students (totaling approximately 10,000) enrolled in colleges and universities throughout the United States. Additionally, Liscio (1986) lists 260 four-year and 287 two-year colleges that provide some level of support services for deaf college students.

The starting point for this chapter, then, is with the history of access on the part of deaf students and a review of contemporary choices students have. Later, the diversity that exists in this large number of programs and the goals that such programming *should* seek to attain when providing services for deaf persons will be discussed.

OPPORTUNITIES FOR POSTSECONDARY EDUCATION

Gallaudet University

On 15 April 1864, Abraham Lincoln signed an enactment that empowered the Columbia Institution for the Deaf, later to be renamed Gallaudet College (changed to Gallaudet University in 1986), to grant degrees. To the present, Gallaudet remains the only liberal arts university in the world specifically for deaf students.

Gallaudet University offers degrees at the undergraduate level in more than 30 majors leading to associate and bachelor degrees, and graduate programs in education, counseling, and school psychology. In addition, students who are not yet academically prepared for college can enroll in a preparatory program to increase their basic skills in reading, mathematics, and science before being admitted to college-level studies.

All classes at the graduate and undergraduate levels are taught using the simultaneous method of communication, employing sign language and fingerspelling in conjunction with spoken English. In addition, Gallaudet provides a range of special programs including a writing center that provides assistance to students who need help with further development of writing skills. Also, a tutorial center provides one-on-one tutorial assistance from both peer and professional tutors. A career center provides a variety of services to students throughout their undergraduate program in helping them to select majors and choose a career direction.

As of May 1989, 7,335 students had graduated from Gallaudet since its establishment, with incalculable benefits to the cultural, social, and economic well-being of deaf people both in this country and abroad. Nevertheless (unlike circumstances for hearing people) higher education remained beyond the reach of the great majority of deaf people until very recently.

Community College Programs

In 1961, the first college program for deaf people outside of Gallaudet was established at Riverside City College in California (Brill 1962). The plan underlying this program, several years ahead of its time, was to establish a unit within an existing two-year, vocationally oriented program to provide special services needed by deaf students that would permit them to take advantage of the full range of courses available to the hearing students in the community. This program began with 12 students and continues to serve students today. It has remained the contemporary model used by many community colleges to offer support for deaf students.

Since the first community college program at Riverside City College, there has been tremendous growth in this type of programming for deaf students. The impetus for this growth has been the passage of Section 504 of the Rehabilitation Act of 1973 (PL 93–112) as amended in 1974 (PL 93–516) – providing for equal access by people with disabilities to college programs. During the 1970s and early 1980s this legislation, in association with the social attitudes accompanying PL 19–142 requiring a 'least restrictive environment' for elementary and secondary school students with disabilities, resulted in a drastic increase in the number of postsecondary institutions establishing programs for deaf students. Since 1973, when 617 known persons were registered in 23 programs, the enrollment and number of programs has grown to more than 3,500 in 134 local programs: better than a 500 per cent increase in the number of deaf persons having access to college programs in their local communities.

Federal Funding for Postsecondary Education for Deaf Persons

In 1965, 101 years after the establishment of Gallaudet, Congress passed the National Technical Institute for the Deaf Act, which, with Lyndon Johnson's signature, became Public Law 89–36. An agreement was reached in 1966 between the federal government and Rochester Institute of Technology (RIT) in Rochester, New York, for the establishment of the National Technical Institute for the Deaf (NTID) on its campus, thereby providing a second national postsecondary institution for the deaf. Unlike Gallaudet College, NTID's mandate called for it to feature technical education. Also, NTID was charged with taking full advantage of the programs already being offered to hearing students through the several colleges of RIT. NTID admitted its first 70 students in 1968, and currently enrolls nearly 1,100 deaf students annually.

Deaf students can earn diplomas, certificates, or associate degrees in science, engineering, business, and visual communication careers from NTID; or, if qualified, earn bachelor's or master's degrees through RIT's eight other colleges: Applied Science and Technology, Business, Continuing Education, Engineering, Fine and Applied Arts, Graphic Arts and Photography, Liberal Arts, and Science.

Students enrolled at NTID receive instruction using simultaneous communication. Those matriculated in one of the other eight colleges of RIT receive support services, through NTID, of interpreting, tutoring, and notetaking. In addition, all students have access to professionals skilled in working with deaf persons in the areas of career counseling and academic advising, and a variety of learning centers that help students develop their skills in communication, mathematics, physics, general education, English, and computer literacy.

Since its beginning in 1968 NTID has graduated 2,725 students: 36 per cent with certificates and diplomas, 45 per cent with associate degrees, 18 per cent with bachelor's degrees and 1 per cent with master's degrees. Approximately 80 per cent of graduates work in business and industry with the rest working in government and education. Examples of positions held by graduates include accounting technician, biomedical photographer, designer, laboratory manager, optical finishing technician, professional artist, teacher, and computer operator.

In 1964, as a logical extension of its federally funded National Leadership Training Program in the area of deafness, California State University at Northridge began providing interpreting and notetaking services to deaf students in regular university classes. These services evolved into the initiation of teacher training programs in 1969 from which more than half of the graduates have been deaf, to the establishment of a 'Center on Deafness' as an administrative coordinating unit for programs housed on campus. Currently, a sub-unit of the national center coordinates the delivery of interpreting, tutoring, notetaking, and counseling services campuswide. In 1988, the program at California State University at Northridge enrolled 215 deaf students.

Another major development in postsecondary education of the

people who are deaf was the establishment in 1968 of regional programs at Delgado College, New Orleans, Louisiana (Wells and Gagnard 1973), Seattle Community College, Seattle, Washington (Traxler and LaFayette 1975), and Technical Vocational Institute, St. Paul, Minnesota (Lauritsen 1974). These regional programs grew out of the initiatives of the Bureau of Education for the Handicapped and the Rehabilitation Services Administration. These two agencies responded to the national priorities of the mid-1960s that emphasized the need for more technical training of deaf persons in integrated educational settings. All the institutions are two-year, vocationally oriented programs. In 1987, 465 deaf students were enrolled in these programs, with funding for the Delgado project being shifted to the University of Tennessee's Postsecondary Educational Consortium in 1983. In the fall of 1988, the Postsecondary Education Consortium reported six affiliate institutions: Central Piedmont Community College, Chattanooga State Technical Community College, DeKalb Community College, New River Community College, St. Petersburg Junior College, and the University of Tennessee.

REPRESENTATION IN POSTSECONDARY EDUCATION

It can clearly be seen that there has been a tremendous growth in the number and types of programs supporting deaf persons attending college – prompted primarily by changing social attitudes, national demographics, and federal and local legislation. The question we must address is whether deaf persons are represented in postsecondary education in proportions equivalent to their hearing peers. In order to address this issue, we apply the methodology developed by Schein and Bushnaq (1962), but update the results with current enrollment numbers. Figure 2.1 graphically compares the relative proportions of deaf and hearing persons enrolled in postsecondary education as a function of the number of students enrolled in elementary and secondary programs. It can be seen that, relative to their hearing peers, deaf students have made significant gains in attending postsecondary education, moving from two college students for every 100 elementary and secondary level students in 1955 to 16 in 100 in 1985. Similar figures for hearing students were eight in 100 in 1955 and 28 in 100 in 1985. The relative number of deaf students enrolling in postsecondary programs still does not match the rate of attendance for hearing persons – lagging behind their hearing peers by 12 percentage points. The gap represented by this difference was greater in 1985 than it was in 1955 when the difference was only 6 percentage points. In short, while the rate of growth has been great, it has not kept pace with the even more rapid growth experienced by hearing persons. These differences might suggest the need for even more support than is currently available. National attention must be focused on the provision of postsecondary educational support for deaf persons if the differences are to be overcome in the future.

SERVICES PROVIDED BY THE PROGRAMS

In the midst of these rapidly expanding postsecondary resources to meet the increasing numbers and a broader range of deaf students, it is vital that the quality of the education to which they have access be maintained and improved. This concern prompted the Conference of Executives of American Schools for the Deaf in 1973 to adopt and distribute a report, *Principles Basic to the Establishment and Maintenance of Postsecondary Programs for the Deaf* (Stuckless 1973). The principles are organized around six topics: planning, administration, staffing, students, curriculum, and support services. These principles should not be considered as a set of standards, but only as a set of guidelines against which to define a program. Additionally, Quigley (1974) has suggested 'a need also to begin studying the higher education programs for the deaf as a system. Most states are beginning to do this with general higher education, rather than allowing the various components to grow in isolation.' Yet little has been done to coordinate the efforts.

A regional survey of the Southeast conducted by the University of Tennessee (Commission on Education of the Deaf 1988) showed that, as a rule, most established programs had no contact with other local, regional, or national postsecondary training; maintained no records specifically about their deaf students; did little, if any, recruitment or placement of their students; and provided services that were generally limited to interpreting, tutoring, and notetaking.

The results of a survey conducted by NTID and Gallaudet University (Rawlings, Karchmer, and De Caro 1988) also show that, while most of the responding institutions have available services in all of these areas, few have personnel with training that permits adequate accommodation for the communication difficulties experienced by the majority of deaf persons. More will be said about this topic later in this chapter.

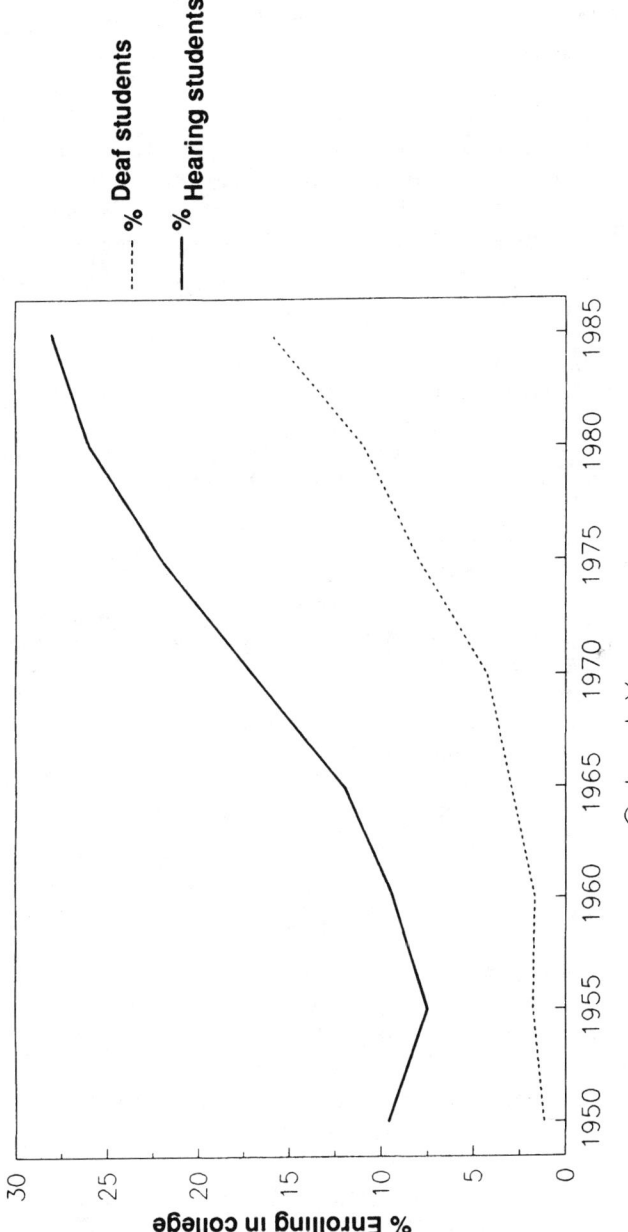

Figure 2.1 College enrollments as a percentage of elementary and secondary enrollments

Source: Schein and Bushnaq (1962)

Demographics of educational programs

In Chapter 1 we saw that, in the United States, deaf individuals graduate from high school with an average reading grade level of about third grade (Allen 1987). Seventy per cent of these individuals cannot access postsecondary education and training, and in general, do not have the competencies to successfully enter or fully compete in the labor force. There is a wide diversity in the reading skill levels of students entering postsecondary education – on the average well below levels of their hearing peers in similar institutions. We have indicated that great strides have been made to provide access by deaf persons to the college environment. The challenge for all of postsecondary education is to find ways to accommodate these individuals so as to improve their chances of success.

What Constitutes a Program?

While the latest edition of *College Career Programs for the Deaf Students* (Rawlings, Karchmer, and DeCaro 1988) lists 156 different programs, it is not easy to define what constitutes a postsecondary program for deaf students. *Principles Basic to the Establishment and Operation of Postsecondary programs for Deaf Students* (Stuckless 1973) provides some guidelines in the definition of a program. These guidelines have been interpreted by the authors of *College Career Programs for the Deaf (Rawlings, Karchmer, and DeCaro 1988)* to mean 'programs' that

(1) have at least 15 full-time deaf students enrolled;
(2) are part of a regionally accredited postsecondary institution;
(3) have a coordinator of services for deaf students who devotes a minimum of 50 per cent of his or her time to directing the program; and
(4) generally comply with the principles proposed by the Conferences of Educational Administrators Serving the Deaf.

In 1988, only 62 (40 per cent) of the reporting institutions met the above criteria. Using these criteria it can be said that many of the institutions offering services to deaf students do not qualify as a program. Obviously a program connotes an organization and a staff, and clearly implies a student population. Additionally, it suggests an array of special services for deaf students. Table 2.1 shows the average size of programs for deaf students listed in the 1986 *College Career Programs for the Deaf*. They range in size from programs with fewer than 10 students (the modal size) to Gallaudet University with more than 1,500 deaf students, the median (including Gallaudet and NTID) being a little fewer than 20 students. The largest programs are the national programs, accounting for about 42 per cent of enrolled students. By far the majority of deaf students are registered in programs in community colleges near their homes.

Table 2.1 Size distribution of programs reporting in *College Career Programs for the Deaf*

Size	Number	% of Total
less than 10	56	40
10–20	32	24
21–50	37	25
51–100	13	7
101–500	3	3
more than 500	2	1

The CEASD *Principles Basic to the Establishment and Maintenance of Postsecondary Programs for the Deaf* (Stuckless 1973) suggest that programs be coordinated by a full-time director. For the programs reported in the NTID and Gallaudet study, 39 per cent reported having a coordinator whose time commitment was less than 50 per cent. This is not surprising when one considers the fact that about 40 per cent of the programs have less than 10 students. Also, only 38 per cent report having a full-time administrator. The combination of the relatively small number of students and the large number of programs without a full-time administrator makes one wonder about the co-ordination of services being offered to students and whether enough attention is paid to justifying an adequate funding level to support the needs of deaf students.

Level of Education

Despite the small size of the service units for deaf students, 98 per cent of the programs are part of an accredited institution, with the majority (61 per cent) associated with two-year junior or technical-vocational programs. This fact denotes a realization by those who established the programs that the handicapping effects of a severe to profound hearing impairment often limit one's ability to compete in a traditional four-year college environment.

In 1987, degrees were awarded to 1,431 deaf students reporting in the *College Career* Programs for the deaf: 48 per cent were at the certificate or diploma level, 22 per cent at the associate level, 19 per cent at the bachelor level, and 11 per cent at the graduate level. The increased number of degrees being awarded annually is the result of the access to higher education afforded deaf persons, and the level of support these persons are receiving from their institution. It is also clear from these numbers that the largest block of degrees are granted as terminal degrees leading directly to employment.

Provision of Support Services

The CEASD *Principles* state that 'Teaching faculty and other professional staff members of the institution should not be expected to cope with the special needs of most deaf students without program support. Nor should the deaf student be expected to adjust readily to a learning situation in which staff are oblivious to his special needs. (p. 6)' Fifty-one per cent of programs indicated no special training was provided for notetakers, 74 per cent required no level of proficiency in manual communication for faculty and staff regularly teaching deaf students without the aid of an interpreter, and fewer than half of the interpreters were certified. These facts, in combination with the large percentage of programs not having a full-time director, lead one to question whether enough attention is being paid to the special needs of deaf students. These staffing questions must have an impact on the number and quality of support services provided and ultimately on persistence at the postsecondary level.

The guidelines specify the types of services that should be available to deaf students. Table 2.2 summarizes these services and lists the percentage of programs having some level of services available to students. It must be pointed out that there is no attempt to make judgments concerning the adequacy of the services provided.

Programs with fewer than 100 students tend not to provide support in terms of special classes, supervised housing, and social programs. At the smallest programs, services often are provided by individuals who are not proficient in communicating with deaf persons. As an example, for programs with fewer than 100 students, only 50 per cent of the individuals providing vocational and personal counseling were listed as able to use sign language when communicating with students. When one considers these facts, in association with the data presented about staffing levels, questions arise concerning whether the staffing at many of the programs is adequate to provide the quality of support services deaf college students need to be successful.

Table 2.2 Support services provided by programs serving deaf students (percentage of programs with services)

	Program size	
Service	<100	>100
Remedial programs	66	87
Special classes	26	65
Tutoring	91	96
Interpreting	98	96
Notetaking	96	86
Vocational counseling	94	96
Personal counseling	98	100
Vocational placement	91	96
Speech and hearing services	69	79
Communication for students	83	100
Supervised housing	38	55
Social programs	45	87

Source: College and Career Programs for Deaf Students

CONCLUSIONS

As we begin the 1990s, the rate of growth for deaf postsecondary students is expected to diminish as it has for hearing college students. The challenge to professionals providing services to deaf postsecondary level students will be to ensure that by gaining access to the college of their choice they are truly able to realize their potential in benefiting from the available learning experiences provided by college.

From the information presented in this chapter, it is apparent that there is a great deal of diversity in the types of accommodations made by colleges and universities in support of their deaf students. The models used run the gamut from no special support provided, to services that only offer sign interpreting in the classroom, to those that offer a full range of services with professionals skilled in communicating with deaf persons. It must be stressed that, by themselves, support services may not necessarily improve the ability of deaf students to understand the content of a textbook or a lecture. The provision of lecture notes or sign langauge interpretation for lectures does not necessarily mean that the 'achievement barrier' created by low reading and mathematics skills has been breached. The communication difficulties of deaf students very often inhibit them from using the avenues most often required for information transfer in college – lecture and reading. We know that access to the classroom is not a problem for these individuals, but integration into the give and take of the classroom and greater college environment often is not achieved. Even for the person with an interpreter, the delay imposed by the task of transferring spoken communication into sign language often keeps the deaf person a step behind the information flow. As a result, questions asked by the deaf student often seem out of place, or interrupting to the lecture. In some cases it may be necessary to modify texts and instructional materials, provide a comprehensive battery of compensatory and remedial programs, or modify the system for delivery of education. Often the needs of each student must be considered individually.

In a similar fashion, the communication problems experienced by most deaf persons make it extremely difficult for them to take part in the usual social activities of campus life. In fact, it may be that social integration is even more difficult to achieve than academic integration, since the former is less amenable to formal intervention and support services. Additionally, problems are often even more pronounced in the social arena, since there is almost total reliance on the spoken word to communicate, whether it be through the telephone, or face-to-face communication. For example, just taking part in a discussion in the cafeteria or hallway is very difficult for the deaf individual. Since so much socialization in our culture occurs through these informal interactions, it is not surprising that deaf persons may have 'physical' access to college but remain excluded from the social mainstream of college life.

This integration into the total educational community should be the goal of any program providing services to deaf persons at the postsecondary level. We should always seek to fully understand the characteristics of both the individual and the institution and the fit between these characteristics. For those of us who work on behalf of special students within a larger educational environment, the problems of integration are enormous. To ensure a successful program requires commitments beyond the special services office and the resources of deaf persons themselves. It requires a total institutional commitment. Tinto (1987) concludes his recent book, *Leaving college*, with the following remarks:

> Regarding the character of effective institutional policy, we must remember that people make a difference. Ultimately, the success of our actions on behalf of student learning and retention depends upon the daily actions of all members of the institution, not on the sporadic efforts of a few officially designated members of a retention committee [or program for deaf students]. Properly understood, institutional commitment is the commitment on the part of each and every member of the institution for the welfare, the social and intellectual growth of all members of the institution. It is a commitment to the notion of education broadly understood which is not limited to either time or place.
>
> (pp. 189–90)

We must, then, look beyond the 'official' services provided by the institution on behalf of deaf students. The services, by themselves, are not the end, but whether the academic and social needs of students are being met within the context of an institutional environment.

While great strides have been made in providing access to postsecondary education for deaf students, it is not at all clear whether institutions have made adequate accommodations to meet the communicative and educational handicaps imposed by a severe to profound hearing impairment. The remaining chapters in this book will discuss the issues of special needs on the part of deaf students and the accommodations necessary to meet those needs.

REFERENCES

Allen, T.A. (1987) 'Understanding the scores: Hearing-impaired students and the Stanford Achievement Test,' in Arthur N. Schildroth and Michael A. Karchmer, (eds), *Deaf Children in America*. Washington, DC: Gallaudet University.

Association for Handicapped Student Service Programs in Postsecondary Education (1987) *Disabled Student Enrollment Survey*. Columbus, OH: AHSSPPE.

Babbidge, H.D. (1965) *Education of the deaf: A report to the Secretary of H.E.W.* Washington, DC: US Dept of H.E.W.

Bigman, S.K. (1962) 'The deaf in American institutions of higher education,' *Personnel and Guidance Journal*, 107, 417–20.

Boatner, E.B., Stuckless, E.R., and Moores, D.F. (1964) *Occupational status of the young deaf adult of New England.* Hartford, CN: American School for the Deaf.

Brill, R.G. (1972) 'An analysis of a group of deaf students in colleges with the hearing,' *Volta Review*, 67, 17–27.

Commission on Education of the Deaf (1988) *Toward equality: Education of the deaf.* Washington, DC: US Government Printing Office, Appendix, L5.

Gallaudet, E.M. (1893) 'The higher education of the deaf,' Paper presented at the World Congress of Instructors of the Deaf, Chicago, IL.

Gallaudet University (1989) *Gallaudet University Factbook – 1989.* Washington, DC: Gallaudet University.

Johnston, W.B. (1987) *Workforce 2000.* Indianapolis, IN: Hudson Institute.

Kronenberg, H.H. and Blake, G.D. (1966) *A study of the occupational status of the young deaf adult of the southwest.* Hot Springs, AK: University of Arkansas.

Lauritsen, R. (1974) *Improved vocational, technical and academic opportunities for deaf persons.* St. Paul, MN: Technical Vocational Institute.

Liscio, M.A. (1986) *A college guide for hearing-impaired students.* Orlando, FL.

Ott, J.T. (1965) *Proceedings of a national workshop of improved opportunities for the deaf.* Knoxville, TN: University of Tennessee.

Quigley, S.P. (1974) 'The deaf student in colleges and universities,' in R.E. Hardy and J.G. Cull (eds), *Educational and psychosocial aspects of deafness.* Springfield, IL: Charles C. Thomas, 95–117.

Quigley, S.P., Jenne, W.C., and Phillips, S.B. (1968) *Deaf students in colleges and universities.* Washington, DC: A.B. Bell Association for the Deaf.

Rawlings, B.A., Karchmer, M., and DeCaro, J. (1983) *College and career programs for deaf students.* Washington, DC: Gallaudet College and Rochester, NY: Rochester Institute of Technology.

Rawlings, B.A., Trybus, R., and Biser, J. (1978) *A guide to college/career programs for deaf students.* Washington, DC: Gallaudet College and Rochester, NY: Rochester Institute of Technology.

Rawlings, B.A., Trybus, R., and Biser, J. (1981) *A guide to college/career programs for deaf students.* Washington, DC: Gallaudet College and Rochester, NY: Rochester Institute of Technology.

Rawlings, B.A., Karchmer, M.A., DeCaro, J.J., and Egelston-Dodd (1986) *A guide to college/career programs for deaf students.* Washington, DC: Gallaudet College and Rochester, NY: Rochester Institute of Technology.

Rawlings, B.A., Trybus, R.J., Delgado, G.L., and Stuckless, E.R. (1975) *1975 Revision of a guide to college/career programs for deaf students.* Washington, DC: Gallaudet College and Rochester, NY: Rochester Institute of Technology.

Rawlings, B.A. and King, S.J. (1987) 'Postsecondary educational opportunities for deaf children,' in A.N. Schildroth and M.A. Karchmer (eds) *Deaf children in America*, San Diego, CA: College-Hill Press.

Rawlings, B.A., Karchmer, M., and DeCaro, J. (1988) *College Career Programs for the Deaf.* Washington, DC: Gallaudet University and Rochester, NY: Rochester Institute of Technology.

Schein, J.D. and Bushnaq, S.M. (1962) Higher education for the deaf in the United States: A retrospective investigation. *American Annals of the Deaf,* 107, 417–20.

Stuckless, E.R. (1973) *Principles basic to the establishment and operation of postsecondary programs for deaf students.* Washington, DC: CEASD.

Stuckless, E.R. and Delgado, G.L. (1971) *A guide to college/programs for deaf students.* Washington, DC: Gallaudet College and Rochester, NY: Rochester Institute of Technology.

Tinto, V. (1987) *Leaving college.* Chicago IL: University of Chicago Press.

Traxler, S. and LaFayette, R. (1975) *Improved vocational, technical, and academic opportunities for deaf persons.* Seattle, WA: Seattle Community College.

Wells, D.O. and Gagnard, R. (1973) *Guidelines for planning postsecondary training programs for the deaf within existing community colleges.* New Orleans, LA: Delgado College.

Wulfsberg, R. and Peterson, R. (1979) *The impact of Section 504 of the Rehabilitation Act of 1973 on American colleges and universities.* Washington, DC: National Center for Education Statistics.

Personal Commentary

Paul Taylor

I started college in 1957 straight from high school. I was the only deaf person in the high school of about 2,000 people and before that I attended the Central Institute for the Deaf from age 3 to age 12. It was the custom at that time for graduates of CID to go to high school without any support services as we know them today. Looking back on that experience, I don't think I would want to do it that way again. To make the transition to a large mainstreamed high school easier, I went to a small private school for the eighth grade. After that I went to the high school I graduated from.

When it came time to choose a career, I wanted to go to medical school. I had all the academic skills, so I talked with several doctors about the possibility and they advised me that, because of my deafness, I probably would not be able to work with people, but could become a medical researcher, since I would not have to see patients in this role. I thought about that and decided that I was not willing to isolate myself from people by working in a laboratory all day. I was really people-oriented and wanted to communicate with people, so I thought that the investment in medical school would not be worth it for me. So I dropped the idea and looked at the area of engineering, because people told me that I had skills in this area. It was not my favorite thing but I had to think about making a living. So I chose chemical engineering because in high school I was good in chemistry and physics.

I went to Georgia Tech, where my first year was almost a rehash of my last year in high school. I was fortunate in high school because I had a very good college prep program so when I went to Tech it was very much of the same in the beginning, but I think this was fortunate, because I needed some time to get used to the college environment.

My classes at Tech were not much different from high school. Most of the teachers stayed close to the book and wrote a lot on the board and I asked other students to copy notes using carbon paper (at that time we didn't have pressure sensitive paper or any other support services). I told the professors that I could not hear in class, but that other students were taking notes, and I would read the book during the class. Most of the professors were very understanding, and told me to come see them if I needed help.

The hardest thing was trying to find out what was going to be on a test. In my sophomore year, I had a harder time because in some of the classes the professors did not use textbooks. They used their own notes and in my third quarter of chemistry class, while the professor used a book, he often departed from the text. Since I did not have the benefit of good notes or listening to the class discussion, I really had no way of knowing what was going on. So I failed that course. I took it again, but with a different teacher, who followed the textbook, and I had a good notetaker. This time I passed the course.

During my years in college, I spent a lot of time outside of class concentrating on learning what I missed during class. I read the textbooks again and again, and had a fraternity buddy who helped explain what I had missed.

As a member of a fraternity I had a lot of support from my brothers. I didn't feel different because I was used to being the only deaf person in the school. Except at Tech, where there was another deaf person, but he was in another major, and not in my fraternity. We got together to talk now and then. I think my fraternity brothers understood what I could and what I could not do. For example, at the fraternity meeting, one of the brothers would jot down what happened so I could get an idea of what was going on. But I couldn't participate as things were happening. What I did was read over the notes, and then talk with the president about what I thought at a later time. I think I was able to train my brothers in how to compensate for my hearing loss. As I think about it now, I wish I had more training in the whole area of social development, and ways to help hearing people adapt to a deaf person. But I didn't know any different at that time.

I think the one thing that I learned from my experience in college, and especially by being part of a fraternity, was how to work in a group. Now, when I went to college, it was very important for me because I had to depend on my fraternity brothers and others to help me fill in the gaps about what I missed. I am not sure that I would do it that way today, knowing what I know about available support services. But despite this, learning how to work in a group with hearing people is very important if a deaf person is to be successful in a mainstreamed environment. Learning how to take part in a group, the give and take that is important for successful group interaction, was a lesson I learned in high school and college, which has helped me all my life. We deaf people cannot always depend on formal support services to provide us with access to what is going on. We must learn how to find out ourselves through communication.

While this is the way I feel, I think we need to provide deaf people with a variety of different options for taking advantage of college life. Not all people will be successful at a school with no support services, such as Georgia Tech. There must be choices. I do feel, however, that it is very important that training in the areas of personal and social development is a priority for all deaf college students. This training must include techniques for communicating in a mainstreamed world so they can interact in the world of work. Often we concentrate our support on providing information in the classroom, and don't do anything about developing support or skills to cope with the rest of the college environment. I think more learning occurs in college outside the classroom than in the classroom. This certainly was my experience as a student at Georgia Tech.

Paul L. Taylor is an Associate Professor in the Data Processing Department at NTID. Mr. Taylor received a Bachelor of Chemical Engineering Degree from the Georgia Institute of Technology, a Master's Degree in Operations Research at Washington University, and professional engineering certifications from the States of Missouri and New York.

Chapter 3
Persistence in college

Michael S. Stinson and Gerard G. Walter

INTRODUCTION

In Chapter 1, we observed that deaf students who seek admission to postsecondary education generally begin their studies with a significant educational handicap, and that without special support, a high proportion of these students drop out of postsecondary education without certification (Walter 1989). Data provided by 156 postsecondary programs serving 7,490 deaf persons in the United States and Canada (Rawlings, Karchmer, and DeCaro 1988) offer some evidence of the withdrawal rate for postsecondary level deaf students. Two-year (junior) colleges supporting programs for deaf students annually take in an average of about nine new students and graduate three. This difference results in an estimated withdrawal rate of about 66 per cent. Similarly, four-year colleges having support programs take in an average of seven new deaf students each year and graduate, on the average, only two, for a 72 per cent withdrawal rate. Withdrawal rates for hearing students average 58 per cent for two-year colleges and 30 per cent for four-year colleges (Tinto 1987). Answers to the question of whether these high rates are acceptable can be addressed both from the point of view of the deaf individual and from that of the institution.

For the individual, the economic benefit of receiving some form of postsecondary certification is considerable. A study by Welsh, Walter, and Riley (1989) indicates that deaf persons with higher degrees report earnings that are more equivalent to those of their hearing peers. On average, deaf persons with no college degree will earn only 68 per cent of what their hearing counterparts earn, while those with a master's degree will earn 89 per cent of what their hearing counterparts earn. Over the course of a work life these differences amount to hundreds of thousands of dollars. Welsh, Walter, and Riley (1988) also have found that deaf students who leave college without certification apparently receive no added economic advantage in the workplace for the time they spent in college; their reported earnings are no higher than deaf individuals who never attended college. For these individuals, the time spent in college results in an additional economic burden because of the wages lost while in college.

Institutionally, increasing yearly persistence rates reduces the pressure on admissions to meet specified enrollment goals. As an example, consider the data in Figure 3.1 that show the effect on total enrollment of increasing persistence rates in the first and second years of attendance. Theoretically, if we were able to improve the first year persistence rate from 77 per cent to 82 per cent, (a total of just five students) and from 80 per cent to 85 per cent in the second year, we would increase the overall enrollment from 331 to 355, with an entering cohort of 100 students. Thus, it would appear that improving persistence has a significant effect on overall enrollment figures.

Another reason for improving persistence is that it is economically advantageous for an institution of higher learning to admit a student and carry that student to graduation, rather than admitting a larger number of students to balance a high attrition rate. The costs of marketing, recruitment, initial assessment, and counseling for a larger number of students can be reduced by the need to admit fewer students each year.

When many students share a common problem such as the failure or lack of desire to persist in college, it behooves an institution, both for its own sake and for that of its students, to learn as much about the factors influencing students' decisions to withdraw from college as is possible so that strategies for intervention can be identified. The remainder of this chapter will focus on understanding the causes of attrition among deaf postsecondary students and approaches to reducing this attrition.

A THEORETICAL MODEL OF PERSISTENCE

Much recent attention has been devoted to understanding student persistence and withdrawal. A theoretical model presented by Spady (1970), elaborated by Tinto (1975, 1987), and tested in various environments (Bean and Metzner 1985; Pascarella and Chapman 1983;

Persistence in college 45

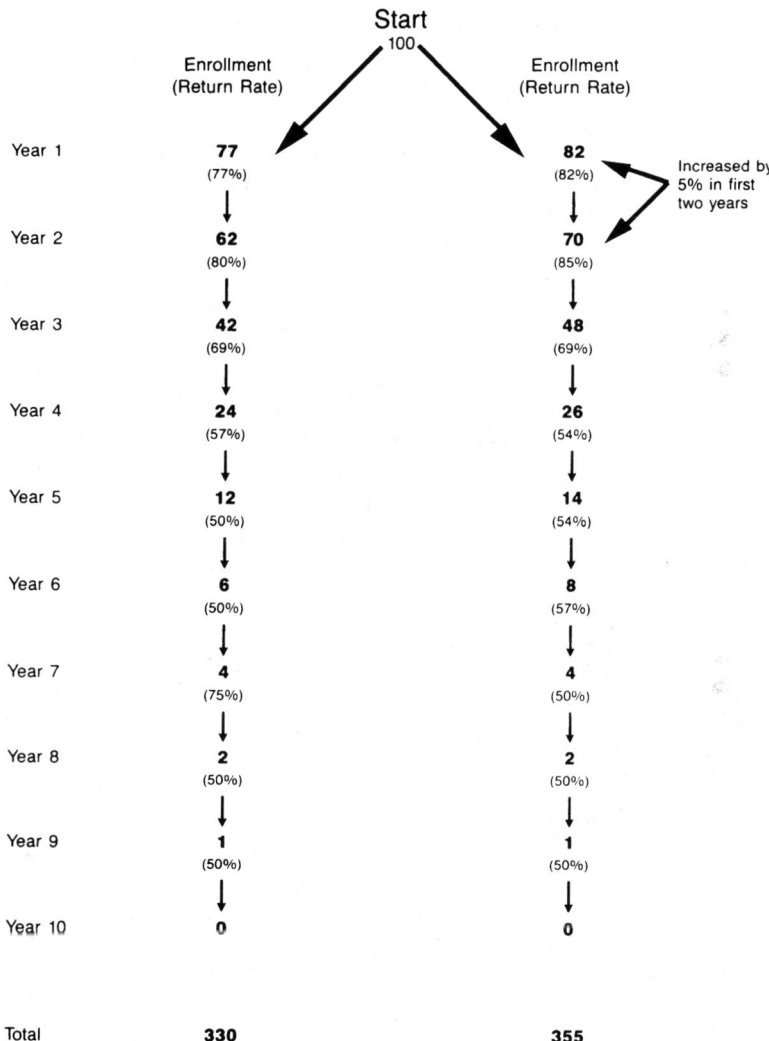

Figure 3.1 Effect of persistence rates on total enrollment
Source: Welsh, Walter and Riley (1988)

Pascarella and Terenzini 1979, 1980) provides an explanatory predictive theory of the persistence/withdrawal process that can be applied, with modifications, to deaf college students. The theory posited by Tinto (1975) considers persistence to be, primarily, a function of the quality of a student's interactions with the academic and social systems of an institution. That is, students come to a particular institution with a range of background characteristics (e.g. achievement, communication, social-economic status, personality), as well as varying levels of commitment to acquiring a higher education. The background characteristics, along with commitment, influence how students will interact with other people in the institution's social and academic systems. When experiences are positive, students increase their sense of being integrated into the academic and social systems of the campus community. In turn, this sense of integration has a positive impact upon commitment to continuing at the institution, and increases the likelihood of persistence until degree completion. When experiences are negative, commitment to the institution and likelihood of persistence decreases. The longitudinal, interactive nature of this model implies that students are continually modifying their sense of academic and social integration and their institutional commitments on the basis of their ongoing college experiences (Tinto 1987).

Any general model for explaining student persistence must be applied with caution to deaf students. Deaf students' academic skills vary more widely than those of their hearing counterparts, and there also is widespread variation in ability to communicate and socialize with both hearing and other deaf students. As the previous chapter indicated, institutions educating deaf students are extremely diverse in the extent of academic support and social opportunities they provide to foster integration. For example, some institutions offer a host of support services, as well as numerous special classes, whereas other institutions offer quite limited support. The particular educational environment will dictate how well a program can provide for the needs of deaf persons matriculating at the institution. Using the theoretical framework provided by Tinto and his colleagues, let us consider some reasons why deaf students drop out of post-secondary education.

WHY DEAF STUDENTS LEAVE COLLEGE

Background Factors

As with hearing students, the background skills, past experiences, and personality characteristics that entering deaf students bring to the college setting have some effect on whether they will persist. These background factors, however, do not, by themselves, fully explain why students withdraw or persist. The effect of background factors is mediated by the social and academic context of the institution (Tinto 1987). Stinson, Scherer, and Walter (1987) developed a model of factors influencing persistence of first-year students at the National Technical Institute for the Deaf (NTID). The model includes background, academic, and social influences, and postulates that the effect of two background factors – performance on high school achievement tests, and extent of high school education in a mainstream setting – is mediated by academic performance at college. Likewise, the background effect of participation in high school extracurricular activities is mediated by participation in activities at college.

These hypothesized relationships are depicted in Figure 3.2, which shows a model of factors affecting college persistence. In this path diagram the hypothesized cause–effect relationships are indicated by the direction of the arrows. Path analysis models hypothesize the causal relationships among a set of variables and the adequacy with which observed correlations fit the hypothesized model. The model was tested through the analysis of data on the persistence of 233 students during their first year of attendance at NTID. Statistical tests supported the hypothesized relations for background factors. The relevant data in Figure 3.2 are the numbers on the paths that can be either positive or negative, and the closer they are to 1.00, the stronger the relationship. These results indicated that experience with mainstreaming and performance on high school achievement tests influenced college academic performance, and participation in high school activities increased the likelihood of participation in college activities. We will address other aspects of this model after considering another study that also identified background factors as relevant to persistence.

Dagel and Dowaliby (1989) also identified background characteristics related to persistence. They defined persistence as whether or not students received academic probation or suspension. They found that NTID freshmen who reported more negative high school experiences on a questionnaire administered during the third week

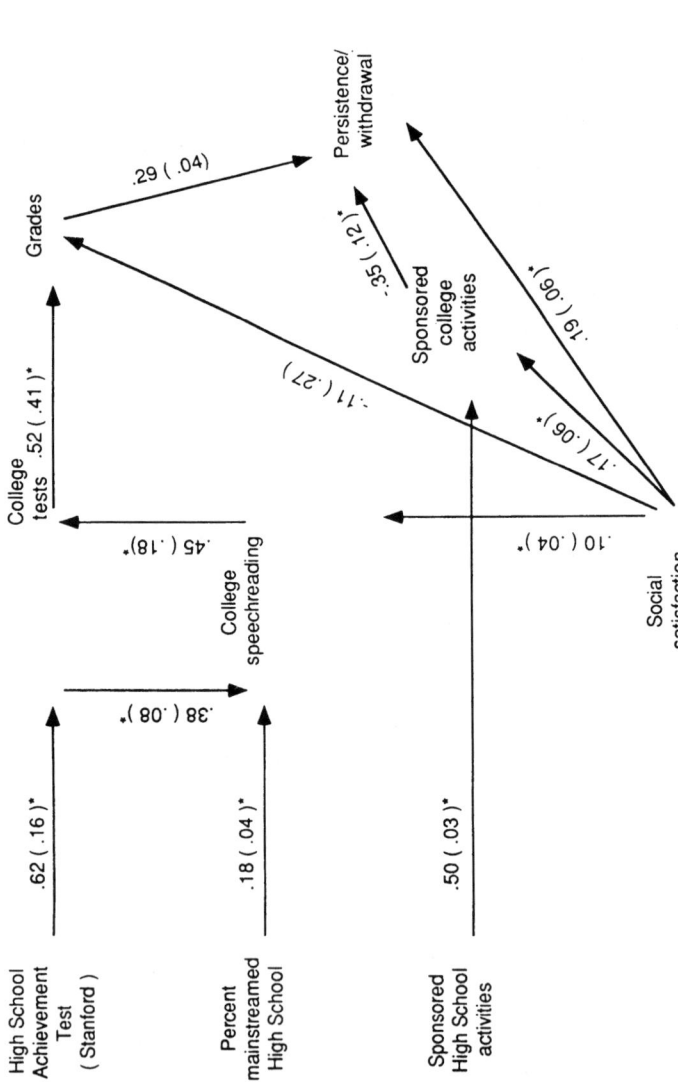

* p <.05

Figure 3.2 **Model of factors affecting college persistence with maximum likelihood estimates and standard errors**

Source: Stinson, Scherer and Walter (1987)

of school were more likely to go on academic probation at the end of the first quarter than were those who reported positive experiences. Items on the questionnaire that indicated negative high school experiences included 'My high school courses were difficult' and 'I did not participate in high school activities (e.g. sports, clubs, honor society).'

Academic Factors

According to Tinto (1987) there are two academic reasons for leaving college: academic difficulty and disappointment with the intellectual climate and learning experiences. The Stinson, Scherer, and Walter (1987) study included measures of academic skills and evaluated the assumption that students with relatively weak basic skills are more likely to experience academic difficulty (e.g. low grades) and subsequently to withdraw. As shown in Figure 3.2, results supported paths in the model that went from college achievement test performance to grades. These results are not surprising and are consistent with previous research with hearing and deaf college students. Achievement test scores are generally good predictors of college grades (Bean 1982).

The path between grade point average and persistence/withdrawal approached but was not statistically significant. While the research literature has provided mixed support for the relationship for hearing students, it is surprising that there was not a significant relationship for the NTID sample. Why wasn't this relationship stronger? This result may be due to the unique set of alternatives and supports provided by the academic environment of NTID. Many students are enrolled in preparatory programs in the first year and, therefore, are not required to take numerous demanding courses in their majors. Furthermore, a diversity of program levels are offered: bachelor's degree, associate in applied science degree, diploma, and certificate. In many majors, students who encounter difficulty at a given level can change to a less difficult program. There also is variation in the difficulty of different majors, and students can make a change in this manner. Finally, there is an unusually extensive program of counseling, tutoring, and remedial instruction for those experiencing academic difficulty.

It also is important to note that the measure of persistence/withdrawal includes voluntary withdrawal as well as academic dismissal. Thus, along with the poorly skilled students, some highly capable ones might leave because the academic offerings do not include the major they desire. Such a bimodal distribution in the academic skills of withdrawing students would attenuate the grade-point-average/persistence relationship. It cannot be safely assumed that there is no relationship between grades and persistence through deaf students' college experience. Grades may very well affect persistence in subsequent years when students more frequently take demanding courses in their majors.

Two other investigations of the persistence/withdrawal of NTID students provide additional support for the proposition that academic difficulty is not a primary reason for leaving. Dowaliby and Dagel (1989) found no relation between measures of mathematics and reading proficiency and likelihood of going on academic probation at the end of the first quarter. In addition, Scherer and Walter (1988) interviewed 320 students who were withdrawing and found that they did not regard academic difficulties as a major reason for leaving. What Scherer and Walter (1988) did discover is that withdrawing students often could not decide on a major area of study. In contrast, they were relatively satisfied with the faculty and outside of class activities.

The results and conclusions reported so far are particularly applicable to environments with a critical mass of deaf students, extensive support services, and a diverse offering of courses taught by signing teachers. From data provided earlier, this is not a common occurrence. More common is the postsecondary setting where there are few other deaf students, limited support services, and few special classes. Research reported by Foster and Elliot (1986) suggests that in such mainstream settings, academic as well as communication difficulties may result in withdrawal. On the basis of interviews with 20 students who had transferred to NTID, they concluded that students had been particularly hampered by communication difficulties even when an interpreter and additional support services were provided. The transfer students complained that teachers frequently moved through material too quickly, were impatient, and treated deaf students as though they could hear. As one student commented:

> Some of the teachers [at mainstream college], they had no experience with the deaf . . . they talk real fast. If I had a question, I'd have to raise my hand and stop the interpreter, stop the teacher. Then they'd explain, and I'd have to turn over here [look back and forth] and it was really a pain.
> (p. 10)

In addition, students stated that lectures tended to be too abstract or theoretical, and the quantity of information presented during the class could be overwhelming. The result was that deaf students often left class confused about the lecture and uncertain of work assignments. Furthermore, some indicated that they had difficulty keeping up with the reading or found the vocabulary difficult. These comments appear to be a reflection of both communication and academic difficulties. They also clearly indicate frustration and disappointment with the learning environment. The reader should keep in mind that these findings are based on students who decided to leave a mainstream college environment. They do not imply that the mainstream setting cannot provide a good education for many deaf students.

These findings are further supported in a study by Franklin (1988), who identified four variables that have a significant relationship with persistence/withdrawal. He studied 246 deaf students attending seven community colleges in the United States. Franklin reported a withdrawal rate during the first year of 55 per cent and found that the students who persisted were generally those who: (a) had better oral communication; (b) attended high schools that offered minimal support; (c) evidenced some type of pre-college preparatory experience, and, (d) made a decision about a major during the first year. The results from this study are consistent with the findings from studies carried out elsewhere.

Thus, both academic difficulties (which were significantly influenced by communication problems) and disenchantment with the learning environment (sometimes related to difficulties in choosing a major) appear to be reasons why deaf students withdraw from postsecondary institutions. While disappointment with the learning environment is a reason why students withdraw from postsecondary institutions specifically designed for deaf students, such as NTID, and from mainstream environments, academic difficulties may not be as significant a factor in the special setting.

Social Factors

Failure to make an adequate social adjustment is a major reason for leaving college, for both deaf and hearing students. There are several reasons poor social adjustment can occur. The student may have difficulty adjusting to living away from home and acquiring the social skills that are appropriate to life at college. There may be incongruence between a student's interests and behaviors and those of others in the social environment. These difficulties can lead to a sense of isolation and dissatisfaction that increases the likelihood of withdrawal. It also is important that the intensity and range of a student's social activities permits adequate integration into the college environment. College life requires investments of time and energy into a whole host of activities, and overextending oneself in certain social activities may make keeping up with other demands of the college system difficult (Tinto 1987).

The Stinson Scherer, and Walter (1987) study included a social satisfaction scale that asked students to indicate their agreement with items regarding the extent they were provided opportunities to meet socially relevant goals. Typical items were: 'A chance to meet people with the same interests as yours' and 'The opportunity to make close friends here.' An important finding was that freshmen students who expressed greater social satisfaction were more likely to persist. This result is consistent with Tinto's (1987) theory that persistence is a function of the students' interactions with the social systems of college, as well as the academic ones. Taking this interactive perspective, social satisfaction is assumed to reflect personality characteristics of students as well as their response to the social environment.

The direct path from social satisfaction to persistence (Figure 3.2) may reflect the importance of the goal of having a quality social life, including opportunities to meet interesting and compatible fellow students and to date members of the opposite sex. Furthermore, students' dissatisfaction with their social life can be a major reason for leaving college (Foster and Elliot 1986; Lang and Stinson 1982). In a national study of deaf students and educators of deaf persons, both groups agreed that the size of the deaf population was the most important factor in attracting students to postsecondary programs (Innes 1985). It can be assumed, therefore, that a major reason for the appeal and attractiveness of large programs, such as NTID and Gallaudet University, is the availability of many social opportunities. The results of this study suggest that considerable attention be devoted to the impact of college socialization on student satisfaction and persistence.

Another finding related to social integration pertains to the frequency of participation in extracurricular activities such as sports, fraternities, and clubs. Students who engaged in more sponsored college activities were more likely to withdraw. One interpretation of this result is that students who participate in many activities in their first year can be overemphasizing their social involvement, which can result in withdrawal. This interpretation assumes that, in order to make a satisfactory adjustment to college, students must first address the tasks of establishing relationships with roommates and hallmates, developing independent living skills, mastering self-management of time for studying, and so forth. If students are involved in many sponsored social activities, they are more likely to devote insufficient effort to addressing the more basic needs they must meet in order to be truly integrated into the college environment.

This reasoning does not imply that participation in extracurricular activities during college is generally undesirable. We, along with most others (Tinto 1987), think that some participation in college-sponsored activities generally facilitates integration into the campus community. The finding does, however, raise a question regarding the wisdom of participating in many extracurricular activities in the first year. Another consideration is that the measure of participation encompassed a variety of activities. A factor analysis of the participation measure indicates that activities can be subgrouped. For example, one subgroup of items pertains to activities such as sing/sign choir and religious groups, and another subgroup pertains to athletic programs. Different kinds of participation may relate differentially to achieving a high grade point average and to persistence at college. For example, preliminary results suggest that participation in special interest groups, such as the sing/sign choir, is associated with attaining high grades.

As is the case for NTID, lack of social integration into the college community appears to be a major reason for withdrawal by deaf students in mainstream settings. Interviews with students who left mainstream programs indicate that many felt they had little or no social life at college. For those living at home, social interaction was limited by the nature of the commuter school. In addition, students spent almost all their free time studying and preparing for class and had little time for social activities. Because of difficulties in communication, deaf students had difficulty making friends with hearing students, as the following quotation attests:

> Social life . . . lousy, lousy, lousy . . . we'd smile at each other. They [hearing students] know that I'm deaf . . . they don't sit down and really get down and talk like [they would ask] 'How are you feeling, how is school, how many sisters and brothers do you

have' . . . tell some jokes and stuff . . . [then] some of the hearing people might come up . . . and they sit there talking and all of a sudden I'm out of the picture . . . then I'll leave and I'll say, 'I'll see ya later' and I can tell just by their expression, their body language, and their movement that they're more fascinated with hearing than me.

(Walter, Foster and Elliot 1987, p. 14)

Furthermore, the deaf students said that there were few other deaf peers to turn to for friendship.

Commitment to College

Individual commitment to attaining a higher education bears importantly on whether students will persist or withdraw. Tinto (1987) makes a distinction between two-goal commitment, which pertains to the individual's educational and occupational goals, and institutional commitment, which refers to the commitment to achieving educational goals within a particular institution. Students who have a strong institutional commitment are more likely to be motivated to do the necessary work and to persist.

In their study to identify NTID freshmen who were likely to go on academic probation, Dagel and Dowaliby (1989) included two measures of institutional commitment. One dealt with negative effect regarding NTID, and comprised items such as, 'I wish I had never come to NTID' and 'I am not happy with my major at NTID.' The other measure was concerned with difficulty at NTID, and included items such as 'I have difficulty paying my expenses to attend NTID' and 'I have difficulty understanding my teachers at NTID.' Students with greater negative affect and greater perceived difficulty at NTID were more likely to go on academic probation than students who had more positive institutional commitments.

Scherer and Walter (1988) also found that institutional commitment was an important factor in their interviews of students in the process of withdrawing from NTID. The most frequently cited reasons for withdrawal were lack of motivation, need for a 'break,' and uncertainty about a career. The responses of these students suggested that this lack of commitment tarnished attitudes toward academic work and classes. Furthermore, the lack of motivation may also have been related to the low utilization of special services that could have most helped them, such as tutoring and counseling.

PROGRAMMING TO INCREASE PERSISTENCE

Much of our understanding of how the four factors: pre-college background, academic integration, social integration, and institutional commitment affect persistence/withdrawal can be applied to college programs to increase persistence. Special programs include admissions screening, basic skill development, career development, early identification, and support services.

Admission Screening

Improving retention of students in college begins by admitting students who match the expectations of the college. Too often programs are concerned with attracting students to the college or university with little thought to the fit between the needs of the student and the expectations of the environment. Contributing to the problem is the 'open door' policy of many community college programs in the United States. These practices are a major reason for the preponderance of what has been termed 'revolving college doors' (Lenning, Sauer, and Beal 1980). It is our feeling that programs have a responsibility to analyze the college environment in sufficient detail to be able to determine the types of students most likely to be successful at their institution. To admit students who are known to have little chance for success wastes resources of the institution, and reduces the lifetime earning power of the individual by both charging them for attending college, and denying them the opportunity to enter the labor market on a full-time basis.

Basic Skill Development

For deaf students entering college, there are a number of variables that may mitigate against their integration into the social and academic systems of the institution. The most notable is their communication and academic achievement skills, especially in the areas of mathematics, science, and reading. For example, Franklin (1988) found that the majority of his subjects who were enrolled in community college programs read below a fifth-grade level. The pervasive low achievement of many deaf persons desiring to enroll in college requires that colleges and universities provide some form of special programming to improve basic mathematics, reading, and science skills. This programming is necessary in order for most deaf students to graduate from their programs.

Career Development

Important reasons for leaving college are the lack of educational and occupational goals and the absence of commitment to the particular institution. In order for such commitment to happen, it is important that students have a sense of direction in their life, and a reason for going to college. As a result, it is important that deaf students develop, first of all, some sense of career objectives, and second, that they select a major in college in keeping with this career area. From research carried on at NTID, the most frequent reason given for withdrawing from college was the inability to decide on a major area of study (Scherer and Walter 1988). While this is typically a difficult decision for most young people, it is an area that is especially difficult for deaf persons because, in addition to lowered achievement levels, they often also have limited knowledge about various occupational possibilities, which reduces their ability to make informed choices about careers. As a result, it is essential that colleges serving the needs of deaf students provide some form of career counseling in order to assist them in making the critical career decisions necessary to further develop commitment to a major area of study.

Early Identification and Intervention

Since the majority of college withdrawals generally occur during the first year of attendance, it is important that close attention be paid to newly admitted students. Many deaf students have the same difficulties that Lee (1974) has described for disadvantaged students who exited from a community college. Such students (a) tend to be poorly motivated; (b) are unrealistic about the time required to complete a degree; (c) have difficulties in developing a positive self image; (d) are poor readers; and (e) depend more on real life experience than on symbolic experience in the learning process. As a result, it is critical that close monitoring occur during the first year of college attendence and that counseling be initiated immediately when difficulties are observed. Generally, problems arise when a student begins to miss class or grades begin to suffer. It is desirable to put in place an 'early warning' system in order to closely monitor progress during the early stages of the postsecondary experience (Dagel and Dowaliby 1989).

Support Services

Traditionally, one thinks of providing for the ready transfer of information in the classroom as the only area in which support services are needed by deaf students in the college setting. However, when one considers that deaf college students generally have little experience in other matters related to college life, there is a need for additional support. Areas such as financial aid, counseling, academic advising, health services, and extracurricular activities all demand support and options for deaf students if they are to become integrated into the college environment. For both academic and social integration, comfortable, effective communication with others is critical. Since deaf persons vary considerably in their communication preferences, individualized adaptations are necessary. Many rely almost completely on sign language for understanding; others rely on speech and sign language together. Still others rely entirely on speech, but need special aids such as FM systems, and need the speaker to produce mouth movements that are easy to lipread. By not receiving support in these areas a deaf student is put at risk of becoming isolated in the college environment and thus in danger of dropping out.

CONCLUSIONS

More deaf students graduated from college in the United States in 1987 than were enrolled altogether just 25 years ago (Walter 1989). Yet this number is only about 30 per cent of those who attempt postsecondary studies. In light of this estimated 70 per cent withdrawal rate, we must ask whether the special needs of deaf students are being met in a manner that provides them equal opportunity to succeed at the postsecondary level.

In trying to understand the needs of deaf students it should first be noted that the same general factors are important in the persistence and withdrawal of deaf and hearing students. For both groups, students who have academic skills and intellectual interests that match the requirements and orientation of the institution are more likely to experience academic integration than those whose skills and interests do not match. It also is important for students to make an adequate adjustment to the environment and to feel socially integrated into the campus community. Furthermore, for both deaf and hearing students, personal goals of completing higher education, together with academic integration, affect institutional commitment.

The greater this commitment, the more likely the student is to persist until completion of a degree.

What is different about deaf students, relative to the 'typical' hearing ones, is that they most often require special social environments and modifications in the academic environment in order to experience social and academic integration. Many deaf students regard contact with a large number of deaf peers as the best opportunity for friendship, dating, and interaction. In this way, deaf students are similar to other ethnic groups. With respect to academic integration, many deaf students do not possess the mathematics, science, and reading skills to function effectively in 'traditional' classes designed primarily for hearing students, even if sign language, interpreting, and notetaking services are provided.

While most programs provide support services of interpreting and notetaking, these services are built upon the notion that deaf students can be 'made equal' to hearing students if they are provided access to regular classroom communication through interpreters, notetakers, and tutors. Once provided these services, deaf students are expected to compete successfully with their hearing peers. If students are not successful, failure is often attributed to a lack of innate ability or effort rather than to the educational environment or method of instruction. Consideration is rarely made of the fact that the provision of lecture notes or sign language interpretation for lectures does not necessarily mean that the 'barrier' created by lower achievement and experiential levels has been breached. It may be necessary to modify texts and instructional materials and provide a comprehensive battery of compensatory and remedial programs to accommodate the needs of deaf students.

In a similar fashion, the communication needs of most deaf persons make it extremely difficult for them to take part in the usual campus social activities of hearing students. Therefore, even though a deaf person has access to college, he/she may remain isolated both socially and educationally from the mainstream. Such isolation, or lack of integration into the educational community, may be an important cause of attrition among deaf persons attending college. This point especially relates to the access students have to the social life of an institution. Research by Walter (1989) points out that very few programs providing support for deaf students make provisions for the social aspects of college life.

Care must be taken to ensure that students are given the opportunity for social interactions. In-depth interviews (Foster and Elliot

1986) with students transferring to NTID from other colleges consistently indicate three reasons for leaving their previous college: inability to communicate with teachers; inadequate support services; and limited opportunities for social interaction with peers. It is integration into the total educational community that we contend must be the goal of any program providing support services to deaf persons. We must look beyond the 'official' services provided by the institution on behalf of deaf students. We must ask whether the academic and social needs of students are being met within the context of institutional environments where the typical hearing student to deaf student ratio is 500 to 1 or worse, and work toward achieving the best possible fit between the deaf student and the college he or she has decided to attend.

REFERENCES

Bean, J.P. (1982) 'Conceptual models of student attrition: how theory can help the institutional researcher,' in E. Pascarella (ed.), *Studying Student Attribution*. San Francisco: Jossey-Bass.

Bean, J.P. and Metzner, B.F. (1985) 'A conceptual model of non-traditional undergraduate student attrition,' *Review of Educational Research*, 55, 485–540.

Dagel, D. and Dowaliby, F. (1989) 'Third-week prediction of incoming postsecondary deaf student probation/suspension,' *Journal of the American Deafness and Rehabilitation Association*, 22, 53–6.

Foster, S. and Elliot, L. (1986) *The best of both worlds: Interviews with NTID transfer students*. Technical Report. Rochester, NY: Rochester Institute of Technology.

Franklin, E.L. (1988) 'Attrition and retention of hearing-impaired community college students,' Unpublished dissertation. Lawrence, KA: University of Kansas.

Innes, C. (1985) 'The national project on higher education for deaf students: Opinion survey,' in J. Gartner (ed.), *Proceedings of the 1985 AHSSPPE Conference*. Atlanta, GA.

Lang, H. and Stinson, M. (1982) 'Career education and occupational status of deaf persons: Concepts, research and implications,' in J. Christiansen and J. Egelston-Dodd (eds) *Socio-economic status of the deaf population*. Washington, DC: Gallaudet University.

Lee, G,E. (1974) *A comparative study of the persistence and academic achievement of "Project 60" and regularly enrolled students at Middlesex Community College* (Technical Report). Bedford, MA: Middlesex Community College.

Lenning, O., Sauer, K., and Beal, P. (1980) *Student retention strategies*. Washington, DC: American Association for Higher Education.

Pascarella, E. and Chapman, D. (1983) 'A multi-institutional path analytic validation of Tinto's model of college withdrawal,' *American Educational Research Journal*, 20, 87–102.

Pascarella, E.R. and Terenzini, P. (1979) 'Interaction effects in Spady's and

Tinto's conceptual models of college dropouts,' *Sociology of Education,* 52, 197–210.

Pascarella, E.R. and Terenzini, P. (1980) 'Predicting persistence and voluntary dropout decisions from theoretical models,' *Journal of Higher Education,* 51, 60–75.

Rawlings, B.A., Karchmer, M., and DeCaro, J. (1988) *College career programs for the deaf.* Washington, DC: Gallaudet University and Rochester, NY: Rochester Institute of Technology.

Scherer, M.J. and Walter, G.G. (1988) *Student-reported satisfaction with college and reasons for college withdrawal* (Technical Report). Rochester, NY: Rochester Institute of Technology.

Spady, W. (1970) 'Dropouts from higher education: An interdisciplinary review and synthesis,' *Interchange,* 1, 64–85.

Stinson, M.S., Scherer, M.J., and Walter, G.G. (1987) 'Factors affecting persistence of deaf college students,' *Research in Higher Education,* 27, 244–58.

Tinto, V. (1975) 'Dropout from higher education: A theoretical synthesis of recent research,' *Review of Educational Research,* 45, 89–125.

Tinto, V. (1987) *Leaving college.* Chicago, IL: University of Chicago Press.

Walter, G.G. (1989) 'Adherence of postsecondary programs to the CEASD principles basic to the establishment and operation of postsecondary education for deaf students,' Paper presented at the International Symposium on Postsecondary Education for the Deaf, Edmonton, Alberta, Canada.

Walter, G.G., Foster, S.B., and Elliot, L. (1987) 'Attrition and accommodation of hearing-impaired college students in the US,' Paper presented at the Tenth National Conference of the Association on Handicapped Students Service Programs in Postsecondary Education. Washington, DC.

Welsh, W.A., Walter, G.G., and Riley, D. (1988) *Value of a college education* (Technical Report). Rochester, NY: Rochester Institute of Technology.

Welsh, W.A., Walter, G.G., and Riley, D. (1989) *Earnings of deaf college graduates in the United States* (Technical Report). Rochester, NY: Rochester Institute of Technology.

Personal Commentary

Dianne Brooks

I became deaf when I was 12 years old. At that time I was attending a public school program in Washington, DC, where I grew up. When I lost my hearing very suddenly I was not aware of any services or programs of support for deaf students. I didn't really consider myself deaf. I was 'having problems' with my hearing, so when I became deaf it was just natural that I stayed in the public schools where I was. I did not know anything about sign language interpreters or anything like that, so the only thing I did differently was to ask people if I could sit in front of them or if I could sit in front of the classroom and do lipreading the best that I could. By the time I was ready to graduate from high school I finally heard about a program for the deaf, Gallaudet College, and I was encouraged by my family to go there. I was worried about the environment of deafness, but I eventually decided that I would apply because for me it was just another college, and I was very excited about going to college. So I applied and was accepted as a freshman.

I grew up with an understanding that I lost my hearing suddenly and therefore probably over time I might get my hearing back, so with this lack of understanding I began attending classes at Gallaudet. Also, I knew nothing about deafness, and nothing about sign language. It was a very traumatic experience because two things were happening in my life at that time. First, I was coming face to face with my deafness for the first time, and second, I was entering a whole new experience that was really somewhat frightening to me.

I didn't do very well personally or socially the first couple of years there because I lacked really good sign language skills and there were so few of us at the college at that time who were not proficient in sign language. There were maybe 10 or 15 of us new persons who were really feeling awkward and out of place. We all found it very difficult to adapt and be accepted into that cultural deaf world. Eventually I left Gallaudet and went to Howard University in Washington, DC. The reason for going there was feeling that I didn't belong at Gallaudet even though I couldn't hear, I still did not become integrated into the environment so I made the transition back to where I felt I belonged.

However, going to Howard University did not solve all my problems, because I was still deaf. At Howard they knew nothing about deafness and provided no support. I learned early on, after I became deaf, to take responsibility for my deafness, and explain it to teachers, to classmates, in order to have them understand what my needs were in the classroom: to have someone take notes for me, to have the teacher let me sit in the front of the class and to stand directly in front of me. To the best of my knowledge I was the only deaf person on the campus and no one ever approached me about my being deaf. Each teacher took it in stride. There were some good attitudes, some not so good attitudes, but I had only met my first other deaf person a few months before I entered Gallaudet so I was in some ways at home in that environment. I still felt the same amount of stress and pressure because of my deafness and the pressure for academic achievement. I didn't have time for socializing or feeling that I belonged, everything became focused on the academic and trying to understand what I was missing in the classroom.

As I reflect now on my experiences in each of these school settings, I think that the years after I lost my hearing were probably the worst years of my school life because I went back to the same classroom a few days after I became deaf to the same friends and the same teacher. I was 12 years old at the time and the thing that struck me the most was the attitude change of those people who knew me, joked around with me, taught me how to be a very good student. Academically I was in school getting B's, that kind of thing. Those people who I knew who had socialized with me, interacted with me, all of a sudden started to slight me and I never was able to understand what was wrong, as if I had something contagious. I became the butt of a lot of jokes and teasing and other things, and most of all the teachers lost patience with me because they were very insensitive, they liked to have the class moving at their own pace. I became a little bit of a thorn in their sides.

The first year of junior high was probably the longest year in my life, but I think a turning point for me in dealing with my deafness. I was in academics with a college-bound group of students and I had a Latin teacher, the kind of person that liked to have the students sit in perfect rows and no clutter on the desk, and most of the day's activities were a recitation on all of the Latin translation. She would call on each person to translate a part in the book and then give you a grade. She called on me one day and I was looking down at the time, so another student tapped me to tell me the teacher was talking to me. When I looked up, she was looking at me very exasperated in a way, and in front of about 34 kids in the classroom she told me she didn't see why I was in that class, I couldn't hear anything, I couldn't understand anything, she didn't really feel that I was going to make it. That was the first time in my life someone had insulted me because of my deafness. At the same time she really hurt my feelings and humiliated me in front of all of the students. I think that day I became a little bit reborn, because when I got through the emotional humiliation I decided one thing – that no one would ever humiliate me again because of my hearing loss, and I was determined that I was not going to drop out of that class, that I had a right to be there.

I think part of that attitude came from my family background because we valued education. From the time I learned to read at a very early age, my family, mostly my mother, always encouraged us kids to study. I think my persistence in the academic environment was because I knew, regardless of what happened to me during the day, that I had family support. I also had a sense of value of the education and I wanted my family to be proud of me.

That doesn't mean that I didn't have any adjustment problems, because I did. I had to learn how to accept the fact of my deafness. Each experience I had, each frustration I experienced, made me a little more confident, a little more determined. In the past I used to apologize to people because I couldn't hear, and then I realized that I had no need to apologize for something that I could not help, and I learned to be more assertive about my disability. I had previously not been able to tell people that I couldn't hear. It wasn't that I was pretending not to hear, I just wasn't using it. And then I became more confident at being able to say, 'I can't hear, would you actually look at me so I can lip read.'

Right now I have no problem saying that, but I think it is a matter of individual confidence, being able to say you're deaf and saying it with confidence, don't say it with shame or embarrassment, say that you need the person to slow down and look at you, be able to ask the person to write out something if the communication becomes really difficult. It took me a very long time to be able to admit that I need that kind of thing, a very long time.

I think that many deaf students coming to college go through similar adjustment crises. When I worked in Psychological Services we had many new students who came in going through this adjustment process. It's not just a communication issue, it's a personal, emotional issue. Who am I, where do I belong, who do I identify with, those are natural questions of the process. For the first time in their lives they come here and they see other deaf people and they have never had the oppor- tunity for socialization, and they're looking, and they're saying, 'Do I want to belong?' Some students make the transition, others do not. Some say they don't belong, they don't want to belong. Some feel that they come to college, and don't want to be associated with deafness, because that will affect their personal perception of who they are.

I think a lot of the motivation to persist in college goes back to the kind of incentive students have for enrolling in the first place. If it is a family value, or if there was someone in high school or outside of the family providing encouragement, then I think that college is a realistic goal for such students, and the issue – like for myself – is what to major in. The college must be supportive in helping with this decision-making process so that the students themselves can internalize the importance of getting through the educational experience.

Dianne Brooks holds a bachelor of science degree in psychology from Howard University and a master of science degree in counseling from Gallaudet University. She has held positions as counselor at Gallaudet University, chairperson of the Department of Psychological Services at Rochester Institute of Technology's National Technical Institute for the Deaf, a Peace Corps trainer, and adjunct member of the faculty of the Phillippine Normal College in Manila. Currently, Ms. Brooks is Manager of the NTID Department of Career Outreach and Admissions.

Part II

The environment of postsecondary educational programs for deaf students

One of the most commonly held assumptions about deaf postsecondary students is that their access to the learning environment is assured by providing them with an interpreter in class. Not only is this assumption incorrect, it is potentially dangerous, since those who hold it may mistakenly attribute the failure or withdrawal of deaf postsecondary students who have used interpreters to inadequacy of the student. We readily acknowledge that some deaf students, like hearing students, enter college without the skills required for success. However, it is very important that program planners and administrators understand fully the range of needs of deaf college students and the kinds of environmental accommodations which may be essential to their success. These needs, considerations and accommodations are the focus of discussion in Part II of this book.

Five areas are addressed in Chapters 4 through 8, each of which focuses on a different aspect of college life. Taken together, they can be used as a blueprint for designing a comprehensive postsecondary environment within which deaf students are viewed as having both *the same basic needs* for academic and social integration as their hearing peers and *special needs*, which reflect the challenges faced by deaf learners enrolled at 'culturally hearing' institutions. The ideas presented in these chapters are perhaps the most easily generalized to deaf populations in countries other than the US, since the concepts are grounded in the often universally shared experiences of deaf people. At the same time, the authors emphasize interaction between the individual and environment, a perspective which suggests that educational planners in other countries should consider the political, social and cultural climate of their institutions when developing strategies to improve the 'fit' between deaf students and the postsecondary programs they have elected to attend.

Given this guiding principle, what specific areas should be considered in creating a supportive postsecondary educational environment for deaf students? First, planners must begin with a thorough understanding of the characteristics and needs of deaf learners, including the backgrounds and experiences which these learners bring to college. As noted in Chapter 4, this knowledge can be used to develop curricula which empower deaf students through incorporation of collaborative learning activities and encouragement of intellectual independence. Second, a comprehensive resource system must be in place which maximizes deaf students' access to information, both within and outside the classroom. Chapter 5 includes a discussion of such a system, including necessary elements, effect of resources, and the need for student involvement in selecting from an array of possible services.

College life involves much more than classroom learning. Students mature, develop new personal as well as social skills, make friends, and interact with other students, faculty, and staff. They also often develop a strong sense of political awareness and identity during their college years. As illustrated in Chapters 6-8, postsecondary planners must consider these dimensions of college life and take steps to insure that deaf students have access to the kinds of co-curricular activities which enhance individual development in these areas. For example, the campus should be organized in such a way as to promote respect for individual differences, and administrative practices should be regularly examined to insure that physical, social and academic segregation of students does not occur. Student development programs should be designed with the goal of helping deaf students develop a strong sense of identity and self esteem. Participation and movement into leadership roles within student organizations should be facilitated. Political activism should be encouraged, both general civic participation, and involvement in specific issues which are relevant to membership in a minority group. Pervading each of these chapters is the idea that deaf role models are critical for student interaction and development, and should include deaf faculties, counselors, administrators, and student leaders.

In summary, the task of designing and administering a postsecondary environment within which deaf students enjoy truly equal participation is challenging and complex. It is not enough to put in place such an environment; routine program evaluation, 'accessibility audits' and critical analysis are also required. Lastly, program planners and administrators must maintain a clear vision of the goals of full integration and realization of individual potential.

Chapter 4

The deaf learner

Harry G. Lang and Bonnie Meath-Lang

INTRODUCTION

When teacher-researchers reflect on the learner in any situation, they are compelled to examine individual behavior as more than the following of some predetermined biological or psychological path. Educators are becoming less prone to define a common, predictable developmental pattern for all students, and less inclined to separate the objective from the personal. Content mastery of particular subjects, while important, is not the only consideration in current work. The interaction between the learner and the world is a topic receiving increasing scrutiny; for such interaction is critical in the formation of identity. We can see a growing awareness of the tension that exists between the self and the world, and between a student's self and others; achieving such understanding may be a primary task in the postsecondary years.

Young deaf adult learners, in particular, strive for increased intellectual and moral authority in a world fraught with misunderstanding, marginalization, and oppression. While pursuing mastery of academic content and professional goals in postsecondary programs, the young deaf adult must simultaneously seek knowledge about power, people, and culture. The dominant role of language and language development in the deaf person's educational history similarly demands exploration, reflection, and resolution. These sometimes-competing priorities for deaf learners in young adulthood are formidable ones. Yet, the perspectives of our students convince us that this work of learning to be-in-the-world is confronted courageously. As one of our deaf students has written:

> I know I have learned a lot lately, it's just this time of the year that I'm willing to learn everything all over again and start from there

to the rest of my life . . . . In fact, I went through a time of experimenting and never cared about school and life. Now I'm out of [that] and focus on myself, my life, school, learn to grow more and learn about anything again from now on – it was before Christmas of this past year when I started to grow up better, and have learned to deal with the cruel realities of life . . . .

Another student, Kim, wrote:

> I always wonder if my life in the future will be like now of what's happening to me. If that's true, how will am I ever going to find much time to take care of more things than I'm going through at this present of time? It scares me a little. I don't know what more to say – all I can say that will I survive real well and will I accomplish my dream one day in my life? I do not want work, work, worry, going though difficult time through the decisions and marriage, (only if I ever release my picky attitude . . .), and piles of responsibilities. Or I can simply climb up the mountain high and turn my life like an eagle – so free. However, I won't reach my dream the way I wanted it to happen, if I avoid the problems like going up the mountain.

Dialogue with young deaf adults provides a powerful text for both teachers and students to examine in exploring issues surrounding learning. The linguistic philosopher Mikhail Bakhtin (Todorov 1984; Bakhtin 1986; Whitson 1988) suggests that understanding one's *own* language, mind, and self comes from the interplay of these factors with the language of others. According to the principle Bakhtin calls 'transgredience,' the thoughts and language of others are reflected in and contrasted to our own. That formative dialogue may result in increasing awareness of similarities and differences, an intriguing idea when we reflect on the lives of deaf students. As Kim wrote in her dialogue journal:

> Can you give me a little of your advise [sic] if you ever experienced this while you were young looking into your life ahead? Did your dream ever come true, yet? If no, did it come out the way you wished? Mind if I become aware of your dreams?[1]

Kim initiated a conversation aimed at comparing and contrasting her life with the experiences of a trusted teacher. As we ponder her questions, and wonder if she could relate to the teacher's response, other questions intrude on our meditation. At the postsecondary level, many deaf students are bilingual in sign and a written/spoken language. How does that bilingualism shape and sort their world – and others' *being-in-the-world* with them? How do deaf students gain access to professional language, and participate visually in the language of 'the system?' How do deaf women and deaf minority students live and learn in the multiple cultures they cross? Unfortunately, there are no economical answers to these questions. The lack of a single 'solution,' however, is all to the good, if we are committed to principles of self-determination for the young women and men we teach. If we accept Bakhtin's idea, we may better understand deaf learners by simultaneously eliciting deaf students' views of their learning, and by examining current thinking on epistemological development in postsecondary education. Our students interact daily with teachers contributing to this thinking. Further, as Bakhtin would add, deaf students themselves are giving 'voice' to these ideas, and are creating their own diverse visions in the process of learning. Our assessment of these influences is derived as much from our dialogue with college-age deaf students as from theory. Following Bakhtin, we must, in the theories we pursue, reflect elements in the language of our students, and we would hope that some of their thoughts reflect ours as well.

At present, we see three dominant themes relating importantly to deaf students' learning in postsecondary environments: (a) the affirmation of reflective and phenomenological orientations in learning and in research on learning, (b) the influence of feminist inquiry on the construction of knowledge, especially in young adults, and (c) the more careful examination of the role of social and political consciousness in intellectual development. These themes are supported by associated work that has important implications for adult deaf students and their teachers. In this chapter, we explore these three orientations and describe their influence on current conceptions of learning. We do so in collaboration with deaf college students who are using writing as one of many tools for making sense of their experiences.

REFLECTIVE AND PHENOMENOLOGICAL ORIENTATIONS

In 1976, Floyd Matson warned of orientations to learning that were predicated on the idea that human beings were either machines or animals. The learner-as-machine idea led to models based on information processing; that is, input to the student would result in very similar or refined output. The assumption here, that the learning environment was largely in the school's control, was reflected for many years in mainstream education. Correspondingly, in programs serving deaf students, correct language models and imitation were also emphasized; a sense of control appeared to be more easily achieved, for the schooling was self-contained or institutional. Deaf and hearing students both were frequently referred to as 'products' of their programs. The second notion, that humans are animals, gave rise to an emphasis on behavioral modification in teaching and the idea of schools as laboratories. Both concepts disregard the fundamental element that makes us *human*, that is, the capacity to reflect.

Reflection on experience and bringing that experience to the classroom has gained increased credibility as a teaching and research tool over the last two decades. Part of this movement has been a reaction to the models mentioned above, but that is a very incomplete picture. The use of personal, biographical experience in the classroom is essential for students and teachers who are from different cultures and backgrounds. At the postsecondary level, the phrase 'experientially deprived,' often applied to deaf learners, is particularly inappropriate. We all have experiences. The *difference* of such experiences among teachers and students, however, suggests the need to elicit those of the students in relation to classroom content. Such a strategy is critical to connection and interpretation, and an important basis for dialogue. Examining how students reflect on their lives and actions also has provided researchers and teachers ways of charting the epistemological development of young adults.

The philosopher Husserl (1976) is generally said to have originated the notion of *phenomenology* as a discipline focused on describing how the world is experienced. Husserl's famous rule: '*Zu den Sachen*' is translated in two ways: 'let us return to the things themselves' or 'a return to what really matters.' The teacher-researcher interested in phenomenology tries to move beyond social norms and structures to essences in the life of the individual's *Lebenswelt*, or lived world. The phenomenological investigator uses interviews, journals, autobiography, and other life-material as data.

One educational researcher whose phenomenological methods have yielded important insights into the epistemological development of young adults is William Perry. His book, *Forms of Intellectual and Ethical Development in the College Years* (1970), is derived from in-depth interviews gathered from students each spring as they completed their undergraduate years at Harvard University. Perry discerned evidence of development in the interview data. When asked to reflect on various questions, students in the early phases of their college educations approached the questions from a position Perry termed *basic dualism*. They saw the world as black or white, good or evil, right or wrong, us or them. These students also tended to be passive toward teaching authority, viewing knowledge as a contained, finite commodity to be given to them by teachers certified with the truth. Gradually, students in Perry's investigation began to acknowledge *multiplicity*, an awareness that authorities may possess different viewpoints on the same question, and that 'right answers' are not always possible. When students began to express their own opinions, and were challenged to support them, the awareness of the multiplicity stage moved to active evaluation of academic knowledge. In what Perry refers to as *relativism*, the learner understands fully that knowledge is constructed, rather than given, not only in school but in other aspects of life as well.

While we must always be mindful that Perry's scheme was formulated from the words of privileged young men, it has been noted as a valuable reference point for the study of other groups as well (Belenky, Clinchy, Goldberger, and Tarule 1986).[2] Some of our deaf college students also echo the increasing sense of multiple perspectives and relativism identified by Perry. In a study of students' perceptions of audiological services (Rohland and Meath-Lang 1984), for example, a graduating student expressed an expansive and tolerant view of a painful past experience:

> I hope that the next time I have to take a hearing test with an audiologist, I hope he or she will have the patience with us because we deaf people have patience to take hearing tests over and over again for the rest of our lives. If people want to become audiologists, they need to understand our sensitivity and our behavior toward them because there are times when we hate to take those hearing tests. To some of us, a hearing test is not important, especially me. Audiologists are wonderful people to work with if they have the time and patience for us . . . .[3]

This student described initial feelings of anger and resistance at the time of his college orientation. He was a fourth-year student when he expressed the measured stance quoted above.

Specific situations, including the cultures in which a person interacts, also have a direct effect on the thinking of deaf learners.

Supporters of situated cognition (Brown, Collins, and Duguid 1989) maintain that some representation of these cultures by educators is critical. If the school does not in some way include work culture or social culture, for example, we cannot expect students effectively to generalize from education to other environments. If cultures other than a 'school culture' (including Deaf culture) are nowhere in evidence, the cognitive transitions will be made even more difficult, and a positive, broad relativism will be harder to achieve.

Brown, Collins, and Duguid (1989) also point out that for creative 'cognitive apprenticeship' to occur, legitimation of students' contexts and experiences must be acknowledged. Deaf postsecondary level students bring a variety of educational backgrounds, languages, cultures, family histories, and other experiences to college and vocational education. This variety of experiences gives them tools for problem solving that teachers can draw upon and use with the students in partnership. (This, of course, presupposes that teachers possess communication skills and techniques to probe the students' implicit and lived knowledge, to build on their strategies, and to offer alternatives.) In so doing, teachers affirm that learning involves more than simple rules and immutable laws. Learning involves, as Perry's phenomenological work suggests, an understanding of different, experienced situations and an evaluation of and respect for the varying ways situations can be approached.

The Process Orientation

Another major trend signifying a more reflective orientation to learning is a current focus on processes and problem solving. While content mastery is still seen as critical to competence in a rapidly changing technological world, there is growing acknowledgment that the *process* of learning is at least as important as the *product*. For deaf postsecondary-level students, this idea is particularly critical; for understanding and defining one's processes of learning is tied inextricably with access to *information*. If students understand how they can, for example, read more analytically or compute more accurately, the likelihood of being able to adapt to changing technology, job responsibility, and social mores is greater. Otherwise, graduates are merely provided with a narrow set of facts and skills that may be rendered obsolete in the next wave of invention.

It is difficult for any young adult to be patient in discerning one's process of learning. A student at Rochester Institute of Technology's

National Technical Institute for the Deaf wrote of a process writing class humorously:

> Some students thought this class was weird. Some joked that you must be lazy to write with us. They thought that was easy. Then they really were mad. They were working all the time. Ha! I'm nervous that you call us as 'writers' all the time, not as 'students' – but I like it, too. Now some of the other students say they never had so much writing in their folder. One girl was surprise that she can write 2 pages in class. She never wrote much before . . . . Sometimes I want you to give more vocabulary tests. Maybe I want an excuse to not write. What do you think?[4]

Analyzing and elucidating one's ways of writing, reading, problem solving, and evaluating do not have the same reassurance of the seemingly measurable gain of a collection of facts. Nonetheless, the emphasis on process approaches and problem solving in areas such as mathematics (Schoenfeld 1985) and writing (Elbow 1973, 1979) with young adults has gained increasing support as a means of developing a more useful, productive knowledge. Seminal work of this nature with deaf students at the postsecondary level (see, for example, Albertini and Meath-Lang 1986; Stone 1989) attests to the possibilities of using personal experience, situated cognition, and problem solving strategies to make knowledge more functional and explicit. Stone (1989) describes the importance of dialogue in particular reference to mathematics problem-solving with deaf students, demonstrating application of both the developmental psychology of Vygotsky (1978) and the pedagogies of Paulo Freire (1970) and other educators who proceed from student experience in the classroom:

> From a constructivist point of view, mathematical representations are not ideal forms to be found on the walls of caves. Instead they are the constructions of people, interacting with each other, and finally agreeing that such will be the mathematical representation of such and such. In this way, mathematical representations are not so different from spoken and written language, yet their use does not seem to be dependent on hearing in the same way that the use of spoken and written language is dependent upon hearing speech . . . . The research on mathematical achievement of deaf students has demonstrated that there is no direct link between the ability to use mathematical representations and the ability to use spoken and written language. However, the extent to which

mathematical representations are consensual and developed out of interactions among people is not all that different from the way in which language develops. It would seem that if we wanted to enhance an individual's ability to understand and use mathematical representations then it would make sense to provide him or her with opportunities to interact with others who understand and use those representations.

(Stone 1989: 565)

FEMINIST INQUIRY AND THE CONSTRUCTION OF KNOWLEDGE

The expansion of thinking about the various ways persons approach knowledge, and the legitimation of those varieties of understanding, has been a major contribution of feminist inquiry and research. Rooted in autobiography, narrative, particularity, and concern for collaboration, the methods and central issues of gender studies contain important implications for teacher-researchers involved with other cultures and groups, including deaf learners. In the last 15 years, feminist and gender studies in education have come to represent an important perspective on teaching and learning. Major research, including Belenky, Clinchy, Goldberger, and Tarule's *Women's Ways of Knowing* (1986), Gilligan's *In a Different Voice* (1982), and Grumet's *Bitter Milk* (1989) point to the importance of redefining educational practice, authority, and knowledge itself. Indeed, in such works the problem of sexism is viewed as fundamental to the world's environmental and arms crises; politics, culture, and economics reflect unequal, stereotyped support of traditional gender relationships. Understandably, writers see schools contributing to these issues through gender-based rules, curriculum, and evaluation (Pinar 1988; Macdonald and Macdonald 1988). Feminist inquiry proposes that we must understand the ways in which boys and girls, women and men, come to know what they know, in order to provide a more complete, accessible education – not to mention ways of working together for a more just society.

There are a number of descriptions outlining the differences in male and female learning, or orientations to learning. The Macdonalds (1988), for example, draw upon Bakan (1966) and other social-psychological theorists in distinguishing between the agency-oriented personality (often male), and the communally oriented one (often female). They note that schools and school systems have historically rewarded the agency-learner for intellectual independence, dominance, and autonomy. The communally oriented learner has been neglected or viewed as dependent; often, perhaps, because it is more difficult to evaluate a team member than an individual. These writers call for a redirection of pedagogy to include, if not emphasize, collaborative, community-oriented, related work in formal educational contexts. These have been seen in the past as 'feminine' modes of work, but are gaining credibility in an increasingly complex world aware of the need to approach its problems collaboratively, from a variety of disciplines.

There are other ways in which writers have characterized the differences between 'masculine' and 'feminine' modes of learning, knowing, evaluating, and communicating. In addition to Bakan's (1966) notion of communal orientation, Gilligan (1982) proposes the idea that moral responses of men and women are made heeding a voice of justice or a voice of care; and that these are frequently gender-specified through socialization, with boys and men putting a priority on justice, women affirming care. Belenky and her colleagues (1986), building on Gilligan's model, speak of the traditional separate knowing, a position focusing on rules and analyses, and connected knowing, an orientation toward relationship. In the Belenky, Clinchy, Goldberger, and Tarvie (1986) study, interviews with women found that both orientations were represented. The separate knowers were often women who attended elite, traditional, patriarchal academic programs, influenced by male professors.

Interestingly, many writers who use feminist perspectives on inquiry regard these contradictions and differences as profound but reconcilable. Like Belenky, others note that these differing orientations can be present in both men and women, although their roots can be traced to differences in biology, socialization, and political power. Some writers, such as Pagano (1988), argue that certain 'oppositions' have been imposed on us erroneously (by Freud and others); that there is no conflict, for example, between nurturance and authority. The problem, as Pagano and others suggest, may lie in restrictive thinking – about production and reproduction, the nature of 'certifiable' knowledge, the value of subjective and objective judgments, and the relative importance of men's and women's work.

Affirming Connected Thinking

One implication of feminist inquiry is that postsecondary education should involve the search for personal connection to what is learned – knowledge that connects the knower to the object or person or idea known. In order to do so, it is necessary for the learner to engage in a variety of tasks, discussions, and types of reflection centered on how one might live and learn given particular experiences, such as the experience of being deaf.

While this appears rather obvious at first glance, it is contrary to some educational experiences of present-day, postsecondary-level deaf students. Many of these students report, for example, that the 'hearing world' has been described repeatedly to them, as a metaphor, goal, and object of desire (Meath-Lang, Caccamise, and Albertini 1982). It is clear that describing the world in this way potentially impedes connection and implicitly excludes the deaf person. There is a need to use texts and materials developed by and about deaf people, specifically those in which education and coming to knowledge are highlighted. The use of such text is especially important in mainstream settings, where deaf students may have minimal interactions with other deaf students and teachers. Interacting with the words and presence of deaf people is crucial for these students.

The Importance of Collaboration

Following the work by Bakan and the Macdonalds cited at the beginning of this section, a second notion found in feminist inquiry is that knowledge is constructed through collaboration. Such inquiry has heightened interest in cooperation vs. competition and working for community good vs. individual recognition. While the experience of the individual learner is certainly elicited and utilized in communally oriented classrooms, that experience is firmly embedded in dialogue. The dialogue that constitutes the text of these classrooms has been currently redefined as teacher–student and peer collaboration. Indeed, the school or class is viewed, through this lens, as a community of learners, accepting responsibility for assisting others in their education. Such communities have been described with particular reference to the learning of writing and mathematics at the National Technical Institute for the Deaf and Gallaudet University (Albertini and Meath-Lang 1986; Staton, Shuy, Peyton, and Reed 1988; Peyton 1990; Stone 1988). These studies parallel a growing body of mainstream literature that asserts that learning is a collection of participatory, guided experiences, where, through mutual activity and dialogue, teachers and students come to share and deepen cognitive functions (Vygotsky 1978).

For genuine classroom collaboration to take place, access to communication is a primary concern, and must be a goal for postsecondary programs accepting deaf students. Interestingly, there have been collaborative learning projects at some colleges and universities, where teachers and peers were tutored in sign language in exchange for content tutoring. While this is a positive statement and strategy, such programs should not be used as a substitute for institutional support of sign language development and/or interpreting services.

Finding 'Voice'

Piaget (1951), Vygotsky (1978), and Luria (1981) have affirmed the critical importance of dialogue in validating the child or adolescent as knower and in contributing to the development of a reflective 'inner speech.' Educators of deaf persons have applied these concepts to teaching, encouraging rehearsal, imaginary monologues and dialogues, and articulated manipulation of objects in a variety of ways. It is entirely consistent with the principles of cognition espoused by these psychologists and educators to build on the ideas with the conception of *voice* in work with young adult learners.

At first glance, the voice metaphor might appear a totally inappropriate one for use with deaf students. Deaf persons themselves, however, are telling us that we should not reach a hasty conclusion. Spontaneous use of the voice metaphor has been used in current and historical work by deaf writers in the Deaf Community such as Padden and Humphries (1988) and Jackson (1895) to indicate emerging cultural and political consciousness, the awareness of bilingual/bicultural people of the repertoire of voices, registers, and languages they have mastered in order to survive. We have found, in addition to spontaneous use of the term 'voice,' that postsecondary-level deaf students are remarkably attuned to the struggle to find a voice, and are capable of defining that search as a cognitive act.

In studies by Albertini, Meath-Lang, and Harris (1987) and Meath-Lang and Albertini (1989), the term 'voice' was put before college-age deaf students in writing classes. Because of the preponderance of the term 'voice' in current writing texts, the teacher-researchers were curious about whether the word had any meaning or value in discussion of writing by deaf people. Without explanation, the young deaf adults were asked what they thought voice related to writing might be. The responses were, for the most part, thoughtful and extraordinarily perceptive. Indeed, the students' notions mirrored those of professional writers.

Students viewed voice as a way to express three basic ideas: that voice was an inner guide; that voice was an expression of personality; and that voice was an individual or political message-to-the-world. We provide an example of each of these below:

> Sometimes I feel like the voice in my head were talking to me. It is usually about good and evil. Like when I was about to do the evil things, the good things in my head tells me not to, 'It is evil if you do this.' It is like thinking of what is right or wrong to do that.... Sometimes I feel like God had put His voices in my head to communicate with me like telling me to do the right thing instead of the evil things. I am a little confused if it was God who controlled my behavior with His voices or just my own voice in my head.... it is like there is a different person which doesn't exist talking to me. I wonder if it is my soul.

> The voice mean to me that when someone is writing on the papers, most of the time, the paper has the voice of that person who wrote. Let suppose when we know someone very well and that person write us the letter without their name on it. When we read that letter and start think who have those feeling, expression, habit of say. All sudden we will know that person who wrote that letter. It can be connected with person's voice to feeling, expression on the paper.

> In the play about disabled people called 'One Voice,' which I was in, people would be aware of how selfish they have, but [different] voices can guide us to be together in a one world....

These categories mirror the thinking of writers as diverse as T. S. Eliot, Virginia Woolf, and Eudora Welty. The definitions of voice proposed by these 18- to 21-year-old deaf students testify to the ability to think metaphorically, inferentially, and authoritatively. Further, they relate such notions directly to their own experiences, forming a relationship to the word-as-object in the way writers advocating 'connected knowing' suggest.

SOCIAL AND POLITICAL CONSCIOUSNESS

As pointed out in the previous section, well-intentioned educators may be making efforts to present reality to the student when they discuss 'the hearing world'; but in so doing they have denied another reality – the student's particular relationship to a world that will never be 'hearing' while he or she is not. The metaphor of 'the hearing world' is facile and incomplete. It may be more productive to engage students in dialogue to elicit, define, and reflect on the various 'worlds' they inhabit: cultural worlds, professional worlds, dream worlds – and to encourage them through writing, career development activities, and discussions of ethical questions to clarify their roles or degree of participation in such worlds. In this course of action, it is all the more important to elicit, consider, and define the deaf learner's 'voices' of teachers as they explore literary, psychological, political, and educational landscapes.

For the purpose of this discussion on social and political consciousness among deaf students, we might borrow a more appropriate metaphor that has been used often in discussions of the education of marginalized learners, particularly with respect to reflections on societal change. In *The Pedagogy of the Oppressed* (1970), Paulo Freire describes the Brazilian peasants as a 'culture of silence,' a class of people without a political voice; and in his call for social change, he emphasizes the importance of dialogue between oppressed people and the authorities. Freire believes such dialogue in the quest of equal opportunity, particularly with an emphasis on the active involvement of the 'culture of silence,' is the essential way for social change to be lasting.

Similar use of the metaphor of silence and voice is provided by Belenky, Clinchy, Goldberger, and Tarule in *Women's Ways of Knowing* (1986). These authors write of a category of 'silent women' who are self-described as 'mindless' and 'voiceless' with respect to external authority. Those identified as belonging to this group of learners are blindly obedient to authority, lack confidence, and feel disconnected. They are characterized by their own perception that they are often seen but never heard. These 'silent women' have drawn abstract, but explicit and startling parallels to deafness and muteness in their autobiographies. They see themselves as voiceless intellects.

As marginalized learners, the metaphor of silence is no less applicable for young deaf men and women in postsecondary educational environments; and the Freirian emphasis on dialogue with 'authorities' is particularly relevant to a discussion of teaching and learning. That deaf learners comprehend the importance of dialogue was made apparent to the 'authorities' at Gallaudet University in 1988 when students demanded greater representation of deaf persons on the Board of Trustees, and called for a deaf president of the University. Challenge to authority is evidence of increased under- standing that knowledge is constructed, not given.

Dialogue can take many forms, both in the context of classroom learning and in the arena of societal change. The common thread, however, is the sense of membership in a community. In the postsecondary-level classroom, it is too common to find the deaf learner isolated by the concommitants of deafness, left disconnected from the community of inquiry of peers and professors. The relatively low incidence of deafness among postsecondary-level learners makes it highly improbable that most institutions of higher education will have a critical mass of such students in a given classroom to be able to establish their own community of inquiry. Reflecting on his days in college, one deaf adult wrote: 'Today, I realize that open and free-flowing communication was missing as I grew up. Hence, I am now more insistent that others sign while talking. . . . It has become important to me, to the point of being fanatic, to have access to ideas and thoughts and to choose conversations as do hearing people.'[6]

This brings us to the crucial question that underlies the discussion of all of these issues: How does a college or university educator, whether familiar or not with deafness as an educational condition, promote the most effective communication possible in situations involving deaf learners? To the less-experienced reader, this may at first appear to be a purely logistical dilemma, the solution being an interpreter or other resource person to facilitate the process of communication. Access to information, however, regardless of the way it is accomplished, does not assure dialogue in its truest form; nor does it guarantee collaborative learning and the development of voice. It does not even assure learning of the basic course content. How then does an educator interested in these goals establish appropriate conditions for deaf learners in a post-secondary-level program? Again, there are no simple answers to such a complex question. But, in terms of political and social consciousness, we do have suggestions from successful deaf learners on possible approaches to this challenge.

The Deaf Student as Change Agent

In the various analyses of the struggles for intellectual voice among marginalized learners, including women and minorities, the authors, in effect, call for learners to serve as change agents in redirecting their destinies. Whether marginalized or not, the need is universal — we must encourage in students the ability to be self-directed learners. For the deaf postsecondary student, the first step toward effective dialogue and self-directed learning is the identification of communicative and attitudinal barriers that may inhibit his or her own learning. In acting on this information collaboratively with peers and/or professionals, the student becomes a 'change agent.'

During a working conference sponsored by the American Association for the Advancement of Science (AAAS) in 1978, deaf science students and deaf scientists participated with people having sensory and physical disabilities in a two-day session to identify obstacles to their learning science in higher education environments. The information collected at this conference may be generalized to any field of learning (Redden, Davis, and Brown 1979). First, 'barriers' associated with communication and access to information were described (including, for example, such situations as foreign language lessons available only on audiotapes). Second, there were financial barriers associated with the extra costs for deaf learners in need of resources such as interpreters. Third, regardless of the physical or sensory disability, the conference participants agreed that the most formidable barrier to successful learning in postsecondary programs was that of attitude. The deaf participants in this working conference described various forms of attitude that they had to face while attempting to become self-directed learners.

These barriers included stereotyping, spread of effect, and patronizing attitudes. The first is the tendency to generalize that all deaf learners are alike. The second was described as problematic in that teachers believed deaf students, by virtue of being deaf, were not capable of learning physics, for example, or even to think for themselves. Teachers often talked *to* interpreters, rather than *to* the deaf students *through* interpreters. Patronizing, or exhibiting an attitude of condescension toward another, takes place in many forms, often unintentional, but almost always inhibiting to the deaf learner in pursuit of communal orientation and dialogue. For many deaf students in college, there is another barrier associated with deafness as a cultural phenomenon. As explained by many deaf college students and faculty at an all-day convocation on 'Attitudes Toward Deafness' at the National Technical Institute for the Deaf at Rochester Institute of Technology in 1988, there is a great deal of unintentional patronizing that occurs when teachers lack awareness of the cultural dimensions of deafness (Lang and DeCaro 1991). The convocation, a response to a student memo challenging these attitudes, was successful in raising the political and social consciousness of both students and teachers. Young deaf adults challenged for breaking down attitudes that inhibit learning, as shown in the following excerpts from the NTID convocation presentations:

> Most importantly, no matter what, I want to emphasize this, no matter what, do not limit or put down students' dreams or goals like I was put down [in wanting to enter a more challenging major]. The USA is a land of opportunity. Let us grab that chance. Don't tell us we can't do it. Let that person find out for himself, if he can't.

> I think often deaf students are brought up always to be learning from faculty and staff, and often, we don't realize that you can learn from us as well. So, I think it's a great idea to be together to learn from each other so that we can learn from you and you can learn from us. Then maybe we can realize what's going on and we can learn from each other and be more motivated.

> Before I came to NTID, I didn't know anything concerning Deaf Culture. I was brought up in a hearing world and then in just one year, I learned a lot. I'm sure that there are some teachers that work here, they've been here 10 years and still don't know that much about the Deaf Culture. It's really important to get in association with the deaf students.

Deaf faculty members also expressed their views on the need for dialogue and collaborative learning. As one explained:

> We need to make sure we understand what our students need. It's possible that there is a relationship between the expectations of students and teachers and their ability to understand the students in the classroom. I suspect that when teachers don't understand the students . . . that becomes a one-way structure, and the expectations are then lowered.

Dr. I. King Jordan, first deaf president of Gallaudet University, joined the NTID faculty and staff for this convocation and he, too, described his personal experiences with unintentional patronizing:

> I worked for years and years, I earned my B.A., M.A., and Ph.D., worked as a faculty member, worked as an administrator. Now I'm president of a university. [Still, when I meet a person,] what does that person want to talk about? My speech. 'You really speak well,' the person said to me. That's very patronizing . . . I try in a very friendly way to explain that . . . there are a lot of things about me that I think are [more] important.

Dr. Jordan also talked of attitudes toward American Sign Language (ASL) as 'poor English' held by those who do not recognize ASL as a language in itself. He noted that such terms as 'deficient' and 'impaired,' which are often applied to deaf students, are not helpful to the development of self-esteem. He concludes:

> One of the basic laws of attitudes is that the first step in attitude change is a higher level of awareness. When you begin to learn more about the community or the people or the thing that you have a negative attitude about, then the more you learn, the easier it is to change your attitude into a more positive attitude.

While a detailed discussion of attitudes is beyond the scope of this chapter, it is important to emphasize the relationship educational researchers are finding between the cognitive and affective. Uguroglu and Walberg (1979), for example, reviewed 40 research studies that contained 232 correlations between motivation and achievement and found nearly 27 per cent of the variance in achievement due to motivational variables and factors relating to the learning environment. These investigations lead us to pause and reflect on the need for students' and teachers' collaborative learning and, in particular, mutual understanding of deaf experience as an educational condition.

If deaf students in postsecondary education, by virtue of communication barriers, cultural or experiential differences, or attitudes of others, are segregated from the community of inquiry, then we have failed in our role as teachers. In the AAAS conference, the students explained that sensory and physical differences are in themselves not 'handicaps.' It is the way that society in general, or teachers in particular, treat persons with differences that introduce the handicap or hindrance to learning and participation. In their quest for increasing social and political consciousness, the participating students suggest that, as change agents, they be approached by teachers (and that they approach teachers) in dialogue about the barriers to learning as well as the course content.

IMPLICATIONS FOR POSTSECONDARY EDUCATORS

Despite technological advances, social change, and increasing acceptance of sign language communication alone and in various combinations with oral/aural communication, the isolating effects of deafness remain, particularly for learners in high-pressure mainstream settings. As a consequence, teachers and support personnel in postsecondary programs need to understand deafness in a fuller educational sense, particularly with respect to psychosocial and cultural factors. The age of onset, the amount of hearing loss, the familial language, and educational backgrounds are a few of the parameters that make a deaf learner unique in both the attitudinal sense and in the way in which learning is approached. Lang (1989) discusses how these and other factors must be considered when reporting achievement and developing assessments for deaf students. We suggest that, as a valuable starting point, the primary source of personal knowledge about these and related issues be acquired through dialogue with deaf learners.

In relation to collaboration and the community of inquiry, communication challenges involving deafness and hearing will be factors to consider, particularly in group situations. Most successful deaf adults look back at their college years with a measure of disappointment that communication in group discussions was frustrating. Part of the reason for this may be linguistic in origin. For some deaf students, English is a second language. For most deaf students, English has been acquired primarily through the sense of vision. Consequently, as with other English-as-a-Second-Language (ESL) learners, some deaf college students will demonstrate gaps in mastery of reading and writing. Pendergrass and Hodges (1976), in a study of younger deaf children in group problem solving settings, found a need for the children to become more proficient in *asking* questions, for example, and recommended that teachers address this need, which is a perspective shift not commonly used in classrooms as a teaching strategy – after all, *we* are the ones doing the questioning. Yet valuable summarization and analytical skills are fostered in this pedagogical practice. For many deaf students at the postsecondary level, the ability to be an active inquirer still requires attention, and addressing this need should be a priority as the teacher promotes collaborative learning.

On the other hand, the participation of deaf learners in the community of inquiry may also be inhibited for purely mechanical reasons. Even deaf students proficient in English language may not be able to join a discussion because of the difficulty in knowing when there is an appropriate pause, the perceived risk of misunderstanding through speechreading, or the lag that occurs when a student is following a sign language interpreter. Stigma associated with speech that is not normal may lead the student to shy away from dialogue. Only a receptive environment will solve this challenge. The participation of deaf college students as members of a mainstream class may be increased through teaching that takes into conscious consideration the communicative needs associated with deafness (Foster and Holcomb, 1990; Saur, Layne, and Hurley 1986) and teachers who, with students, develop routine classroom communication protocols. In regard to the delivery of support services, in fact, the deaf learner should be involved in every step of the planning. Collaborative planning of resources will also encourage self-directed learning. In search of ways to have postsecondary educators experience some of the isolating effects of deafness and discuss the implications for collaborative learning environments, the National Technical Institute for the Deaf has provided opportunities for hearing persons to be fitted with 'tinnitus maskers,' hearing aid-type devices that produce a static sound, effectively simulating a hearing loss. Some faculty members wearing these maskers immediately noticed the challenge of learning primarily through vision. 'Small tasks like passing papers and listening to oratory simultaneously become impossible,' wrote one teacher in a journal they were asked to keep throughout the day. 'When I focused on the papers, I could not see what was being said.' Another wrote of eye fatigue 'My eyes felt tired from concentrating on everyone's lips. . . , I wanted to close my eyes, but then I would be able to understand nothing!' And a third teacher described the need constantly to attend to visual forms of communication for fear of missing important information: 'I really was struck with how often I missed the first few words of what people were saying whether they were signing or not. The amount of concentration it takes to keep informed and in tune is enormous!' One professor not wearing a masker took notes on his observations of his colleagues who were 'deaf,' commenting on how the hearing loss immediately changed his judgment of their abilities: 'Some people that I would classify as "excellent" suddenly became "average" or even "poor".'

Social aspects of hearing loss also became apparent to these college educators. 'One of the most surprising reactions was my unwillingness to "stick out,"' wrote one teacher. 'I'm not sure what I was afraid of – embarrassing myself, having other people feel awkward – I'm sure a mixture of these plus others.' The journal of another colleague provided some very poignant emotions: 'It is very difficult for me to express my feelings in words, when I think about it I could cry because it was so meaningful to me. . . . I feel that the experience will make me a better person for my job and for my relationship with my deaf friends.'

Such experiences create an empathy through which collaboration becomes more possible. Balancing collaborative learning and intellectual independence, however, requires judicious reasoning, regardless of whether the learner is hearing or deaf. For the classroom having both deaf and hearing learners, there may be distinct advantages in both kinds of activities. Collaborative learning experiences will promote sharing of cultural information and help to dispel a notion of deafness as pathological in character. Such activities will help all students to shift from dualism to relativism and multiplicity of perspectives. Political and social consciousness come with such changing viewpoints.

On the other hand, course assignments that encourage intellectual independence will lead the deaf student, as well as hearing peers, toward self-directed learning. The balance of these two approaches is especially critical in one sense – the more the deaf student participates and collaborates in the community of inquiry and develops self-direction, the sooner the stigma attached to difference is lifted, self-confidence is nurtured, and the students' own goals and dreams are reached.

That yearning toward self-directed learning must be attended to in every marginalized learner, as is prophetically stated in the first words found in the African-American writer Ralph Ellison's book, *The Invisible Man* (1952):

> It goes a long way back . . . . All my life I had been looking for something, and everywhere I turned someone tried to tell me what it was. I accepted their answers, too, though they were often in contradiction and even self-contradictory. I was naive. I was

looking for myself and asking everyone except myself questions which I, and only I, could answer.

NOTES

1 These quotations are from an article on reconceiving curriculum based on deaf students' texts (Meath-Lang, 1990).
2 The work of Mary Belenky and her associates (cited in the References) has concentrated on women's ways of learning and modes of knowing. This work also references the work done by Professor Belenky with deaf learners at the National Technical Institute for the Deaf (USA).
3 Student quoted in Rohland and Meath-Lang (1984).
4 Student quoted in Meath-Lang (in press).
5 Students quoted in Albertini, Meath-Lang, and Harris (1987).
6 'Essays on Deafness,' Unpublished collection of autobiographical reflections of deaf faculty. National Technical Institute for the Deaf, Office of Faculty Development.

REFERENCES

Albertini, J., and Meath-Lang, B. (1986) 'An analysis of student-teacher exchanges in dialogue journal writing,' *Journal of Curriculum Theorizing*, 7, 1, 153-201.

Albertini, J., Meath-Lang, B., and Harris, D. (1987) 'Voice in writing: The views of writers, teachers, and deaf students,' in D. Copeland and D. Fletcher (eds) *Removing the writing barrier: A dream?* New York, Lehman College, 222-46.

Bakan, D. (1966) *The duality of human existences*. Boston: Beacon Press.

Bakhtin, M. M. (1986) *The dialogic imagination: Four essays by M. M. Bakhtin*, translated by C. Emerson and M. Holquist (M. Holquist, (ed.). Austin, TX: University of Texas Press.

Belenky, M. F., Clinchy, B. M., Goldberger, N. R., and Tarule, J. M. (1986) *Women's ways of knowing: The development of self, voice, and mind*. New York: Basic Books.

Brown, J. S., Collins, A., and Duguid, P. (1989) Situated cognition and the culture of learning,' *Educational Researcher*, 17, 1, 32-42.

Elbow, P. (1973) *Writing without teachers*. London: Oxford University Press.

Elbow, P. (1979) 'Trying to teach while thinking about the end,' in G. Grant, P. Elbow, T. Ewens, Z. Gamson, W. Kohli, N. Oleson, and D. Riesman (eds.) *On competence*. San Francisco, CA: Jossey-Bass, 95-137.

Ellison, R. (1952) *The invisible man*. New York: The New American Library, Inc.

Foster, S. and Holcomb, T. (1990) 'Hearing-impaired students: A student-teacher-class partnership,' in N. Jones (ed.), *Special educational needs review: Vol. 3*, 150-69. London: The Falmer Press.

Freire, P. (1970) *The pedagogy of the oppressed*, translated by M. Ramos. New York: Herder & Herder.

Gilligan, C. (1982) *In a different voice: Psychological theory and women's development.* Cambridge, MA: Harvard University Press.

Grumet, M. (1989) *Bitter Milk: Women and teaching.* Amherst, MA: University of Massachusetts Press.

Husserl, E. (1976) *Ideas,* translated by W. R. Boyce-Gibson. Pittsburgh PA: Humanities Press.

Jackson, B. F. (1895) 'Voices,' *The Buff and Blue,* 3, 5, April 12, 66–8.

Lang, H. G. (1989) 'Academic development and preparation for work,' in M. Wang, M. C. Reynolds, and H. J. Walberg (eds), *Handbook of special education: Research and practice.* Oxford: Pergamon Press.

Lang, H.G. and DeCaro, J.J. (1991) *Attitudes Toward Deafness: Proceedings of The Second Convocation of Faculty and Staff.* Rochester, New York: National Technical Institute for the Deaf.

Luria, A. R. (1981) *Language and cognition.* Cambridge, MA: Harvard University Press.

Macdonald, J. and Macdonald, S. C. (1988) 'Gender, values, and curriculum,' in W. F. Pinar (ed.). *Contemporary curriculum discourses.* Scottsdale, AZ: Gorsuch Scarisbrick Publishers, 476–85.

Matson, F. (1976) *The idea of man.* New York: Delacorte Press.

Meath-Lang, B. (1990) 'The dialogue journal: Reconceiving curriculum and teaching,' in J. Kreeft Peyton (ed.), *Teachers and students writing together: Perspectives on journal writing.* Alexandria, VA: TESOL Publications.

Meath-Lang, B. (forthcoming) 'A lesser loneliness: Marginalization and the formation of the writing community,' *Journal of Curriculum Theorizing.*

Meath-Lang, B. and Albertini, J. (1989). 'Authenticity in writing: A reflection on voice, imagination, deafness, and teaching,' in A. Martel (ed.) *To pedagogy and what matters.* Edmonton: University of Alberta Curriculum Praxis Series, 7–13.

Meath-Lang, B., Caccamise, F., and Albertini, J. (1982) 'Deaf persons' views of their English language learning,' in H. Hoemann and R. Wilbur (eds), *Interpersonal communication and deaf people.* Washington, DC: Gallaudet College, 295–329.

Padden, C. and Humphries, T. (1988) *Deaf in America: Voices from a culture.* Cambridge, MA: Harvard University Press.

Pagano, J. (1988) 'The claim of philia,' in W. F. Pinar (ed.), *Contemporary curriculum discourses.* Scottsdale, AZ: Gorsuch Scarisbrick Publishers, 514–30.

Pendergrass, R. A. and Hodges, M. (1976) 'Deaf students in group problem solving situations: A study of the interactive process,' *American Annals of the Deaf,* 121, 3, 327–30.

Perry, W. G. (1970) *Forms of intellectual and ethical development in the college years.* New York: Holt, Rinehart & Winston.

Peyton, J. K. (1990) *Students and teachers writing together.* Alexandria, VA: TESOL Publications.

Piaget, J. (1951) *Play, dreams, and imitation in children.* New York: Norton.

Pinar, W. F. (1988) *Contemporary curriculum discourses.* Scottsdale, AZ: Scarisbrick Publishers.

Redden, M. R., Davis, C. A.,and Brown, J. W. (1979) *Science for handicapped students in higher education.* Washington, DC: American Association for the Advancement of Science.
Rohland, P. and Meath-Lang, B. (1984) 'Perceptions of deaf adults regarding audiological services,' *Journal of the Academy of Rehabilitative Audiology,* 17, 130–50.
Saur, R. E., Lane, C. A., and Hurley, E. A. (1986) 'Dimensions of mainstreaming,' *American Annals of the Deaf,* 131, 4, 325–30.
Schoenfeld, A. H. (1985) *Mathematical problem-solving.* Orlando, FL: Academic Press.
Staton, J., Shuy, R. W., Peyton, J. K., and Reed, L. (1988) *Dialogue journal communications: Classroom, linguistic, social and cognitive views.* Norwood, NJ: Ablex.
Stone, J. (1988) 'The pedagogical implications of normalization and representation in mathematics learning,' in M. Weinstein and W. Oxman-Michelli (eds), *Critical thinking: Language and inquiry across the disciplines.* Montclair State College, NJ: Institute for Critical Thinking.
Todorov, T. (1984) *Mikhail Bakhtin: The dialogical principle,* translated by W. Godzich. Minneapolis, MN: University of Minnesota Press.
Uguroglu, M. E. and Walberg, H. J. (1979) 'Motivation and achievement: A quantitative synthesis,' *American Educational Research Journal,* 16, 375–89.
Vygotsky, L. (1978) *Mind in society.* Cambridge, MA: Harvard University Press.
Whitson, J. A. (1988) 'The politics of non-political curriculum: Heteroglossia and the discourse of 'choice' and effectiveness,' in W. F. Pinar (ed.), *Contemporary curriculum discourses.* Scottsdale, AZ: Scarisbrick Publishers.

Personal Commentary

Jane Mullins

I was born into a hearing family that consisted of a college professor for a father, a mother who later became a town librarian, and a brother two years older than I. The cause of my deafness is unknown, although it is thought that high fever resulting from a bad case of chickenpox at age 1 ½ might have caused the profound deafness. My parents confirmed my deafness when I was 4, and like many parents at that time, they wanted me to be as 'hearing' as possible. So they immediately had me fitted with monstrous body hearing aids, which were always banging me in the chin everytime I played. My parents also arranged for speech therapy which was to continue all the way through to high school. I started school in the local kindergarten program, but could not participate in class activities such as listening to a story or discussing ideas with other children. So my parents enrolled me in a day oral program for deaf children, which was an hour's drive away in Philadelphia. I happily attended this school from ages 6 to 9, then my father got a new teaching job in Iowa. The nearest program for deaf students there was a good two hours' drive from the town to which we were moving. My parents were emphatic about not wanting me to live away from home. They collaborated with the Philadelphia school to 'test' me in a mainstreamed environment. This consisted of being escorted twice a week across the street to another public school to attend a math class. Looking back, that was a pivotal class to select. Math happened to be one of my favorite and best subjects (having a math teacher for a father helped, too). It was a class where I could easily learn on my own, watching the blackboard examples and following the examples in the book. I did not have to rely so much on lipreading and guessing as I did in other classes. Based on that 'success,' I was transferred back to third grade at my local school. Being mainstreamed was bewildering. I would quietly sit in the classroom, oblivious to the discussions going on around me, lost in my own daydreaming. But when it came to homework assignments, I'd figure out the answers on my own or ask for help. I continued to be mainstreamed in public school after we moved to Iowa, all the way through to high school.

While there were no support services at the public school in Iowa, I performed quite well academically, in part because my classes were very small (we lived in a small rural town), and in part because I had very supportive parents who literally were my life-long teachers. They compensated for the many learning opportunities I missed by virtue of not being able to follow classroom discussions. They taught me how to seek out new ideas on my own.

I credit my mother (and her stubbornness) for opening new worlds to me. When it was time for me to learn how to read, I refused to do so. I would not cooperate. Nothing could convince me to read. But my mother was persistent. She would patiently take me to the library, week after week, to select new books even if I had not opened the ones we checked out earlier. Finally, my curiosity got the better of me, and I began to peruse the pages. I started soaking in Greek mythology, *Little Women*, life on the prairie with Laura Ingalls, Charles Dickens. I became a voracious reader.

Through extensive reading, I also improved my writing and explored many new ideas and my language skills developed rapidly. My family encouraged me to grow in these areas, too. As I began to experiment with writing stories and journals, I got nothing but positive reinforcement and support for these endeavors. I'd play 'schoolhouse teacher' with my mother, grandmother, and great aunt, requiring them to reiterate deliberately misspelled words. In addition, once or twice a week for a few years, my family would play vocabulary games at the dinner table. I cherish this particular memory, because within this activity, I felt equal to the rest of my family, and for once, could fully participate in the discussions. But at all the other times when we were not playing the games, I would get so bored (and frustrated!) at the dinner table, not being able to follow the general discussions going on. This same boredom was true of the classroom activities, for I could never keep up with what was being discussed.

On my own, I was able to learn a lot. I also had certain supportive teachers, such as my Spanish teacher. She would give me additional reading materials while the rest of the class would listen to audiotapes. My math teacher had an agreement with me that I would always sit in a certain place, and she in turn would always face me directly as she used the blackboard to do examples. This was not unique to the school I was enrolled in. I had similar experiences in England, where I lived for six months with my parents when I was 15. There I attended an all-girl's school, again being the only deaf student. This school's Headmistress set up an individualized program for me, where three of my classes consisted of just me and the teacher. I benefited a lot academically from this set-up. Together with supportive teachers and family, I thrived as a student.

But, I did not thrive as a person. I was trying so hard to hide my deafness, thinking this would help me to better 'fit' into the crowd. But when it came to extracurricular activities, particularly those involving groups, I constantly felt isolated and lonely, because I could never follow conversations. I was afraid to be assertive, for fear of revealing my deafness. One incident stands out clearly in my mind. I was quite involved in a church youth group, and one evening we were sitting around talking about mutual concerns and issues. The room grew darker as the evening wore on, until all I could see were the silhouettes of the people with me. After quite some time, the youth leader turned on a light and asked me, 'How are you doing?' 'Fine,' I replied passively. The leader then turned off the light, and the discussion continued around me. I was very hurt by this exclusion, yet I did nothing, out of fear of further imagined rejection from these people. Things came to a head when I attended a private, four-year liberal arts college in Illinois for two years after high school graduation. Again, I had no support services. While I was performing satisfactorily (mostly C's, a few B's), I was not satisfied with the way I was learning. I did not like having to sit for long periods in any one class, not being able to follow class discussions. So I decided to ask for permission to skip classes, and be responsible for my own work. I was reluctantly granted this permission by teachers, who, while not pleased with the idea, did not offer alternatives for me to consider. After trying out this experiment, I found I still was not satisfied. I ended up with even less contact with my peers, in and out of class, and felt more isolated from the mainstream of things. I decided to join a sorority, thinking that I'd develop valuable resources to help me with classes as well as other activities. That didn't work either, because I still could not fully participate in sorority activities, be they informal get-togethers or business meetings. In other campus activities, I'd go to plays and understand only a small portion of the performances. I'd go to seminars such as a presentation by the late well-known sociologist Margaret Mead, and find myself admiring her countenance and dignity, but losing out on the valuable exchange going on between her and other students. I shied away from majoring in psychology, because there were too many seminars where I wouldn't be able to keep up with discussions. I focused on history, thinking at best I could be a librarian, and besides, history has many facts I should be able to keep up with. Still, even with a subject like history, something was missing. I needed to know what others, like the professor and classmates, saw in historical facts. I needed to try out my own ideas with them. Even in my favorite subject, math, I was having trouble keeping up with my calculus professor because there were a lot more class discussions than there were visual examples on the blackboard itself. The growing discontent I had experienced in high school with feeling like less than a whole person was escalating at college. While I felt so much isolation, loneliness, and frustration during my junior high and high school years, I had the strong support of my family to cushion me. But here at college, I no longer had that cushion of support. I was very miserable. Above all, I needed the confidence to assert myself in learning situations and this thought dwelled in my consciousness.

It was about this time that I learned about Gallaudet University and I decided to give it a try. This decision became another significant turning point in my life. At first, I had to undergo a significant personal adjustment to the 'cultural shock' of being in a 'deaf environment' and learning sign language for the first time. I was forced to see myself as a deaf person, after trying so hard to pretend to be 'hearing' for so long. I felt very alone and vulnerable at first at Gallaudet, stuck between the hearing world and that of the deaf. But with a great deal of time and patience on my part, I slowly became assimilated into the deaf culture. Sign language became my 'inner voice' along with the English language.

At the end of my first year at Gallaudet, my father commented on how he had never seen me so happy as then. This motivated both my father and stepmother to enroll in a sign language class. I was so pleased and touched by this gesture. But at the same time, I found myself sadly wishing that my whole family, including me, had learned sign language when I was still a very young child. If we had communicated in sign language while I was growing up, I would have felt much more accepted and included in group activities, thereby averting much of the loneliness and isolation I actually experienced as a child.

While my personal adjustment at Gallaudet was a traumatic

but profound experience, I had an easier adjustment as a student. I still remember clearly the first class I attended. Out of instinct, I sat in the front row. I geared myself up to talk to the teacher about my own needs. Then all of a sudden, the teacher began to lecture, and I was pleasantly surprised to find that I was following almost every single word (even though I was not yet skilled in sign language). The teacher was so easy to lipread, and the discussion pace was such that I could keep up with everyone; I could even relax! It was so wonderful to be able to more fully exchange ideas and thoughts in the classroom discussions. I returned to my original idea of majoring in psychology, and graduated with a degree in this field.

After working as a research assistant at Gallaudet for one year, my desire to be with and help others led me to enroll in the Gallaudet graduate counseling program. While the number of deaf students in that program was disproportionately small, I found the classes very stimulating and challenging. By then, I had become quite fluent in sign language, and all my professors and classmates were good signers, too. Being able to access information 100 per cent allowed me to learn directly from people, which was the missing element in my earlier mainstreamed experiences.

Many of the tensions I once harbored within myself are now gone. As a counselor, friend, colleague, and, especially, as a learner, I felt more 'balanced' with my acquired knowledge and skills, and I continued to thirst for new knowledge and experiences.

I will always be a learner. I am still learning about the deaf culture, and I am now experimenting with what it is like to be without hearing aids after over 30 years of wearing them. For one thing, silence is so peaceful! I realize that I don't have to be completely responsible for ensuring that communication succeeds between another person and myself. Rather, through a kind of collaborative assertiveness, I am finding that others will meet me halfway in order to make the communication work. And, through my personal experiences, I find I have become more and more an advocate for making information fully accessible to deaf students in the academic environment. I find myself unwilling to receive information in a 'hit-and-miss' fashion, whether this be in the form of poor or sporadic signing or no captions on television. I find myself wanting to see deaf culture made an integral part of young deaf children's education. In my work with deaf college students, I try to plant 'seeds' of inquisitiveness and pride in their minds. I encourage them to explore new frontiers of knowlege, to take the initiative and challenge their teachers in the classroom. I firmly believe that with the right environment, deaf students can, as Carl Rogers so eloquently puts it in his *Freedom to Learn for the 80's* book, 'respond with an avid interest in learning, with a growing confidence in self, with independence, with creative energy.'

Jane Mullins is an associate professor and career development counselor at Rochester Institute of Technology's National Technical Institute for the Deaf. She holds a BA in psychology and an MA in counseling the deaf. Her job responsibilities involve personal, career, and academic counseling with deaf students, and teaching courses. She has also been involved in NTID's Outreach Project for Deaf Adults. Prior to her employment at NTID, Mullins worked as a research assistant in the Office of Demographic Studies at Gallaudet University. Jane and her husband, Artie, reside in Rochester with their dog and three cats.

Chapter 5

Resources for deaf students in the mainstreamed classroom

Rosemary E. Saur

INTRODUCTION

In the past 25 years there has been a growing recognition and acceptance of the need to provide resources for deaf students who are in a mainstreamed classroom environment. These resources are intended to provide such students with access to the information being presented in the classroom. Ideally, resources make it possible for deaf students to compete and cooperate with their normally hearing peers by removing some of the communication barriers that inhibit their participation in academic life. More recently, persons working with deaf students have come to look at resources as more far reaching than the immediate classroom situation. Resources available outside of the classroom focus on developing skills in students that will enable them to cope more effectively during their educational experience and throughout the rest of their lives, as well.

This chapter is intended to focus on those resources that are necessary or desirable in a post–secondary educational environment, on ways to maximize the positive effect of such resources, and on the need for active involvement of the deaf student in planning.

Before describing a model of resource services, it is necessary to consider the terms used to describe such services, as well as the impact those terms may have on our attitudes and, ultimately, on the way we deal with students. It is also important to consider the reality of providing services and its dependence on available resources. Finally, an approach to delivering resources is suggested that avoids the concept of resources as being simply a collection of interpreting, notetaking, tutoring, etc. The following sections deal with the basic assumptions underlying this chapter.

SOME GUIDING PRINCIPLES AND PHILOSOPHIES

Services: Support or Resources?

The use of the phrase 'support services' is firmly ingrained in the culture of special education, particularly at the postsecondary level, despite the negative connotations that might be associated with such usage. What follows is not likely to change this practice. However, the old query, 'What's in a name?' should be considered before one begins, so that the perspective from which these services are viewed is very clear.

What is wrong with the use of the term 'support' to identify the services we provide to students? It is not the accuracy of that term but the connotation that is objectionable. Using the words 'support services' can easily foster a view of deaf students as passive and dependent, receiving what they need from protective, all-knowing support providers. If one carries this definition further to the common use of the terms 'support team' or 'support department' to indicate the agency or office providing the services, one creates a further picture of institutionalized passivity on the part of students and benevolent providers working together to make up for what students lack.

At a time when deaf persons are beginning to assert their rights to self-determination and full participation in society, a long-used but patronizing term, such as support, might well be seen as a barrier rather than as an aid to the full growth of students. Clearly, no one has ever intended to patronize students or imply that they are helpless by using the words 'support' and 'support team' or 'support department.' However, to the extent that our words shape our thinking, the unexamined use of such terms is thoughtless and requires scrutiny, especially in view of the current *Zeitgeist*.

If well-worn labels could be easily changed it would be preferable to use the term 'resources' rather than 'support' to identify the educational services provided to deaf students. This was done in the introduction to the chapter. The term 'resources' tends to shift the perception of control and responsibility from the service provider to the student. That is, students *use* resources but they are *provided* with support. By employing the term 'resources' one focuses more on the individual rights and responsibilities of deaf students themselves in receiving services rather than on support providers. It should be acknowledged that at times the use of the word 'support' is entirely appropriate and the concept just discussed should not be carried to extreme.

Empowering Students

The point of all of this discussion over the word 'support' is to take the philosophical position that the ultimate goal in the provision of services is to empower students. We need to provide the means for deaf students to take control over their own destinies, whether that be short-term in the classroom or long-term, throughout their lifetimes. These individuals will always need a variety of resources in order to contend with the demands of the hearing world. They must learn to know for themselves exactly what their rights are, what resources they require, and how to obtain those resources. Clearly, students do not learn these skills all at once. Therefore, what is being suggested is a developmental perspective that recognizes students' entry-level skills and also their needs at particular times in their lives. This approach assists students in moving on to greater self-knowledge and assertiveness and, hence, to greater independence. At graduation one hopes to see students who no longer need advice and mentoring but are aware of their own needs for resources and able to obtain them as required.

The Ideal v. the Real

In the best of all possible worlds deaf students would receive a full range of resources that would completely eliminate their inability to hear as a factor in their educational experience in the mainstreamed classroom. This is never really the case. In the here-and-now world we do not have wide flexibility because of limited fiscal and human resources as well as the lack of technological advances in some areas. Where then, is the necessary balance between what is possible and what should be?

Students have the right to adequate resources. In the United States the concept of reasonable accommodation was set forth in Section 504 of the Vocational Rehabilitation Act of 1973. However, except in extreme cases, a legal requirement or limitation is rarely the issue. We need to ask what are the needs of the student and what are the resources of the community? We must think of what the community can provide, given that resources are an important priority. Those resources are not always what might easily or willingly be provided. Nor should they be funded by what is left over after needs in other areas have been met. We also need to ask what resources students must have in order to be competitive and successful and what would be helpful but not essential. Thus, those who provide resources for deaf students will often find themselves in the role of advocate. In this regard we are, of course, speaking of students who have the potential – aptitude and academic background – to be successful in postsecondary education.

The Top-Down Approach to Providing Resources

The resources needed by deaf students in the mainstreamed educational setting are not simply collections of independent resources. Therefore, there is a need to look at what an organization must provide in order to successfully manage those resources. This is not an attempt to specify organizational structure as such, since what might exist and function well in one academic setting may have no applicability in another area. Some general requirements can, however, be described.

Ideally, an office or department providing resources will act as a homebase for mainstreamed students. This is more than simply a place to go to sign up for resources, to get notes, to receive advice. A homebase is a place where students are known, understood, and valued as individuals. This office may very well be looked on as a refuge from the storms of academic life and the special pressures it imposes on one who is deaf. At the very least it is a place where deaf students can expect other persons to know how to communicate with them.

The office or department providing resources will also be a link to the academic community. It will provide resources to the teaching faculty and others in the community by explaining the needs of deaf students and offering suggestions for accommodating them in the classroom and elsewhere on campus. Thus, the organization is an advocate for its students to the larger community but is also a resource to assist the community in carrying out its responsibility to the students. This is a large order for any organization but a necessary one if students are to be integrated into the academic community and receive all the benefits thereof. In small departments, this assignment is likely to be a matter of 'winning the world, one person at a time.' In other words, such liaison occurs with individual teachers and departments as need arises and continues to exist. In larger organizations representing more deaf students the efforts will likely be more far reaching.

Key to the success of any department providing resources to

mainstreamed deaf students is the person or persons who provide guidance to those students throughout their academic careers. These individuals may have various titles and statuses. They may be regarded as counselors, advisors, or mentors. They may or may not have faculty rank. More will be said of this important position later in the chapter.

The following section will focus on the most commonly provided resources. The discussion just completed was an attempt to give a picture of how services should be organized for students. We move on to focus more specifically on the resources themselves.

A MODEL FOR PROVIDING RESOURCE SERVICES TO DEAF STUDENTS

What will be presented here is a model of the many resources that may be provided to mainstreamed deaf students. The model is intended to be descriptive rather than prescriptive in that all resources may not be provided to all students in all settings. However, it is directive in the sense that concerns for high standards and quality control are expressed for each component of the model. The standard in-class resources of notetaking and interpreting will be described along with out-of-class resources such as advising, counseling, and tutoring. Other, less common resources such as developmental courses and technological advances in providing services will also be dealt with, albeit briefly.

In-classroom Resources

Interpreting and notetaking are the visible resources that are popularly associated with providing services to deaf students within the classroom. Of the two, interpreting is by far the most costly in both human and fiscal terms. However, the important point is that both resources provide students with access to the information presented by an instructor in the classroom.

Interpreting

In addition to content information, interpreting provides access to other people and to the immediate communication environment. Therefore, it offers increased opportunity for class participation to deaf students and strengthens in them the feeling of being fully involved or equal members of a class.

It is well to begin with a definition of what is meant by interpreting in this chapter. In its narrowest sense the term is used to mean changing the spoken language, English, into American Sign Language (ASL) or vice versa. In a more general sense, interpreting is used to indicate any way in which the spoken word is changed in form to be understandable to deaf students. The general use of the term includes oral interpreting where English words are clearly emphasized on the mouth. When interpreters use Signed English it is known as transliterating. Signed English borrows signs from ASL but signs are presented in English word order. The English words are also clearly emphasized on the mouth, making it possible to speechread. 'Interpreting' is used in its general sense in this chapter.

It is beyond the scope of this chapter to go into great depth on interpreting as a profession. However, there are several points that should be made. It is currently recognized that there are special skills needed for those who interpret in the educational setting. Thus, educational interpreting is becoming defined as a profession in and of itself. For more information on educational interpreting see the definitive report of the National Task Force on Educational Interpreting (Stuckless, Avery, and Hurwitz 1989). Other issues that pertain more specifically to interpreting in the postsecondary setting will be dealt with briefly. These include, hiring, managing, and the evaluation of interpreters.

It should be made very clear from the start that if interpreting is to be provided to deaf students, it should not be done in a piecemeal fashion. Poor quality or inconsistent provision of service may be little better than no service at all in a demanding college classroom. Most large communities have an interpreting referral service or agency from which interpreters may be hired. This may be the only option for a fledgling service provider or situations in which only a handful of students require interpreting resources.

If interpreting is to be provided by an in-house staff of interpreters it will be desirable to first hire a manager/administrator skilled in interpreting and knowledgeable of providing the resources in the classroom. It is essential that interpreters be hired with the proper skills and certification and with the ability to interact favorably with the students and faculty being served. The interpreter manager will be able to determine who has the proper skills and attitude during the hiring process. The manager will be able to encourage the development of the interpreter as a professional employee, increasing skills and certification in a way that will ultimately benefit the students receiving the resources. What is most important, the manager will be able to exercise quality control in the provision of service by providing proper scheduling for interpreters, maximizing their effectiveness and protecting their health and well-being.

Notetaking

Despite the importance of the interpreter in ensuring full participation in the classroom, many students, if given the choice of either a notetaker or an interpreter, will select the notetaker. Why is this so? It is probably because getting the content of the material presented in class is the primary objective for most students. They must pass tests on that content in order to receive credit for the course. Few deaf students feel able to take complete notes for themselves while watching the interpreter nor do they feel able to remember everything presented without notes. For most students a notetaker is a must for success in class.

Notetaking involves recording the main points of what is said in class during lectures, discussions, reports, and so forth. Notes are clearly not intended to be a complete record of everything said in class. Rather, they should be a comprehensive summary. When taking notes the notetaker highlights important main topics or themes in the lecture, defines new or difficult vocabulary, and organizes the material to best present the class information.

Important as it is, notetaking can never replace deaf students' efforts to gather their own information in the classroom; it can only support or supplement that effort. It is vitally important that all deaf students take their own notes to the best of their ability whether they have a notetaker in the classroom with them or not.

Why make such a strong statement? In the first place, much research has shown the cognitive and educational benefits of taking notes for students in general (Beecher 1988; Anderson and Armbruster 1986; Dubois 1986; Carrier 1983). Notetaking helps to focus attention and requires the writer to process and integrate information as it is presented. All of this activity seems to result in better learning. Self-generated notes also act as cues for recalling more information than is written down. In the second place, deaf students will need some skill in notetaking all of their lives in situations where they will be unable to have a notetaker or borrow someone else's notes. The more that can be done to encourage and foster the development of notetaking skills the greater the benefit to deaf students. It must be acknowledged that students will vary greatly in their ability to adapt and to take useful notes. All should be encouraged to do so, although few will become totally self-sufficient. The notes provided by a trained notetaker will amplify, supplement, and expand any notes that deaf students have been able to take for themselves. By comparing their own notes with those of the notetaker, students will be able to determine whether their understandings are correct and can seek out information to reconcile any discrepancies. In short, notes are a vital link to the information presented in the classroom. They are most effective when they come from two sources, the students themselves and a trained notetaker.

There are a number of issues that must be considered in hiring notetakers. A notetaker is a resource person/service provider knowledgeable in the academic content of the course and trained in proper notetaking techniques. Anyone can serve as a notetaker if they have the proper knowledge and training. However, this task is performed more frequently by hearing students hired for that purpose than by professional service staff.

Students who are hired to take notes for deaf students should have previously taken the course and received a good grade in it. It becomes advantageous to develop a pool of notetakers in a given major area such as mathematics, accounting, liberal arts, and the like. This pool of students may be tapped to take notes for a variety of courses in that major. Moreover, their interest and expertise in the content area will add to the quality of the notes they produce. Reality dictates, however, that it will often be necessary simply to recruit a student who is taking a course for the first time and is willing to take notes.

Notetaking is a deceptively simple activity that becomes complex and exacting when done properly. A person who is able to take adequate notes for his/her own use may be unable to produce notes that are useful to another individual. Therefore, training is an important aspect of providing a notetaking service. It is beyond the scope of this chapter to describe in detail the notetaker training process. However, suggestions for conducting a training program are available from a number of sources (Lewis 1985; Osguthorpe, Wilson, Goldmann, and Panara 1980a,1980b; Wilson 1986).

A group of student employees hired as notetakers becomes another opportunity for liaison on the part of resource providers. Hearing students can become sensitized to the abilities and needs of their deaf peers through the contact they have with those students and with others who provide resources. Including notetakers in social activities with deaf students can promote understanding and mutual respect as well as friendship. A second benefit to notetakers is the fact that taking notes helps them to review course material and strengthen their own knowledge in the content area.

As with interpreting, quality control is an important aspect of notetaking. All persons involved with the notetaking process must evaluate the quality of the notes and the skill of the notetaker on a regular basis. The assistance of the classroom instructor must be sought in accomplishing this goal. Only the instructor can be the final judge as to the accuracy and completeness of the notes. At times it may be difficult or impossible to secure such cooperation. However, most instructors are concerned about the accuracy of the information being received by their students. If they are regularly supplied with copies of the notes this task should be little trouble. The deaf student receiving the notes should also be a part of the evaluation process, being able to reflect on the usefulness and completeness of the notes along with the dependability of the notetaker. The resource person who serves to manage notetakers should review the notes for format, presentation, and accuracy of content as much as possible.

Resources Outside the Classroom

The visible resources provided to deaf students within the classroom must be guided and supplemented by resources outside of the classroom. These less visible resources provide students with the means to tie educational experiences together and fully benefit from instruction given. It should be pointed out from the start that one person may serve in more than one of the roles being described. This is especially the case with small programs and few resources.

The Advisor or Mentor

The role of the resource advisor has been highly developed over the years. The combination of content expertise, knowledge of resources, and understanding of deafness makes this a unique position. Advisors who work on behalf of deaf students must carry out an intensive liaison effort with the academic community around them to benefit students. They must also work continually with students to foster growth and development.

What are the characteristics of an individual who is successful in the role of advisor or mentor to deaf college students? Beyond the skills required by the typical job description, an advisor for mainstreamed students must be flexible, tolerant, and a good decision maker. In fact, the decision-making capacity is of primary importance for a person in this role. Many times this person will be required to tread in unknown territory when trying to optimize resources for students. In dealing with new departments or organizations within the academic community, the person must be able to balance the needs of students with the adaptability of the organization. Every new student presents a unique history and a set of needs that will require a different approach to providing resources. Knowing when to individualize and when to take a common approach is often a difficult task.

The advisor has the ability and opportunity to act as a bridge and advocate for deaf students in the academic community. But the advisor also interprets the community to the student. The community does not always understand, nor is willing to take the time to understand, the needs of deaf students. The advisor to such students has the opportunity to help them learn to cope in such an indifferent or even hostile world. Learning how and when to assert one's rights is difficult. Learning how to adapt and survive is essential to success in college and later on in life in the working world. The advisor/mentor has the unique opportunity to help students build these skills as they negotiate their academic hurdles.

The advisor also has the opportunity to make a small difference in the frequently indifferent or hostile academic world. In providing liaison to the classroom instructor, the advisor/mentor has first of all the opportunity to make learning more accessible to the deaf student. Second, the advisor has the opportunity to sensitize the instructor to the needs of all deaf persons and offer specific strategies for communication with the deaf student. Again, the decision-making and interpersonal skills of the person are of utmost importance as one must win the confidence and acceptance of the instructor before any suggestions for changes can be made.

Counseling

Counseling is related to the work of the advisor and can at times be combined in one position. Minimally, a person who works as an advisor must know when to refer a student to counseling personnel.

Often it will be necessary to piece together resources or seek them out for students. Many counseling resources may not ordinarily be accessible to deaf students because of communication barriers. A counselor who is knowledgeable of the special needs of these students and who has the communication skills to work with them is an invaluable addition to any resource unit.

Tutoring

As with other resources, tutoring is a means for providing student access to information presented in class. By definition, tutoring is an umbrella term used to describe re-teaching that is focused on a particular course content generally taught by another person. Most often, tutoring is conducted on a one-to-one basis, although group tutoring may be held when several students are taking a class together. Contrary to a common misconception, students do not always come for tutoring because they are poor students, because they don't understand what is being taught in class, or because they have performed poorly on an exam.

It is recognized that deaf students typically do not get as much information from an interpreted lecture as do hearing students (Jacobs 1977). A good set of notes clearly helps to close this gap. Even so, the majority of deaf students benefit from tutoring provided outside of the classroom. Of great importance to students' academic success is the ability to tie together and integrate the information of the course content. Tutoring may facilitate this process. Thus, tutoring may include remedial, supplementary, review, or expansion of the course content.

In the course of tutoring some students may need to learn study skills or problem-solving strategies. By addressing such specific needs, a tutor focuses on the development of the individual student vis-à-vis the course content. Tutoring, therefore, adds to and reinforces what has been presented in the classroom but also goes beyond to influence the growth of the student as learner.

Tutoring may be provided by different kinds of people in different situations. A professional tutor is a person who is an educational as well as a content specialist and who is able to communicate well with deaf students. This person is important for tutoring students with critical needs and in the most basic, fundamental courses. If a program is not large enough to hire tutors who are content specialists on a permanent basis, it is desirable to hire on an adjunct basis those in the community who have the skills. The advantage of the professional tutor is having an individual who can diagnose student difficulties and prescribe appropriate interventions. They can also monitor progress of students. However, there are also advantages to the peer tutor. Professional or faculty tutors may not have the time to address all of the students' tutoring needs. They may also be limited in the range of their content expertise in different subject areas. Peer tutors, hearing or deaf, can provide tutoring resources to students that will supplement what is provided by the professional. Student tutors have the advantage of having taken the course recently. In the case of the tutor/notetaker they will actually have been in the class with the deaf student. Hearing student tutors can provide the student with the chance to interact with a hearing peer in a positive setting. Deaf student tutors can provide role models for younger, less experienced students as well as help with the course. As with other resources, quality control is a concern for tutoring. It is usually less of a concern given a professional or faculty tutor than with a peer tutor. Student tutors must be carefully supervised and evaluated by both the student being served and by the student tutor's manager.

At some institutions it has become the custom to hire hearing students in the combined position of tutor/notetaker. This student goes to class with the deaf student and takes notes. Then the tutor/notetaker provides tutoring to the student outside of class as needed. The tutor/notetaker manager is responsible for supervising the quality of the notes and the effectiveness of the student as a tutor.

Other Resources for Students

Deaf students may need resources beyond those directly related to specific courses in their academic programs. Two of these will be discussed briefly. The first is the teaching of developmental courses; the second is social activities as an integral part of a resources program.

Courses in orientation to college, learning strategies, study skills, problem-solving skills, and the like may be very important in giving deaf students a needed boost for success. Many special-needs students come to college with developmental lags caused by the hurdles of overcoming a handicap and trying to keep up and succeed academically. Deaf students are equally subject to these difficulties, particularly where language development is linked to skills such as reading comprehension. Certainly not all deaf students are faced with such challenges, but for those who are, special courses outside of the regular academic curriculum may help to ensure a fair chance at achieving postsecondary career goals.

On the surface, social activities may appear simply to be relief from the regular routine and something for deaf students to do together. However, properly handled they are excellent tools for developing peer groups among students with similar needs. They may well become an extension of the advising process if students are encouraged to take part in the planning and execution of such activities. Helping students to become a functioning part of a peer group is an important educational goal and one that a department providing resources can encourage in deaf students. Formation of a student advisory group can further encourage the development of self-advocacy skills in students. The goal in any of these activities is the development of an informal network that provides mutual support to all of its members.

Technological Advancements as Enhancing Services

Technological developments carry some promise for advances in the provision of needed resources to deaf students. Only a few will be mentioned in this chapter. The first of these, which has been tested and used in a limited manner at the National Technical Institute for the Deaf (NTID), is Real Time Graphics Display (RTGD)(Stinson, Stuckless, and Henderson 1988; Stuckless 1983). RTGD is a sophisticated, computer-supported system that converts a spoken lecture to the written word, which appears on a CRT (Cathode Ray Tube) screen in front of the student. Central to the operation is a court stenographer who follows the lecture and feeds codes to the computer, which carries out the rest of the operation. The RTGD system also produces 'hard copy' of the lecture, which can be corrected as needed and provided to students. RTGD does not as yet completely replace the need for an interpreter or even for a notetaker.

However, despite its seeming advantage for capturing classroom information, the extreme expense of RTGD confines it mostly to limited and experimental use at the present time. The system cannot handle notation or mathematical equations, thus there are also content area limitations in its use. Even so, the mere existence of such a system, no matter how limited, expensive, and cumbersome at the present, offers real hope that future developments in the area of speech recognition will enable deaf students to participate more fully in their mainstreamed educational experiences.

Other, low-tech methods have been considered for improving the resources available to students. A notetaker using a laptop computer is able to take notes more rapidly than one using the standard handwriting method. Notes on a computer disk can be easily revised and printed out for students. Whether there is real advantage to this system is an open question and it is currently a topic of research.

Adjustments to the communication environment of the classroom also benefit students. In large lecture halls where amplification is used, the addition of an inductive loop system will enable deaf students to hear a speaker with their hearing aids. This addition may not benefit all students, but significantly enhances the environment for others. Institutions interested in enhancing the listening environment for all students might conduct an acoustic evaluation of all classrooms with the goal of improving poor acoustic situations.

IMPACT ON THE MAINSTREAMED CLASSROOM

Thus far, the concern of the chapter has been on the needs of mainstreamed deaf students and the resources necessary for their success. In this section the focus shifts from a description of possible resources to an analysis of the way those services (and the students who use them) impact on the students and the classroom.

The Instructional Process

The resources provided to deaf students may at times seem to separate them from their instructor. With notetaking and tutoring available, deaf students may not appear to need any contact at all with the person who teaches the course and grades them. Resource providers and deaf students must be aware of this danger and take the initiative to prevent its occurrence. In order to benefit truly from their educational experience, deaf students must be encouraged to contact their instructors on a regular basis. As their development continues, students will eventually turn to instructors for assistance outside of class rather than a tutor.

Professional/faculty tutors must keep in contact with the instructor to be sure that their tutoring is in keeping with the instructor's goals in teaching. This contact may also give the tutor an opportunity to influence positively the way instruction is delivered in class. This positive influence can benefit the hearing as well as the deaf students. For example, by recommending that the instructor use transparencies on an overhead projector to help the deaf students receive more information, instruction may become more visible to all students. The tutor, in fact, becomes a partner of the instructor with positive results for both hearing and deaf class participants.

The resources available to deaf students may cause resentment among their hearing classmates unless an attempt is made to inform these students of the reason for such resources. Thus, a program of education is needed to create understanding and sensitivity to the needs of deaf students. Beyond that, however, it is often possible for resources to be shared in some way that will benefit hearing students. The indirect benefits to hearing students of improved instructional strategies have already been mentioned. A hearing student who misses class because of illness might be provided with notes on the request of the instructor. Other adaptations for deaf students, such as captions on films, may assist the hearing as well.

The impact of deaf students on the general classroom environment may be subtle. If deaf students have an interpreter, they will need to sit together in a place where they can see instructor, board, and interpreter at once. This tends to be either the left-front or right-front of the room, creating a 'deaf-corner,' which in turn emphasizes the differences in people and affirms separateness. Therefore, it is as much a disservice to hearing students as to deaf students. Instructors who are unaware and/or insensitive will sometimes treat this corner as 'no-one's' land, teaching to the hearing majority and letting the interpreter take care of the deaf students. Integration of the classroom takes a concerted effort on the part of the instructor to include everyone in the instruction process. This does not happen easily or without effort, but is absolutely essential if deaf students are to be fully a part of their own educational process (Saur, Layne, Hurley, and Opton 1986).

Finally, creative solutions to instruction in the mainstreamed classroom tend to grow from necessity. Some of the best classroom strategies have come from regular teaching faculty who have felt a concern for all of their students and have sought solutions from their own perspective. Hearing and deaf students put into situations where they must communicate to be successful find ways to communicate on their own. The resources provider can facilitate the integration of students but can also learn from those who take the time to work with all students and to understand them.

Direct Instruction

This term refers to the practice in which an instructor uses both speech and sign language (signed English). Clearly this is not a common skill or practice and would likely not be used except in situations where there is a fairly large population of mainstreamed deaf students. The advantages to deaf students of direct instruction should be obvious. Deaf students who have been taught this way say that the instructor's use of sign makes them feel more a part of the class, closer to the instructor and more sure of the information they are receiving. There seem to be few distractions for hearing students; the general opinion expressed is that it doesn't bother them after they grow accustomed to it (Saur, Layne, and Hurley 1981). In fact, many hearing students prefer an instructor who signs because it slows down their speech, making it easier to understand them and take notes.

It is not likely, whatever the benefits, that instructors who use sign language will become common anywhere in our postsecondary schools outside of specialized programs for deaf students. The amount of time required for acquiring the level of sign skill necessary becomes almost prohibitive in the life of a busy, academic person. However, considering the benefits to students, instructors who do have the interest and facility for acquiring sign language skills should be encouraged to do so and rewarded for their efforts in the tenure/promotion/salary processes of their institutions.

CONCLUSION

Ultimately, the resources provided to deaf students will be driven by the requests and determined needs of the students themselves. Therefore, the success of any system of services or resources will rest on having an educated, knowledgeable consumer. Students must be fully a part of any system that purports to provide them with resources. Before they can be effective contributors to the process, however, they must know their own needs and be able to articulate them. Thus, the degree of student control in the process will necessarily be determined by student experience and maturity. At one time this process was known as 'dependency reduction.' Today the term seems paternalistic and negative. As stated earlier, we should look at our efforts in this area as fostering the empowerment of students, helping them to realize their own capabilities and gain confidence in their ability to self-advocate and get whatever resources they need.

Sometimes it is necessary to provide resources to students on a very limited budget and with few personnel resources, in which case it is doubly important to involve the student in planning and setting priorities for what can be provided. Creative solutions to problems can come from such collaboration. The resource person or service provider may have to act in a number of roles such as interpreter/advisor/tutor. If an interpreter is not available, students must have strategies for surviving in the classroom without one. This might mean sitting next to the notetaker and following what is written or getting extra notes from the instructor. It might be possible to take a tape recorder to class, record the lecture, and have the lecture transcribed by a typist. If no notetaker is available, notes might be obtained from an instructor or from another student in the class. The volunteer notetaker could be provided with pressure sensitive paper so that he/she could keep his/her own copy of the notes.

The key to providing good resources to students is to clearly identify a need first and then to identify the needed resources, rather than to plug students into already existing services. The standard methods of providing resources have clearly withstood the test of time in giving most students the resources they need to be successful. However, it is possible to provide good support in a less elaborate fashion.

In this chapter, many things have been written about empowering students, of making them aware of and responsible for identifying their own needs for resources. It has been pointed out that the provision of resources to students provides the opportunity to positively influence the hearing community as to the capabilities and needs of deaf persons. The need to identify properly the kind of resources a student needs has been emphasized. Finally, it was noted that quality control of a service, however large or small, is critical to student success. Thus, there is a need to train and monitor carefully the people who provide the resources.

At this time in history deaf persons are becoming increasingly aware of their rights as citizens and members of the larger society. Changes will have to occur in the way the hearing majority deals with these persons, accommodates their needs, and gives them the opportunity to contribute to society. Those who provide resources to mainstreamed, deaf students in postsecondary education will find themselves in the difficult but challenging position of offering encouragement and helping to open opportunities for young, deaf leaders of the future.

REFERENCES

Anderson, T.H. and Armbruster, B.B. (1986) *The value of taking notes during lectures*, (Technical Report No. 374) Illinois Univ., Urbana, Center for the Study of Reading. Cambridge, MA: Bolt, Beranek and Newman, Inc.

Beecher, J. (1988) 'Note-taking: What do we know about the benefits?' *ERIC Digest No. 12*, ERIC Clearinghouse on and Communication Skills. Bloomington, IN.

Carrier, Carol A. (1983) 'Notetaking research: implications for the classroom,' *Journal of Instructional Development*, 8, 3, 19–26.

Dubois, N.F. (1986) 'A review of the research on notetaking from lecture: some new directions to investigate,' Paper presented at the Annual Convention of the American Psychological Association, Washington, DC, August 1986. (ERIC document Reproduction Service No. ED 274 896).

Jacobs, L. (1977) 'The efficiency of interpreting input for processing lecture information by deaf college students,' *Journal of Rehabilitation of the Deaf*, 11, 235–47.

Lewis, J.P. (1985) 'Nota bene: a good notetaking program for successful postsecondary mainstreaming,' Paper presented at Association on the Handicapped Student Service Programs in Postsecondary Education, Columbus, OH.

Osguthorpe, R.T., Wilson, J.J., Goldmann, W.R., and Panara, J.E. (1980a) *The Tutor/Notetaker*. Washington, DC: Alexander Graham Bell Association for the Deaf, Inc.

Osguthorpe, R.T., Wilson, J.J., Goldmann, W.R., and Panara, J.E. (1980b) *Manager's Guide:The Tutor/Notetaker*. Washington, DC: Alexander Graham Bell Association for the Deaf, Inc.

Saur, R.E., Layne, C.A., and Hurley, E.A. (1981) 'Naturalistic research on mainstreaming at the National Technical Institute for the Deaf,' (Paper Series #43). Rochester, NY: Department of Educational Research and Development, National Technical Institute for the Deaf (ERIC Document Reproduction Service No. ED 209 910).

Saur, R.E., Layne, C.A., Hurley, E.A. and Opton, K. (1986) 'Dimensions of Mainstreaming,' *American Annals of the Deaf*, 131, 5, 325–30.

Stinson, M.S., Stuckless, E.R., and Henderson, J. (1988) 'Perceptions of hearing-impaired college students toward real-time speech to print: RTGD and other educational support services,' *Volta Review*, 90, 7, 339–48.

Stuckless, E.R.. (1983) 'Real-time transliteration of speech into print for hearing-impaired students in regular classes,' *American Annals of the Deaf*, 128, 5, 619–24.

Stuckless, E.R., Avery, J.C. and Hurwitz, T.A.(eds) (1989) *Educational Interpreting for Deaf Students*, Report of the National Task Force on Educational Interpreting, Rochester, NY: National Technical Institute for the Deaf.

Wilson, J.J. (1980) 'The tutor/notetaker as a support service for hearing-impaired students: The training program,' Paper presented at the meeting of the Association on Handicapped Student Services Programs in Postsecondary Education, Denver, CO, May 1980.

Personal Commentary

Thomas L. Callaghan

The following pages focus on my personal experiences in schools and colleges with and without resources such as interpreting and notetaking. Before doing so, I will describe a little of my background. I have been deaf since birth with an approximate loss of 100 dB. Because of my hearing parents' desire to have me develop oral communication skills, my family moved to Massachusetts from New Jersey in 1951 to enroll me in the Clarke School for the Deaf.

After 12 years in the Clarke School, I carried on the Clarke tradition by attending a hearing high school. In this case the school was Williston Academy, a private preparatory school in Easthampton, Massachusetts. The first year at the prep school was immensely difficult for me. One of my resources was the Clarke School Alumni Association which offered, and still does, to myself and recent Clarke graduates, opportunities to mingle with successful alumni two or three times a year. This was an ideal way for me to gain a respite from the demanding world of academics, recharge my depleted batteries, and exchange information and ideas to assist myself to better cope with academic pressures.

Classes at the prep school were small, no more than 12 students in a class. Formal support services were nonexistent for the Education for All Handicapped Children Act of 1975 (commonly referred to as PL 94-142), was some 10 years away from its enactment. Support in classrooms varied from teacher to teacher. Some would demand that I participate in class discussions; others would arrange with my classmates to take notes for me in exchange for a percentage of the student's grade. Sometimes one or two classmates volunteered to be my 'ears.' This was a necessity in my Latin classes for it was almost impossible for me to lipread a Latin-speaking instructor.

During my senior year at Williston I chose the University of Massachusetts at Amherst (UMass), because of its excellent engineering programs, particularly the civil engineering program. A combination of my desire to specialize in areas associated with transportation and my love for nature was the reason for my selection of civil engineering as a major. I was not daunted by the nonexistence of special support services for deaf students at UMass because of my success at Williston and the constant fostering of positive thinking by the Clarke School.

My first year at UMass was a very difficult struggle because the college environment was a totally new experience. My previous education, from preschool to preparatory, had not adequately prepared for this unstructured setting. This compelled me to learn how to use available resources and establish my own support system. One of my early moves was joining the UMass freshman football team, a much needed, although temporary, structure for me to rely on. It did bring to me a sense of belonging to the collegiate community and opportunities to develop friendships with peers from many parts of the campus.

In order to get as much information from classes as possible my first strategies were to copy notes from classmates sitting on both sides of me and to hold semi-weekly meetings with faculty. This worked well only in engineering and science courses, not in liberal arts classes because of the inability (or unwillingness) of my classmates to record enough of the information given out by fast-talking professors. Skipping liberal arts classes and appearing only for tests were my solutions to that problem, much to the dismay of the teachers and my parents. My frequent absences from classes were at first tolerated and then discouraged by my faculty advisor and professors who tried to work things out with me. Some of the solutions we tried included solving problems on the blackboards during class and giving short presentations to class. They were practical due to the small size of my engineering classes. However, my experiences of making presentations to the class were something I wanted to forget completely.

Sometime in the spring semester of my third year, still frustrated despite my increased class participation, I arranged with my mother to transcribe course notes. The setup was that I would record a class with a cassette and then send the cassette along with class notes collected by several means to my mother who would, in turn, transcribe the notes. It could be from one to three days before I would get the transcripts because of a combination of her unfamiliarity with course content, the average time of three hours required to transcribe one hour of class, and transportation difficulties. One immediate benefit was that I had the privilege of deciding which classes should be recorded and whether a cassette should be transcribed in its entirety or in part. Another benefit was that the transcripts gave me a chance to know exactly what happened in class, but they could call for time-consuming readings.

The next two years at UMass witnessed some refinement of my support system. In May 1972, I received a bachelor's degree in civil engineering and embarked on an 11-year career as an engineer in Massachusetts, Washington, DC, and the Commonwealth of Dominica.

In the spring of 1982 I returned to UMass to study for a master's degree in computer science, the vogue at that time. It was my first opportunity to take advantage of PL 94–142. Support services which UMass provided were limited to either notetaking or interpreting, not both. Due to my strong desire to know what was happening in class I chose the latter. Getting notes was more difficult than anticipated; the first few students I asked responded to the effect that having an interpreter should suffice. Diplomacy, persistence, and humor helped me resolve this situation. My rapport with teachers and students were no different from my experiences in the early days.

By the fall of 1982 my interest in computer science fizzled out due to my growing reluctance to devote more of my time to computer programming. Thus, the reawakening of my long-dormant interest in energy technology caused me to switch my major to mechanical engineering.

One year later I changed schools and got a new job. I began leading the double life of support faculty and part-time student in the mechanical engineering program at Rochester Institute of Technology (RIT). With full support services in place, RIT is like a communication paradise. I knew that I could sit in any class and get the same amount of information my classmates were receiving, and then get the class notes a few hours later. Also, I could get assistance with problems that bedeviled me from time to time. The quality of notes and interpreting was consistently excellent.

Having interpreting services does definitely facilitate my communications with faculty members and students; it represents the removal of a huge obstacle which many students face daily in their pursuit of higher education. I, however, sense an underlying bias on the part of RIT faculty and students toward the deaf students. It may be my own bias or both theirs and mine. It seems that once some of the obstacles are removed, the remaining obstacles become, or at least appear to become, more pronounced and deaf students double the effort to succeed in college. For example, some may find themselves under pressures by others to articulate their ideas or participate more frequently in class. They would prefer not to get involved due to their lack of self-confidence and self-esteem. It could be their lack of experience in competing with their hearing peers; many are uncomfortable in being 'put on the spot' after years and years of near-isolation in classrooms. At the same time I have a concern that deaf students may develop a dependency on support services which may deprive them of developing the necessary skills to utilize resources to their advantage.

In the last 20 or more years I have observed tremendous progress in narrowing the information and communication gaps for deaf students and placing them in a better position to compete with their hearing peers in the demanding college environment. My experiences have demonstrated that one will have a better chance of succeeding in college if he/she takes the initiative to establish his/her own informal network of resources and learns to utilize effectively the resources provided by others.

Thomas L. Callaghan is a faculty member at the Rochester Institute of Technology/National Technical Institute for the Deaf. He has received two degrees in civil and mechanical engineering – from the University of Massachusetts at Amherst and the Rochester Institute of Technology, respectively. Before coming to RIT he worked as a civil engineer for several firms in Massachusetts, Washington, DC, and Dominica. He was born with an approximate 110 dB hearing loss and attended the Clarke School for the Deaf in Northampton, Massachusetts.

Chapter 6

Interaction between deaf and hearing students in postsecondary educational settings

Patricia Mudgett DeCaro and Susan B. Foster

INTRODUCTION

The creation of social settings and the shaping of individual and group relations is a uniquely human activity. Much of this activity is done within educational contexts. This chapter is about the creation of educational and social environments on college campuses serving both deaf and hearing students. The actual shape of the arrangements of everyday life on these campuses contains strong messages that reinforce and shape people's perceptions regarding deafness and the relationships between deaf and hearing people.

The chapter is divided into three sections. In the first section, we trace the history of models used in deaf education by reviewing major trends in the social management of differences and assumptions about the nature and value of deafness. In the second section, we use an ecological model as a way of describing and explaining interaction between hearing and deaf students in mainstream postsecondary settings. The chapter concludes with thoughts regarding the creation of a college campus that provides maximum access, choice, and empowerment for both deaf and hearing students.

HISTORY OF EDUCATIONAL MODELS USED IN DEAF EDUCATION

In order to understand the history of the education of deaf people, it is first necessary to locate this history within the larger context of social trends regarding the management of individual differences and the social meanings that are ascribed to the characteristic of deafness. Examination of these themes explains how major educational models for deaf people have been conceived and implemented.

Melting Pot or Mosaic? Assimilation v. Pluralism as Guiding Social Philosophies

The United States as a society has had a very strong ethic of assimilation. Celebration of the United States as a 'melting pot' has come to symbolize the belief that people from other lands should be brought into the mainstream of American culture as quickly as possible, leaving behind their national languages and cultures. Underlying this philosophy is the idea that in order for people who are different to be successful, they must become as much as possible like the norm. Within this framework, differences are, in general, devalued and those who cannot or will not conform treated as outsiders. In fact, success has sometimes been measured in terms of the degree and speed with which the new citizen sheds all those characteristics that made him or her 'different.'

While there has always been some resistance to assimilation, such resistance has increased dramatically in recent decades with the celebration of ethnic, religious, racial, and gender differences by various groups. For example, blacks, Hispanics, and women are rediscovering, celebrating, and attempting to preserve those characteristics that are special to them as a group (Belenky, Clinchy, Goldberger, and Tarule 1986; Omi and Winant 1986). Within this pluralistic vision, differences are valued and the 'melting pot' becomes a 'mosaic.'

Conceptions of Deafness and Deaf People's Educational Ability

From antiquity to the present, deafness has been perceived by the majority of hearing people as an undesired deficiency (Gannon 1981; Lane 1984; Moores 1982; Reagan 1989). Such a view is reflected in the term 'dis-ability.' Variations on the theme of deafness as a problem run through much of the history of western civilization. Deaf people were first thought to be incapable of rational thought, education, or contribution to normal society (Lane 1984). The advent of Christianity, with its ethic of caring for those who are in need, led to educational efforts and the belief that deaf people could learn and come closer to the norm, with help. Developmental psychology contributed to the concepts of deaf people as 'developmentally delayed' as a result of experiential and linguistic deficiencies (Furth 1966), and/or 'psychologically stressed' due to problems of isolation and rejection associated with their difference (Myklebyst 1960).

In a reconceptualization of deafness and deaf people in society, an opposing set of assumptions held predominantly by deaf people asserts that while deafness is certainly a disadvantage in a society controlled by hearing people, deafness itself is a 'different ability,' rather than a 'dis-ability.' This marks a shift from the perception of deaf people as deficient (and therefore inferior), to that of 'different but equal' (Kyle and Pullen 1988; Reagan 1989). As Reagan states, deaf people have called for 'reconceptualizing deafness and the deaf as a sociocultural, rather than as an audiological and pathological phenomenon' (1989:46). The affirmation by linguists (Klima and Bellugi 1979; Stoke 1960) that American Sign Language (ASL) is a language rather than 'poor English and mime' marked the 'professional' beginning of this new perspective on deafness. The protest at Gallaudet University in 1988, which ousted a hearing president and the president of the Board, forced reforms in college policy, and insisted upon a deaf president, brought that struggle into the open. Celebration of deaf heritage (Gannon 1981) and studies of deaf culture (Padden and Humphries 1988) consolidated the view that deaf people are not only equally able to learn, but also have new and different perspectives to bring to hearing society. Along with this comes the suggestion that the academic delays, so often associated with deafness, may be largely a problem of hearing people's difficulties in communications, and associated rigid and controlled forms of teaching (Wood 1990) and cultural misunderstanding.

Society's Response to Deafness

The notions of assimilation versus pluralism, in combination with changing definitions of deafness, provide a framework for analyzing societal responses to deafness. Historically, in western cultures, deaf people were either left to the care of their families or put into asylums, at least in part a reaction to the belief that deaf people *could not* become enough like hearing people to assimilate into the larger society and should therefore be removed from society. However, once people understood that deaf people could in fact be educated and even potentially 'cured,' the disciplines of medicine, psychology, education, and linguistics, as well as the weight of technological inventions, were brought to bear upon the 'problem of deafness' with the hope that deafness could be prevented or its effects ameliorated. This view has often been called the 'medical model' of disability in that deafness is seen as a disease to be cured. It is grounded in the philosophy of assimilation with a focus on individual normalization.

> This [medical] model has the assumption that differences in physical, sensory, or mental capabilities necessarily produce a defective member of society. Such a situation then requires remediation or treatment. Indeed, *not to treat*, given the knowledge of difference, offends against an implied 'Hippocratic oath' shared by all members of our enlightened society.
>
> (Kyle and Pullen 1988: 50)

Indeed these efforts have made a tremendous difference in the lives of many deaf people. Advances in technology have made possible the prevention of deafness in many cases (antibiotics), the elimination of some types of deafness (surgery), and opportunities for access to and integration with a hearing society (hearing aids, captioning). A 'psychology of deafness' was elaborated (Myklebyst 1960) to describe psychological and developmental problems and to develop strategies to help both deaf students and their parents deal with these. Indeed, Bender (1981) titled her book, *The Conquest of Deafness* in anticipation of advances yet to come.

However, despite these significant contributions, some aspects of deafness were never addressed due to the focus upon assimilation through normalization. Most people making decisions regarding the development and application of new technologies and medical advances have been hearing, and relatively unaware of the societal and cultural contexts within which deafness is defined, as well as political issues related to distribution of power. The possibility of a deaf community, culture, and pride was rarely recognized; therefore, the analytical power of the disciplines was not brought to bear upon such positive aspects of deafness as the close-knit deaf community, ASL poetry, differing cultural norms, nor upon such issues as the possible advantages of learning sign language in school, or empowerment.

Regardless, much of what was intended to bring deaf people into the mainstream was also empowering. For example, much of the communication technology, laws regarding interpreting and affirmative action, and increased educational opportunities are empowering to the deaf community and also increase access to the world of hearing people. However, it was not generally recognized that there might be a view of deafness within which society might be asked to change to ensure access, choice and empowerment of deaf people as 'different but equal' partners in America. It is interesting to contemplate what differences we would see in the technology, the literature and knowledge relating to deafness, and in education, if deaf people had had a greater voice in decision making, and society had focused upon the goals of empowerment, access, and choice.

Educational Models

Four different educational models can be described that reflect different sets of assumptions about deafness and views of society's role with regard to deaf people. These models are illustrated in Figure 6.1 as an interaction between settings (segregated or integrated) and conceptions of deafness (disability or different ability). The models reflected by Cells 1 and 2 are grounded in the assimilationist perspective; those represented by Cells 3 and 4 fall within the pluralist tradition.

Much of the history of education of people who are deaf can be described in terms of the first two cells. As Moores and Kluwin (1986) point out, many elements of what today is called 'mainstreaming' were practiced by early educators of the deaf. In this spirit, some of the earliest schools for the deaf were established as day schools and located in cities in order to enable students to live at

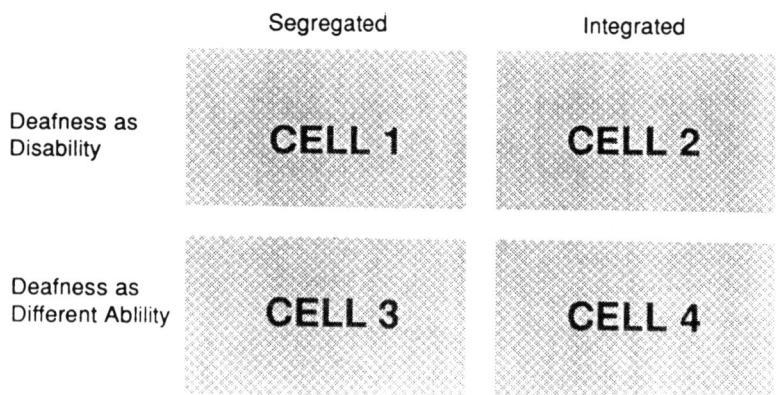

Figure 6.1 Models used in deaf education

home with their families and associate with hearing children outside the school. Other deaf children attended school with hearing peers, with varying levels of support. In general, this period was characterized by optimism and belief that people with disabilities could (and should) be assimilated within the larger society.

Toward the end of the 19th and beginning of the 20th centuries, however, the optimism dimmed. This period, sometimes referred to as the 'genetics period,' was characterized by the belief that many people with physical and/or mental differences were a threat to society (Deutsch 1949; Wolfensberger 1975). During this time, residential schools for deaf students were established in rural or isolated places, that is, 'out of the mainstream.' Interestingly, while the reason for removal from the regular school was grounded in the belief that the deaf person could not be taught within these settings, the goal in many of the separate institutions remained normalization and eventual return of graduates to the hearing world. Both removal from and return to the hearing world are based in the assimilationist perspective, since acceptance in this world is often based on one's ability and/or willingness to conform.

It is critical to note differences between the experience of deaf people and those of other people with a physical or mental difference vis-à-vis congregation and segregation in special institutions. The experience of the latter was almost always one of abuse and isolation (Blatt and Kaplan 1974). In contrast, Gannon (1981) suggests that such segregation was often beneficial to deaf people, since it provided an escape from the isolation they experienced in the hearing world, an opportunity to communicate freely for both social and academic purposes, and the chance to participate in a broad array of activities. These schools offered many deaf people their only opportunity to engage in the professional activity of teaching and provided deaf role models for students.

Despite these advantages, educators cited problems with the separation of deaf people from the mainstream of American education. Most often, these problems were associated with the inability of separate systems to ensure the assimilation of their students into society and the corresponding belief that attending school with hearing peers would promote normalization. One common argument is based upon the belief that there are pathological and social problems that accompany physical disabilities. Green (1976) discusses the low self-esteem and devaluing of self that may come with the failure at communication. She goes on to state that, 'Given the normal model, given the chance to emulate a peer group, given realistic expectations, hearing-impaired children can develop social skills as adequately as their hearing peers' (Green 1976: 79).

Other arguments against separate schools for deaf students are grounded in the principles of civil rights and the belief that separate *is not equal* when segregation is involuntary and based on a devalued characteristic. Following the reasoning used to support racial desegregation of the public schools, residential schools for students who are deaf came to be seen by the hearing public as shameful and discriminatory, a strategy for keeping deaf people out of society and denying them their rights as citizens. As a result, the last twenty years have witnessed a return of many deaf students to public schools. This practice, generally referred to as 'mainstreaming,' was operationalized through Public Law (PL) 94–142, also known as The Education for All Handicapped Children Act of 1975, which states that disabled students have a right to a free, appropriate education in the least restrictive environment. Although the law recognized that some exceptions could exist, the mainstream is normally considered to be the least restrictive and therefore the preferred option. Again, as the term 'mainstreaming' suggests, the goal is assimilation:

> We as administrators, supervisors, teachers, and parents need to view mainstreaming both as a *goal* and a *process* – a goal for every hearing impaired child to enter the mainstream of life and a process by which each child will reach that goal.
>
> (Froehlinger 1981: 43)

The results of mainstreaming have been mixed. For example, while deaf students in mainstreamed programs tend to show higher levels of academic achievement than their peers in separate classes and programs, it is not clear whether this difference can be traced to their integration status alone (Allen and Osborn 1984; Kluwin and Moores 1985). Moreover, there is evidence to suggest that mainstreamed deaf students experience problems in the areas of personal and social development (Farrugia and Austin 1980; Foster 1989; Mertens and Kluwin 1986). Foster (1989) describes this as 'the trade' between academic and social opportunity by setting.

Both the educational models described so far (Cells 1 and 2) are grounded in the presumption that deaf people are deficient. Both are based on the premise that to succeed in society, one must be as much like hearing people as possible. The educational strategies employed within these kinds of programs mirror this philosophy, in that deaf people are treated in ways designed to minimize differences related to deafness and/or removed from society. Foster (1989) refers to this as the 'hidden curriculum' that underlies both settings.

Currently, there is a growing interest in providing deaf people with educational experiences that are based on the philosophy that deafness is a *different ability*. Within this framework, deaf culture, language, and community are interpreted as variations on the general themes of ethnic diversity, multiculturalism, and bilingualism. Thus far, most proponents of this approach have suggested that it can only be achieved in reorganized separate institutes administered by deaf people, corresponding to Cell 3. Indeed, it would appear to be much easier to attain goals of personal empowerment in settings with clear leadership opportunities and access to educational content facilitated through instruction in sign language by people familiar with and respectful of deaf culture and norms. Reagan summarizes this position as follows:

> In a sense, what we are now seeing is the development of a very different debate within deaf education, one between those advocating a separate and distinct education for deaf children based on their unique social, cultural, and linguistic needs, and those who seek to mainstream deaf children into the regular classroom as a way of ensuring cultural and linguistic conformity. In short, the debate between the assimilationists and the pluralists in American education is coming, somewhat belatedly, to deaf education.
> (Reagan 1989: 46)

This position often assumes the impossibility of attaining the desired goals in an integrated setting. Yet a great number of young deaf persons will continue to be placed in predominantly hearing settings despite any increase in respect for the role of schools for deaf students. Nor is it sufficient simply to say that deaf students should be divided into those for whom the mainstream is best and those for whom a separate school is best, without discussion of alteration of these settings for empowerment and access. Both settings require alteration.

Thus a very significant question facing educators today is whether the philosophy that deafness is a different ability rather than a disability can be conceived and implemented within educational settings serving both deaf and hearing people (Cell 4). Can the goals of accessibility, choice, and empowerment replace those of normalization, remediation, and cure within integrated school settings? Can a pluralistic philosophy replace that of assimilation in these educational communities? The current climate of pluralism, combined with growing interest in multicultural and bilingual education, has made such an approach *conceivable*. Making it happen is another thing entirely, and requires both commitment and skill from those responsible for the creation of educational settings. One of the first steps is to examine carefully the existing educational setting for indications of practices that foster or interfere with access, choice, and empowerment.

AN ECOLOGICAL MODEL OF INTERACTION

Interaction between deaf and hearing students within postsecondary educational settings is a complex phenomenon. To explain or influence it, one must understand the range of factors that influence interaction, including individual as well as environmental factors. An ecological model of human behavior can be used to illustrate and discuss the ways in which the individual interacts with his or her environment (Bronfenbrenner 1979). Briefly, this model, depicted in Figure 6.2, is grounded in the idea that in order to understand the behavior of the individual, that individual must be seen as existing within social settings, institutions, and cultural systems, each of which interacts with and therefore influences (and is influenced by) the individual and the other systems. This 'nesting,' or location of the individual within one or more social and cultural settings, is perhaps best conceptualized as a series of concentric circles, with the individual represented at the center of the circle(s).

Systems can also overlap, in which case the representation would include two or more environments intersecting or touching at some point. In considering the case of the postsecondary campus, such a diagram should include the various kinds of settings within which students routinely interact, as well as the larger culture and organization of the institution. In the following pages, we describe each of these elements, and how they influence the interaction of students within specific campus settings. This model does not explore differential distribution of power and the resulting effect upon knowledge, programming, setting, resources, and organization. Such issues must and will be explored in subsequent work.

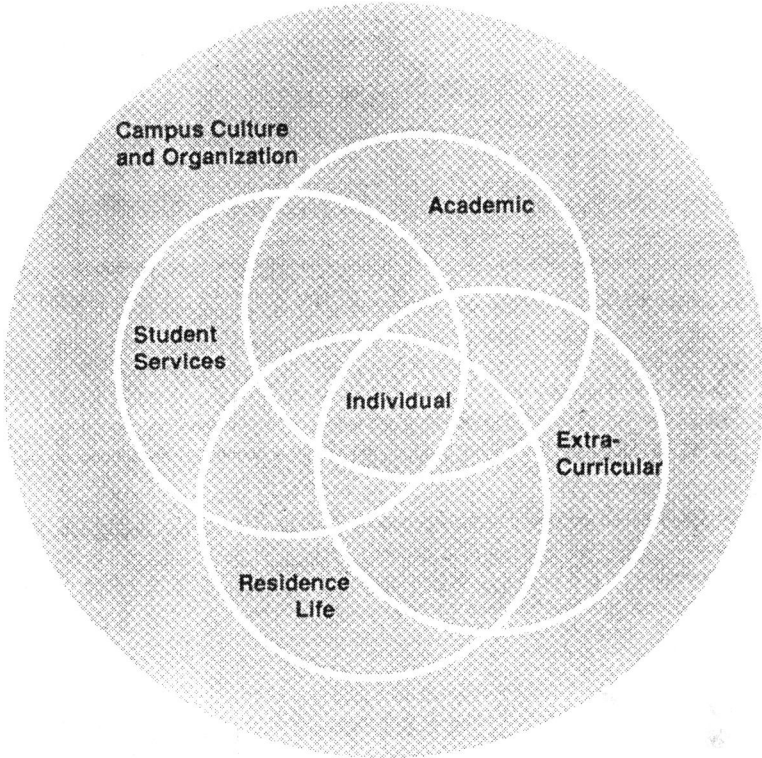

Figure 6.2 An ecological framework for analyzing interaction on a postsecondary campus

Source: Bronfenbrenner (1979)

Individual Characteristics

Students bring with them to college a host of attitudes, skills, beliefs, assumptions, expectations, and goals. Whenever they enter a specific campus setting or interact with another person, they interpret and analyze their experience in light of these highly individual characteristics. Questions that can be used to describe and analyze individual characteristics relative to interaction between deaf and hearing students might include the following: What kinds of knowledge does the student have about deaf (or hearing) people, and how accurate is this knowledge? What kind of communication skills does the person have? What are their reasons for being in this setting or participating in this activity? What are students' attitudes and feelings about deaf (or hearing) people?

Specific Campus Settings

Every campus is made up of specific settings where students meet and interact with one another. The goals and functions of these settings, the rules that govern behavior within them, their physical location and design, and the ways in which they are organized and administered all shape the types of interactions that are possible. We have identified four broad categories of campus settings: (1) academic settings (for example, classes, labs, and academic clubs); (2) extracurricular activities (sports, parties, student government, social clubs, and fraternal associations); (3) residence life (dining halls, lounges, residence halls); and (4) student services (mental and physical health services, religious centers, libraries, financial aid, special support services, admissions, and job placement). Campus settings frequently overlap, as reflected by the intersection of circles on the diagram.

Campus Culture and Organization

Factors related to campus culture and organization include the goals and purpose of the institution, distribution of resources, program administration, physical layout of the campus and appointments of the buildings, academic calendar/pace of campus life, and number of deaf students on campus. Analysis of the culture and organization of the campus includes a description of these factors and the ways in which they influence (both intentionally and unintentionally) the behavior of those who live, work, and study within it.

In the following pages, we illustrate the complexity of the ways deaf and hearing students learn about one another on a mainstreamed campus by telling a story of two students attending 'State College (SC).' Through the eyes of Nancy and Jack, we examine the web of interactions between deaf and hearing students in the contexts of the individual, a range of campus settings, and the overall campus culture. Much of this story is based on research on interaction between deaf and hearing students at Rochester Institute of Technology (Foster and DeCaro 1990). However, we have been careful to include only those findings that can be reasonably generalized to other postsecondary settings. In this sense, State College is not a specific campus, nor are Nancy and Jack 'real' people; rather, they are 'composites' that include the features of many postsecondary institutions and students.

State College: A Composite Case Example

State College is a liberal arts school with a wide variety of academic programs available to the 5,300 students on campus. The College provides the 50–75 matriculated deaf students with special services designed to facilitate their integration on campus. These services are coordinated through the Handicapped Student Services Center (located in Jackson Residence Hall). The Center offers deaf students assistance with registration, resource services (including interpreting, notetaking, and tutoring), and counseling. The Center also serves as a sort of 'home' for the deaf students who often meet there to collect their mail, use the TDD (telecommunication device for the deaf), and just to socialize. For reasons of economy and safety, State College renovated two floors of Jackson Hall with strobes for each room to accommodate the deaf students. Each floor has some hearing students as well, some of whom requested this placement, and others who were put there because other floors were filled. Nancy (who is hearing) and Jack (who is deaf) are freshmen at State College.

Pre-college Experience

Nancy arrives at SC with very little previous experience with deafness. She has some concept of 'deaf' and 'hearing' gained through movies, an aunt who taught sign, and an older neighbor who is becoming deaf. She received a brochure about disabled students on the SC campus but doesn't really understand the numbers or the exact situations in which she might find herself with deaf students. Nancy hasn't really thought much about deafness, but feels that the only difference between deaf people and her is that *they* can't hear. She assumes that they can all lipread and speak fairly well, and expects that some use sign, which she thinks of as a sort of combination of English and mime. Finally, she feels sorry for them and assumes that they wish they could be normal (that is, hearing).

Jack, on the other hand, has been around hearing people all his life. He is quite 'used to' hearing people and feels that he understands them. He has spent a few years in a school for deaf students but for most of his education has been in mainstreamed programs where he was one of only a handful of deaf students. His experiences with hearing people have been both positive and negative. He is well aware of the communication barriers between deaf and hearing people, and believes that it requires a positive attitude and much effort on everyone's part to get past it. As he says, 'It is very easy for hearing and deaf people not to bother with each other because it [communication] is something you both have to really fight for.'[1] Jack knows about the anxiety associated with deaf and hearing interactions; for example, he will tell you that a lot of hearing and deaf people are afraid to try to communicate because they believe they might fail or be ridiculed. With other deaf students Jack uses signed English and a little ASL, but he is highly skilled in manipulating a wide variety of methods of communication, including writing, gesturing, varieties of sign, and speech.

Early Campus Experiences

Both Nancy and Jack attend the first day of Student Orientation, in which a great deal of information is presented to new students about registration, campus organizations, and academic programs. However, they go separate ways the second day, because Jack attends a program for students with disabilities, while Nancy continues in the general orientation. There is actually nothing said in the general orientation about deaf people, but on the second day Nancy does overhear some side comments from the student orientation staff about the immaturity of the deaf students, all the government money that pays their way, and their '6th-grade math level.'

Jack learns a lot at the general orientation, but during the second day in the special orientation for deaf students he really enjoys being in an environment where he can interact and easily communicate with other deaf students; he says that he feels at home and in control there. Already he has the feeling that he will spend a lot of time at the Handicapped Student Services Center.

Residence Life

Nancy has been placed on a mainstreamed floor. Although she noticed the sign pointing to the Handicapped Student Services Center and knows there are a few deaf students on campus, she has no idea at all about how to interact with them and is immediately overwhelmed by a situation in the residence hall when she goes to get her room key only to find that her Student Resident Advisor (SRA) is deaf. As she writes home, 'I asked her a question and she didn't even answer, then she turned around and started talking to me but her voice is so weird, its just so different it makes me really nervous.'

As one of only 64 deaf students on campus, Jack is also surprised to find so many deaf students on his floor. While he has braced himself for the social isolation he has come to expect with hearing people, he also believes that it would be a good experience for him to live with them since this might better prepare him for a career in 'the hearing world.' He is relieved to find that he is not the only deaf person on his floor, and looks forward to the opportunity to meet deaf *and* hearing people.

Both Nancy and Jack are pleased to discover that their residence hall is in some ways the nicest on campus. The hall, called 'Hotel Jackson' by the older students, is designed in suites of three rooms sharing a private bath. Further amenities include modern 'stackable' furniture, cable television outlets in each room, and air conditioning! While Jack and Nancy agree that the private rooms are great, they also find that the hallways and television lounges are institutional and uninviting. Fire regulations prevent much decoration on those walls and require that students' doors remain closed. Lighting in the hallways is too dim for good visual communication, and the television lounge is bare except for a sofa in poor condition and a television that is chained to the wall and too high to reach or watch comfortably. Jack says it is hard for him to strike up conversations in the hall because it is too dark to read people's lips. Nancy, who describes her initial impression of the floor as one long corridor of closed doors, recalls the difficulty she had getting to know other floor residents. As she puts it 'Some of the people on my floor, it took them the longest time to even say "Hi" to me because they weren't sure if I lived there or if I was just visiting.'

Not surprisingly, both Nancy and Jack learned that a number of the second- and third-year hearing students on the floor are people who value their privacy and are not particularly interested in an active social life or interaction with other students. On the other hand, some of these students are quite friendly and comfortable with deaf students *because* they have been there more than one year and have become really 'used to it.' These students are also the best signers in the hearing group.

Nancy finds she is not in an integrated room (housing policy stipulates that hearing and deaf students are only placed in the same room when a specific request is made). However, there are two deaf students in the suite, so they share the bathroom. The noise is her only real complaint about them. The deaf girls turn their music up really high to hear it and then sometimes leave the room and forget the music is on. Jack's hearing suitemates complain about his habit of slamming the doors but one of them can sign a little and has told Jack about the problem. The two of them devised a way to pad the doors so that it will be quieter, since Jack can't tell when it slams.

In the second week of school the two SRAs (one deaf and one hearing) arrange an interesting floor program about deaf and hearing interactions that makes everyone feel optimistic about working together to overcome the communication barriers. However, as students establish friendships and become immersed in schoolwork, enthusiasm for these programs wanes and students become reluctant to attend events that they perceive as forcing interaction. As Nancy says, 'It would be nice to have more interaction between hearing and deaf students, but the more the SRA's push us together, the more we pull back – anyway, we have to want to do the same things first.' Despite these difficulties, some activities do continue to be successful. One of the favorites is the Sunday night practice of renting a movie and showing it in the lounge, with free pizza. The movie is captioned, and as hearing and deaf students drift in to eat and watch the movie, conversations sometimes occur. Jack recalls striking up a conversation with a hearing student at one of these events in which they wrote page after page of dialogue to one another.

Just as Nancy and Jack are beginning to get to know a few students on the floor, people start changing rooms, often leaving the floor entirely in the process. Mostly, this is due to the College's efforts to redistribute students and to relieve the overcrowding that occurs at the beginning of the year, when students are sometimes assigned three to a double room. Jack had begun really to enjoy two hearing students across the hall and even went to their parties, but now that they have moved he has lost track of them and is not really motivated to put so much effort into a new relationship with other hearing students on the floor.

In fact, Jack attends mostly all-deaf parties now. Actually, he and Nancy find that mixed parties are tough. People go to parties to relax, not to work hard at communicating, and anyway Jack and his friends love to be very active at parties and need the lights on full, while Nancy and her friends prefer the lights lower, and quiet chatting. Jack thinks hearing people are pretty boring at parties, and Nancy's friends think deaf students are immature.

Everyday Campus Learning

Both Nancy and Jack notice support services on campus like the captioning on campus televisions and the TDD in the Jackson Hall lobby, but it is quickly obvious that these services are limited. For one thing, there are not enough interpreters to adequately cover extracurricular activities. Nancy recalls the time when both she and Jack showed up for the first meeting of the ski club; since there was no interpreter, Jack couldn't understand what was going on and left. As Nancy describes it, this was 'another lost opportunity' for interaction between hearing and deaf students. Of course the dining, bookstore, library, bursar, and other staff don't know signs and it took Jack three times as long to get his books as it should have. Jack and the woman at the counter were both really frustrated. Nancy, waiting in line behind him, became irritated and decided not to get in line behind deaf students again if she could help it. She also formed the opinion that communicating with deaf students was a really, really hard thing to do.

Jack and Nancy both recall that they must note whether or not they are disabled on almost every campus form they fill out. Jack asked about this and was told that this is because the College needs to keep a record of what they are doing and spending for the deaf and other disabled students. Jack says he wishes students were not routinely required to make this distinction, since it reinforces his sense of being different and separate from the other students.

Nancy and Jack are in the same biology class. Nancy is fascinated by the interpreter at the front of the room. Although she understands that Jack sits up front to see the interpreter, she also says that this further isolates the deaf students, since they are always in a group at the front of the class. Jack is more pragmatic – he says he couldn't function in the class without the interpreter and, anyway, he prefers to sit with other deaf students because then he has someone to talk with before class starts, adding that even when he is the only deaf student in class the hearing students still don't often approach or make casual conversation with him.

Later in the Year

By the end of the fall semester, Nancy has begun to notice that friendship patterns on her floor tend to reflect compatible communication methods. She is sure now that communication is the *only* barrier between deaf and hearing people. She decides to learn to sign so that she can at least go across the hall to borrow a book or converse with the deaf student in her gym class. Some of her hearing friends feel that they get along really well with deaf students and that they understand each other, but Jack says that it is all just saying 'Hi' and other surface communication only. Everybody has a lot of uncertainty at each encounter about who is deaf or hearing, what kind of communication they prefer, and what is meant by certain actions or looks. Neither Jack nor Nancy is very aware of the extent to which they are misreading facial expressions and behaviors because of differing communication modalities, experiences, and cultures. Nancy has talked with her roommate about the deaf students' rudeness in refusing to let her through when they are talking in the hall, not knowing that Jack has complained to his deaf friends about how hearing students seem to insist on interrupting the signed conversation rather than politely just walking right through!

Nancy was the only first-year hearing student on her floor to take the sign language course offered at SC, and as she became more skilled, her desire and interest in interacting with deaf students increased a lot. She became less awkward around deaf people and good enough at sign to have a few 'real' conversations. Her contact with a deaf counselor at the Center who was her sign teacher impressed her tremendously as she began to realize how much deaf people could do. Jack started coming to ask her if she would call for a pizza for him, or interpret what someone else was saying. Eventually, they began to stop by each other's rooms during study breaks and walk over to the dining commons together.

It is now almost the end of the year. It has taken Nancy a whole semester just to get used to having 'hands fly around,' but now she has developed some communication skills, and has some idea that not all deaf people are alike, nor do they all wish they could hear. Equally important, she has already found herself in several situations in which she has gone out of her way to defend or explain deafness to other hearing students.

Jack spends more and more of his time at the Handicapped Student Services Center and is emerging as something of a leader in the deaf student group that routinely meets there. He says this is the first time in his life that he has felt he can be a leader, since it was so hard to compete for these kinds of positions in high school, where he was the only deaf person. He and the other deaf students have decided to start a fraternity on campus, and have been instrumental in convincing the administration to increase the number of full-time interpreters at SC. He has also become a student assistant to a deaf counselor at the Center. Jack says that this person was instrumental in helping him through some rough coursework at the beginning of the year, adding that he has developed a new sense of pride and membership in what he refers to as the deaf[2] student community at SC as a result of this relationship.

Although most of his closest friends are deaf, Jack considers Nancy to be a good friend, too. He says that her willingness to learn sign language was critical to the development of their friendship, and greatly respects her efforts to communicate with him and other deaf students. He looks forward to the next year at SC, and hopes that he will be able to find more hearing students like Nancy.

CREATION OF AN EDUCATIONAL PROGRAM ON A PREDOMINANTLY HEARING CAMPUS

Earlier in this chapter we posed the question of whether it is possible to construct an integrated educational setting that is accessible and empowering for the deaf students. Our attempt in this chapter to describe and better understand what fosters or impedes attainment of such goals is a first step in addressing this question. The story of Nancy and Jack illustrates some of the possible experiences, both positive and negative, of deaf and hearing students on a specific campus, as well as the complexity of their interactions.

Each campus situation and setting is different and requires custom-designed practices. Nonetheless, some guiding philosophies have emerged from our work, which we present below, along with a few specific practices and recommendations that may be useful to the reader.

Creation always begins with a set of assumptions and a goal, whether examined or unexamined. For a long time the creation of educational settings for deaf people rested upon assumptions derived from the hearing world that did not take into account the full spectrum of possibilities and choices that may comprise any one deaf person's views, community, and aspirations. Deaf people have now made it clear that this is no longer sufficient. Deaf people have called for a redefinition of deafness as a valued and different characteristic, within which empowerment, access, and choice replace the goals of assimilation and normalization. This focus requires that proposed or existing programs be examined in light of the question, 'In what ways does our program promote or impede empowerment, access, and choice by deaf students?' This question cannot be answered by hearing people alone. It must be addressed with and by deaf post-secondary students and faculty, based on their day-to-day experiences as deaf people in a hearing-dominated world.

Both Nancy and Jack found that many activities and settings on campus were inaccessible to deaf students, or promoted distinctions that set deaf students apart from their hearing peers. One strategy for evaluating and improving accessibility for deaf students is a campus-wide 'audit,' in which forms, rules, signs, physical facilities, offices, and so on are examined for access to a variety of people. These items can then be prioritized for importance and practicality of action. For example, an audit of SC would probably yield recommendations that interpreter coverage of campus events be increased, lighting be upgraded in the residence halls, faculty, professional, and support staff be required to learn at least basic sign language and become creative as well as flexible in alternative methods of communication, and the development of alternative ways of identifying students as disabled on campus forms if it is truly necessary (for example, asking all students for social security numbers and then programming the computer to sort students on this basis).

In creating or evaluating a program, the designers must also keep in mind the ecological complexity of interaction on campus. This approach is consistent with a consensus forming across disciplinary fields that seeks to situate individual experience within the social context in all its complexity. Each practice must be understood in terms of individual characteristics and experiences as well as external realities such as time, administrative practices, fire regulations, and other rules. For example, Nancy's decision to learn sign language is due to many factors acting in combination, including her experience on the mainstreamed floor, the Sunday pizza and movie parties, and her frustration at being unable to communicate with her deaf suitemates. Similarly, Jack's statement that 'communication with hearing students is limited' is a reflection of communication barriers, inadequate resources, the physically isolating environment of Jackson Hall, and the pervasive sense that deaf students at SC are somehow different, and therefore set apart from hearing students.

Not only are these interactions complex, there are also many decisions designed to attain one goal that have serious *unintended* consequences that undermine efforts to reach the same or another goal. For example, the residence hall in our story, while undoubtedly a nice place to live, also posed many serious physical obstacles to the very interaction that the establishment of mainstreamed floors was intended to encourage between hearing and deaf students. Likewise, the labeling of the service center the 'Handicapped' Services Center, and the listing of deaf students separately on office forms for accounting purposes had the unintended effect of emphasizing 'otherness' and 'dis'ability of deaf students. On the other hand, the center provided Jack opportunities that he might not have had without it. The involvement of deaf faculty and students is critical in identifying the unintended consequences of campus policy and practice upon their daily lives. Critical issues that are often avoided include differential power relations, the consequent allocation of resources, and the cultural definitions of what's 'right' or 'wrong' that are woven into the system of interactions. Rowe best describes the problem:

> Micro-inequities are woven into all the threads of our work life and of American culture. . . . Micro-inequities are of a fiendish efficiency in maintaining unequal opportunity, because they are the air we breathe, the books we read, and because we cannot change the personal characteristic which leads to the inequity. Micro-inequities are omni-present in our work and educational lives.
>
> (Rowe 1981: 155)

In recent years, multiculturalism and pluralism have become increasingly important and discussed themes in education. Even though the numbers of deaf students may be small on any one campus, working with other minority groups as one of several who share general concerns and who are often misunderstood and mislabeled, may not only positively influence perceptions of deafness but also increase chances of accommodation. For example, Weis (1985) discusses how time is controlled by the white majority in ways that may be detrimental to minorities due to their needs or to cultural differences, and the negative stereotypes and labels such as 'immature' and 'lazy' that often accrue to the minority student who does not fit or conform to these standards. Similarly, hearing students often consider deaf students 'rude' for using 'too much space' in conversing, and 'overly emotional', judging by their facial expressions, despite the linguistically encoded and necessary nature of both spatial use and facial expression in sign language. Although the specifics are different, various minorities share a similar sort of problem. Working toward the goal of understanding and gaining access for all students helps to derail arguments that any one group is too small to justify attention or accommodation. Administratively, deaf students have traditionally been placed with groups of students with other disabilities, when in fact there might be a better case made for placement with minority affairs.

In some cases, differences between groups must be addressed directly, given that assumptions often lead to misunderstandings, stereotyping, and even hostility between people who are different. Knowledge often fosters respect. Courses relating to minorities in general, or specifically to deafness and sign language, should be offered for credit and open to all students. Faculty and students who come in direct and frequent contact with deaf students should be encouraged, if not required, to take such courses. Student Resident Advisors on integrated floors should take specific coursework not only in communication methods, but also cultural differences and attitudes toward deafness, since their role is to educate students and facilitate cooperation and dialogue. Some kinds of information may best come in little 'bytes,' offered at appropriate moments by knowledgeable authorities; one strategy is a 'culture booth' staffed by a deaf and a hearing student, to answer frequently asked questions such as, 'Why do all deaf students seem to be so emotional?' or 'Why are hearing students so reluctant to walk between deaf people who are talking in sign language?' Finally, campus publications can be used to discuss issues directly. For example, an article in the RIT newspaper *Reporter* used the facts to challenge the widespread perception on that campus that deaf students were babied and got a practically free education (Tiffany 1990). Students can be encouraged individually, or as part of a class, to discuss their differences and their points of view.

Another way to increase knowledge of and respect for deaf people on campus is to encourage deaf and hearing faculty and students to work together on projects. Note that it *must not* always be a hearing person who takes the lead. Interdisciplinary work across majors might be interesting. For example, a physical access problem on campus can be addressed as an engineering project or competition.

Drama productions can incorporate deaf and hearing actors who sign. Students on one of the mainstreamed residence hall floors can be given a modest budget and encouraged to pool their ideas and expertise in order to design more inviting and interactive lounges and hallways. Working cooperatively in teams is an aspect of scientific and business work that is seldom practiced in competitive school settings. Giving groups of students (deaf and hearing) more decision-making power regarding problems and programs not only increases the dialogue between them and creates interesting solutions, but enhances commitment and involvement with each other. This approach also achieves interaction between hearing and deaf students without focusing upon deafness per se; as Nancy said, students enjoyed doing fun things together but resisted activities that were contrived or forced.

Weis (1985) notes the critical need to have a substantial number of minority faculty in the academic areas (or any other responsible, decision-making capacity on campus) as role models since their absence signals the possession of prestigious knowledge by the majority only and deprives the institution of alternative points of view. Nancy's increase in respect for and expectations of deaf people, as well as Jack's sense of pride and membership in the deaf community, both are the result of interactions with deaf role models on campus.

Finally, particular attention must be given to the advantages and disadvantages of both integrated and separate activities and groups. As Jack's experience illustrates, there are significant roles for separate settings on mainstream campuses. For example, essentially segregated settings can mitigate some of the unintended negative aspects of mainstreaming (such as isolation and personal rejection). Every student needs a 'home,' or a place in which he/she feels comfortable and in control. Two possibilities described in the SC case example are the Handicapped Student Services Center and the fraternity. Others include special interest houses for students (deaf or hearing) who want to learn about deaf culture and ASL, and clubs or political groups that organize campus-wide activities related to deafness and perhaps send members to the campus-wide student government to represent the interests of deaf students. It is important to stress that the need for, and development of separate social and political groups should not be used as an excuse to avoid creating complete access to campus-wide activities. Only when a full array of options is truly available can we ensure access, choice, and empowerment for all students.

Can an empowering, accessible postsecondary educational setting be created where both deaf and hearing students are equal and valued participants? The possibility is conceivable within the current climate of a changing attitude toward deafness and a general discussion regarding multiculturalism, but the realization of such an environment is a challenging task requiring creative and thoughtful planning. While there is no single strategy that works everywhere, the ideas of pluralism, multiculturalism, empowerment, access and choice should be guiding principles for the development of programs for deaf students. As strategies and interventions are planned, they should be examined in light of these principles, with careful attention to unintended as well as intended consequences, and with consideration of who has the decision-making and resource allocation powers. Deaf people must be participants at all times and at all levels in order to identify problem areas and participate in the creation, implementation, and evaluation of solutions. In each case, the goal should be the creation of a campus where *all* services, settings, and activities are fully accessible to all students, and decisions about when and how to participate made by students from a position of choice and equal opportunity.

NOTES

1 Quotations are taken from interviews with deaf and hearing students conducted as part of the RIT research project mentioned earlier (Foster and DeCaro 1990).
2 The use of the uppercase 'Deaf' is used to refer to 'a particular group of deaf people who share a language – American Sign Language (ASL) and a culture,' as opposed to the lowercase 'deaf,' which refers 'to the audiological condition of not hearing.' (Padden and Humphries 1988)

REFERENCES

Allen, T. and Osborn, T. (1984) 'Academic integration of hearing-impaired students: Demographic, handicapping, and achievement factors,' *American Annals of the Deaf*, 129, 100–13.
Belenky, M.F., Clinchy, B.M., Goldberger, N.R., and Tarule, J.M. (1986) *Women's ways of knowing: the development of self, voice, and mind*. New York: Basic Books.
Bender, R.E. (1981) *The conquest of deafness* (3rd ed.). Danville, IL: Interstate Printers & Publishers, Inc.
Blatt, B. and Kaplan, F. (1974) *Christmas in purgatory*. Syracuse, NY: Human Policy Press. (1st publication by Allyn & Bacon, 1966).
Bronfenbrenner, U. (1979) *The ecology of human development: Experiments by*

nature and design. Cambridge, MA: Harvard University Press.
Deutsch, A. (1949) *The mentally ill in America: A history of their care and treatment from Colonial times* (2nd ed.). New York: Columbia University Press.
Farrugia, D. and Austin, G. (1980) 'A study of social emotional adjustment patterns of hearing impaired students in different educational settings,' *American Annals of the Deaf,* 125, (5), 535–41.
Foster, S. (1989) 'Reflections of a group of deaf adults on their experiences in mainstream and residential school programs in the United States,' *Disability, Handicap and Society,* 4 (1), 37–56.
Foster, S. and DeCaro, P.M. (1990) 'Mainstreaming hearing-impaired students within a postsecondary educational setting: An ecological model of social interaction,' Paper presented at the annual meeting of the American Educational Research Association, 16–20 April, Boston, MA.
Froehlinger, V. J. (1981). 'Why mainstreaming?,' in V.J. Froehlinger (ed.), *Today's hearing-impaired child: Into the mainstream of education: A practical guide for teachers, parents and administrators* (40–8). Washington, DC: Alexander Graham Bell Association for the Deaf.
Furth, H. (1966) *Thinking without language.* New York: Free Press.
Gannon, J. R. (1981) *Deaf heritage.* Silver Spring, MD: National Association of the Deaf.
Green, R. R. (1976) 'Psycho-social aspects of mainstreaming for the child and family,' in G.W. Nix (ed.), *Mainstream education for hearing impaired children and youth* (75–85). New York: Grune & Stratton.
Klima, E. S. and Bellugi, U. (1979) *The signs of language.* Cambridge, MA: Harvard University Press.
Kluwin, T. N. and Moores, D. F. (1985) 'The effects of integration on the mathematics achievement of hearing-impaired adolescents,' *Exceptional Children,* 52, 153–60.
Kyle, J. G. and Pullen, G. (1988) 'Cultures in contact: Deaf and hearing people,' *Disability, Handicap and Society,* 3 (1), 49–61.
Lane, H. (1984) *When the mind hears: A history of the deaf.* New York: Random House.
Mertens, D. and Kluwin, T. N. (1986) 'Academic and social interaction of hearing-impaired high school students,' Paper presented at the meeting of the American Educational Research Association, San Francisco, CA.
Moores, D. F. (1982) *Educating the deaf* (2nd edn.). Boston, MA: Houghton-Mifflin Co.
Moores, D. F. and Kluwin, T. N. (1986) 'Issues in school placement,' in D. Lutterman (ed.), *Deafness in perspective.* San Diego, CA: College Hill Press.
Myklebyst, H. R. (1960) *The psychology of deafness* (2nd edn.). New York: Grune & Stratton.
Omi, M. and Winant, H. (1986) *Racial formation in the United States.* New York: Routledge & Kegan Paul Inc.
Padden, C. and Humphries, T. (1988) *Deaf in America: Voices from a culture.* Cambridge, MA: Harvard University Press.
Reagan, T. (1989) 'Nineteenth-century conceptions of deafness: Implications for contemporary educational practice,' *Educational theory,* 39 (1), 39–46.

Rowe, M. (1981) 'The minutiae of discrimination: The need for support,' in B.L. Forisha and B.H. Goldman (eds), *Outsiders on the inside: Women and organizations* (155–70). Englewood Cliffs, NJ: Prentice-Hall Inc.

Stoke, W. C., Jr. (1960) 'Sign language structure,' *Studies in Linguistics Occasional Papers*, 8. Buffalo, NY: University of Buffalo Press.

Tiffany, M. (1990) 'NTID: The reasons behind the big bucks.' Rochester, NY: RIT *Reporter*, (66), 20, April 20, 1990, 10–11.

Weis, L. (1985) *Between two worlds: Black students in an urban community college*. Boston, MS: Routledge & Kegan Paul.

Wolfensberger, W. (1975) *The origin and nature of our institutional models*. Syracuse, NY: Human Policy Press.

Wood, D.J. (1990) 'Cognition and learning,' Plenary session presentation at the 17th International Congress on Education of the Deaf, Rochester, NY.

Personal Commentary

Solange C. Sevigny-Skyer

I was born profoundly deaf to hearing parents. My older deaf brother had been sent to a state residential school for the deaf. School became his family, deafness his culture, and American Sign Language his language. He came home only on weekends where communication was strained since my parents' primary language was French and his was sign!

Nine years after his birth, I was born. From the moment my deafness was diagnosed at age 2, my rearing took a completely different route. This time my parents were determined to see their deaf child totally integrated and sent me to an experimental mainstreamed program, where I was the only deaf student. Only during outdoor recess play could I interact with the hearing students, because that did not require as much communication as classroom interactions. Total integration and the 20 mile daily commute took a tremendous toll on me emotionally, socially, and academically. In spite of my profound hearing loss, I was expected to learn to lipread, develop clear, understandable speech, and keep up with classes. This was such a difficult challenge. I lagged behind my hearing peers in reading, writing, and speaking. I remember one day in second grade when my teacher was explaining subtraction via the borrowing method. Very frustrated, and seeing that my classmates were able to understand and do their math assignment, I panicked. I frantically tried to figure out my own subtraction system so that I could do the required assignment, too. It was not until years later that I discovered that I had taught myself to subtract via the 'complementary addition' system. Mistakenly attributing my academic struggles to lack of intelligence, I blamed myself for not being able to keep up easily. The idea that my struggles might be due to not being able to hear never entered my mind.

Again in junior and senior high school I was the only deaf student. Shy and insecure, I had very limited interactions with my classmates. Although I really wanted to, I couldn't participate in after school activities because of transportation limitations. I wanted and needed to attend sports events or other fun activities like my hearing friends. There was a speech therapist who visited my school once a week. On her scheduled visits I would avoid walking by her office, because I did not want her to see how isolated I really was. I walked between classes alone. I ate in the large cafeteria alone. I pretended indifference, yet inside I was crushed and rejected. Once I risked running for class treasurer. I remember giving my speech in front of a filled auditorium. The crushing blow was hearing the election results . . . out of 150 students, I had only two votes. It was the ultimate rejection. I felt very 'different,' and blamed myself for not being normal enough to be accepted as an equal. Education-wise I struggled. Nobody had ever heard of support services such as interpreters or notetakers . . . I was on my own. Despite having no help, I graduated from high school with honors and was recognized by the National Honor Society. Yet still I felt that I did not quite measure up to my hearing peers . . . wasn't quite good enough.

One year before I graduated from high school my counselor told me I was not college material. I attended a hearing college and proved him wrong! Once again, though, I struggled with no services, and I was too ashamed to admit the need for notes or ask for help, so I had to constantly figure out ways of keeping up. There was no other alternative. There was no social life . . . I barely had time to do my work. I was so tired trying to guess what was said on televised math lectures while examples and illustrations were demonstrated. I did pass that math with a C, but I could have done better. Lipreading conversational French was so difficult. My final music appreciation exam required me to play 'Mary Had a Little Lamb' on the piano and flute, so I memorized which notes went with which keys, but had no idea if it sounded correct. While classical music records played, I watched the records going round and round and round. No one understood the frustrations of being the only deaf student on campus. I felt alone, isolated, and misunderstood. I felt as if I was living inside a glass room where I could see things happening, yet I was isolated from everyone and everything around me. There was no one to look up to, and no other deaf person to ask for advice. My brother and I were too different and too far apart to understand or help each other.

I graduated with a bachelor of science in education and above average grades, and went on to three years of odd jobs until I decided to continue my education at Gallaudet University, the world's only liberal arts college for the deaf. I was excited. At last, I thought, education was going to be easier for me! I vividly remember my first day on campus. My taxicab dropped me off at the entrance of Gallaudet University. Struggling with my three pieces of heavy luggage and unable to find my dormitory, I asked for help from the first student I bumped into. Her immediate response was an angry and sarcastic expression and her two arms signing (mimicking) my being an 'oral' deaf. I was dumbfounded. I was crushed. I had never expected to be rejected by people who were deaf like me. As the weeks passed, I learned more about deaf students at Gallaudet, sign language, and the stigmatism associated with being an 'oralist.' I was torn between two opposing worlds – the hearing world I was raised in and the deaf world on campus. Many of these students were proud of their deafness. This was so different from my own view of deafness. During all my growing years I had been ashamed of my difference; now I struggled to learn that I could be proud of my 'differentness.' I remember going shopping with three deaf friends who were all signing. I was so happy to be invited to go, yet it was so hard to allow myself to be seen signing in public! I wanted so badly to be a part of the deaf world and be accepted, which meant learning sign language and suppressing my shame, yet I also wanted badly to hang onto my familiar, feigned normalcy role. Standing at the crossroads, feeling torn by a kaleidoscope of conflicting thoughts and feelings, I decided to immerse myself in the 'deaf world.' I shunned everything associated with the hearing world. I desperately needed to be accepted by my own people, yet I was still struggling with accepting myself. At Christmas I went home excited about showing off my new sign language skills to my brother. For the first time we were able to hold a conversation! We signed non-stop without voice for almost two hours. While we conversed my mother repeatedly interrupted to ask what we were talking about. I would say: 'I'll tell you later,' or 'It's not important.' The tables were turned; I was no longer an outsider in my own family. Finally there was someone who understood what being deaf and left out meant.

Slowly I began to adjust to being in a deaf environment. Once I felt comfortable with using sign language, I found my academic experience exhilarating. I was finally able to follow class discussions and understand *every* word of a professor's lecture. I literally became a 'sponge,' absorbing new information. My new socialization experiences were overwhelming. I went out with new friends, went to parties, attended basketball games, and relished the experience of talking late into the night. For the first time I realized the social isolation that had encompassed me in the hearing world. Toward the end of my graduate studies, I found it very difficult to leave Gallaudet for my internship assignment. I was so accepted and included there, and had such kinship with others like myself that I wanted to hang onto that.

At the completion of my internship, I was employed as a Career Development Counselor at the National Technical Institute for the Deaf, and there I had yet another kind of educational experience taking post-graduate courses. This time I was in an all-hearing class with an interpreter and notetaker. I was concerned and uncertain about how this would work out, but wanted to try it. The first time I felt very self-conscious about having an interpreter, which would draw attention to me and my 'special needs,' yet the instructor was understanding and empathetic. He included me in all the class discussions. My opinions were valued. What a comforting and surprising thought it was for me to find out that hearing students sometimes ask irrelevant questions or have difficulties understanding a class lecture, too! I remember one particular class discussion where a hearing student shared a humorous incident. I broke into a belly laugh . . . it was the first time I had ever been able to laugh along with everyone else in a hearing class, because now I understood what was happening. Having an interpreter made that experience possible.

My experiences clearly point out the struggles and frustrations that even a highly motivated, self-disciplined, and determined deaf person faces in a mainstreamed educational setting without support services and the benefits of those services. So much of my academic difficulties and social isolation could have been averted with the appropriate support services. Like anyone else, deaf students need to feel included wherever they are, as well as the specific need to talk with and share experiences with each other. Instead of a shameful disorder, deafness is a 'difference to be accepted.'

Solange C. Sevigny-Skyer received her BS from Rhode Island College in 1973, and her MA degree in Counseling the Deaf from Gallaudet University in 1978. She has taken postgraduate courses at the University of Rochester, State University of New York at Brockport, and at the Rochester Institute of Technology. Currently, she is a career counselor and a faculty development coordinator. In addition to her counseling responsibilities, she also teaches 'Psycho-Social Aspects of Deafness' to NTID students. Her involvement in the deaf community includes working with deaf parents of hearing children. She has written several articles about her work with deaf students, deaf parents, and her own personal experiences in various publications and professional journals. She is married and has two hearing children.

Chapter 7

Student development

Thomas Holcomb and Judith Coryell

INTRODUCTION

Student development requires a unified approach encompassing the systematic integration of experiences that produce the most effective development of students (Creamer 1980). This approach supports the concept of the development of the 'whole person' – intellectually, emotionally, physically, and socially. Winston, Bonney, Miller, and Dagley (1988) noted that student development has grown out of a cluster of human development theories including psychosocial development (e.g. Erickson 1968; Chickering and Associates 1981; Havinghurst 1972), cognitive development (e.g. Piaget 1932; Perry 1970, Kohlberg 1963), person–environment interaction (e.g. Astin 1977; Banning and Kaiser 1974; Clark and Trow 1966), and typological theories (e.g. Kolb 1974; Gross 1979). The goal of student development is to integrate these theories into a consistent practice that will assist college students in achieving complex developmental tasks while becoming self-directed and independent (Miller 1982).

According to several experts in the field, one of the main purposes of colleges and universities should be to encourage and enable intentional development throughout the life cycle (Chickering and Associates 1981; Miller and Jones 1981; Winston, Bonney, Miller, and Dagley 1988). Fertile ground for this development is created when purposeful experiences are provided for students, including deaf students attending postsecondary programs. It is the task of professionals involved in student development to create these experiences, both inside and outside the classroom (Creamer 1980).

The purpose of this chapter is to discuss theories of student development and point out their applications to activities that are intended to promote overall development of deaf college students. To accomplish this goal, historical perspectives of student development are traced, followed by a presentation of developmental tasks. Next, issues specifically related to deaf students are discussed as well as strategies for the design and delivery of an effective program for fostering total development in postsecondary settings.

HISTORICAL PERSPECTIVES OF STUDENT DEVELOPMENT

From its earliest beginnings, higher education has been involved in more than mere intellectual development (Hoetling 1980; Miller and Jones 1981). Unlike current practice, university faculty had the responsibility of providing experiences outside the classroom. In addition, faculty members were given the charge to mold each student to meet an image set forth by the institution. As a result, students in the university system were subjected to rigid indoctrination of ideals and morals beyond the scope of their academic pursuits. For example, religious objectives were often a dominant theme of earlier postsecondary education, a clear indication of an interest broader than the intellectual domain (Shaffer 1970). This approach to college life created an environment that promoted moral development yet was limited by the emphasis on obedience and uniformity among the student body (Fley 1970; Miller 1982).

As the country evolved from an agrarian to an industrial society, higher education became increasingly desirable and accessible to the middle class. Following this trend, there was a considerable increase in college enrollment, making it difficult for faculty to attend to students' needs outside the classroom (Fitzgerald, Johnson, and Morris 1970; Miller and Prince 1977). Additionally, the characteristics of students became more diverse, making it difficult to fit students into a mold prescribed by the university. For this reason, universities became less involved in non-classroom (co-curricular) functions, and students were left with the task of meeting their own developmental needs (Fitzgerald, Johnson, and Morris 1970). By the early 20th century, there was a distinct separation between academic and cocurricular components of university life. One approach to resolve this gap was for students to organize secret underground social/literary organizations, commonly known as the Greeks, to meet their needs for enrichment outside the classroom (Miller and Jones 1981).

As early as 1938, the American Council on Education recognized the importance of the total development of students. Four basic assumptions about the importance of student growth were identified. They included: 1) the individual student must be considered as a whole; 2) each student is a unique person and must be treated as such; 3) the total environment of the student is educational and must be used to achieve his or her full development; and 4) the major responsibility for a student's personal and social development rests with the student and his or her personal resources (Williamson 1949).

Realizing the necessity of these components, efforts were initiated to merge the various aspects of intellectual and personal/social development within the educational community. These efforts resulted in the development of structured opportunities for student growth. This focus was to make student involvement more meaningful and all aspects of campus life more relevant (Johnson 1970). However, there was a notable shift away from the earlier practice of the faculty being responsible for the developmental needs of students outside the classroom. Instead, a new group of professionals emerged who specialized in promoting the total development of students. Once again, student development became a legitimate mission of higher education (Berdie 1970; Johnson 1970; Miller 1982; Winston, Bonney, Miller, and Dagley 1988).

By the 1960s, the role of students on campus shifted from a passive, disciplined status to a more assertive and self-determined approach. With student movements emerging across the country, paternalistic policies within the institutions were challenged, resulting in a shift in the perspective of college students from dependents to responsible adults (Butler 1970; Miller 1982). Instead of *in loco parentis* policies and practices, the development of self-direction, self-control, and self-discipline was promoted as the ultimate goal of college discipline (Butler 1970; Fley 1970; Johnson 1970; Miller and Jones 1981; Shaffer 1970).

As a result, higher education began to assume the challenge of providing a more balanced environment that intentionally promoted development across all domains. These areas were identified in a model of student development put forth by Chickering and Associates (1981) and graphically represented in Figure 7.1. The model includes the following dimensions: developing competence, managing emotions, developing autonomy, establishing identity, freeing interpersonal relationships, developing purpose, and developing integrity.

150 The environment of educational programs

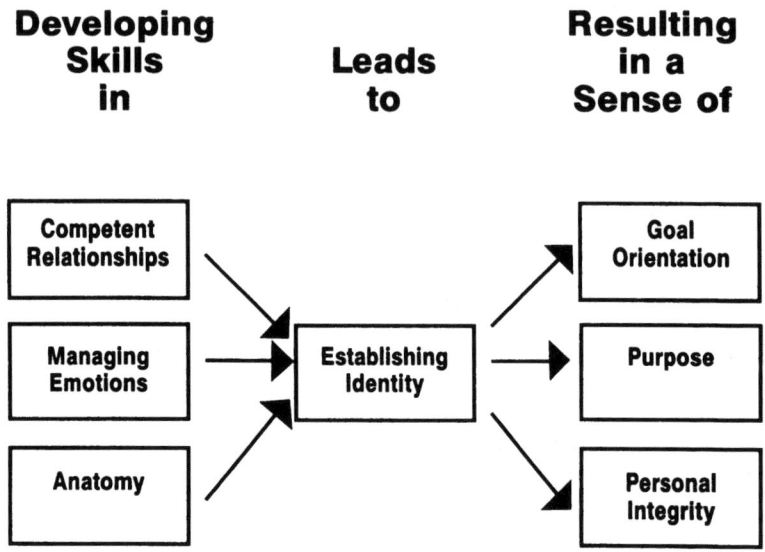

Figure 7.1 Chickering's model of the domains of student development
Source: Chickering and Associates (1981)

This model specifies that growth in competent relationships, the management of emotions, and the development of a sense of autonomy are important for the formulation of a self identity. In turn, the formation of identity is a prerequisite for development of goal orientation, a sense of purpose, and personal integrity.

Following the national trend, student development practices were adopted in the 1970s by postsecondary institutions serving deaf students. Both Gallaudet University and Rochester Institute of Technology's National Technical Institute for the Deaf (NTID) began to apply theoretical perspectives of student development in their administrative structure and programmatic efforts. As part of the approach, deaf students were provided with intensive training to function as paraprofessionals within the university environment (e.g. resident advisor, student development assistant, and community aide). Many of these individuals have gone on to pursue professional degrees and are now assuming leadership positions in the field of student development.

Dr. Frank Turk, formerly of Gallaudet University, is credited as the first deaf person with a doctorate in student development. He was instrumental in translating student development theories into effective practices and innovative programs designed specifically for deaf students at the secondary and postsecondary levels. At NTID, similar efforts were initiated to link student development and deafness in the mainstream environment. In 1986, the First National Conference on Student Development for the Deaf was jointly sponsored by NTID and Gallaudet University's Model Secondary School for the Deaf. Professionals and researchers from across the country convened in Rochester, New York, to review state-of-the-art applications of student development models to the deaf student population. A second national conference followed in 1990 at Gallaudet University.

DEVELOPMENTAL TASKS FOR COLLEGE STUDENTS

The literature abounds with developmental task hierarchies. Perhaps Erickson's (1968) definition of 'crisis' best describes the developmental tasks for college-age students. He used the word 'crisis' to designate a necessary turning point, a crucial moment when development must move one way or another, marshaling resources of growth, recovery, and further differentiation. It then seems reasonable that development can best occur when there is a balance between the challenges of a crisis and the support of university personnel.

At college, students are frequently faced with crises as they move from being young, naive teenagers beginning their academic career to poised, mature adults as they leave the university setting. During these years, students are confronted by many issues and exposed to people of various backgrounds. Perhaps they have never before experienced a multicultural environment that encourages diversity and appreciates individuality among people. This environment forces students to examine their own values and determine how their beliefs as an adult may or may not blend into the ideals held by their families (Berdie 1970; Coons 1971; Kuh, Whitt, and Shedd 1987).

Finding a balance between crisis and support ensures optimal growth at the various developmental tasks. Deriving from the six domains identified by Chickering and Associates (1981) earlier in this chapter, these tasks include: 1) breaking psychological ties/ establishing emotional independence; 2) establishing identity and developing a value system; 3) adjusting to life on one's own; 4) handling peer relationships; 5) choosing and preparing for a career; and 6) preparing for marriage and family life/managing home.

The support needed to manage crises must be intentionally designed to provide students with an opportunity to learn and examine the various developmental dimensions. If not, a negative collegiate experience can result. Students can be so overwhelmed by all of the polarization going on in their life that they are unable to deal with the crisis. For example, they might become involved in abusive situations such as getting heavily involved with drug usage or becoming trapped in an unhealthy relationship. However, if students are provided with support and an optimal learning environment, they will discover the positive side of human diversity, and be better equipped to grow to their full potential.

Like hearing students, deaf students begin their college careers at different levels of development. The developmental tasks of deaf students can be diverse and dependent on several unique factors such as their educational and communication backgrounds. However, for many deaf students, gaps in their development are often a result of insufficient access to information and opportunities for personal and social growth, not only at school but often at home and in the neighborhood. For instance, the inability of teachers, parents, friends, and other family members to communicate effectively with the deaf young person may result in superficial and inadequate opportunities for successful completion of developmental tasks at appropriate age levels. Many of these gaps may be a result of missed opportunities for incidental learning that hearing children obtain automatically. Examples of incidental learning include the development of problem-solving skills by overhearing parents discuss and resolve difficulties at home; exposure to strategies for handling delicate issues such as dating and sexuality often gained through television programs, locker room discussions, and subtle messages from adults; and development of assertiveness techniques from observing adults negotiate with one another. Since these experiences are often lost to deaf children and adolescents, it is crucial that the personal/social needs of deaf college students be aggressively addressed.

To more carefully examine the unique experiences encountered by deaf students, each of the six developmental tasks identified earlier in this chapter will be explored.

Breaking Psychological Ties/Establishing Emotional Independence

The transition from the safe and comfortable surroundings of home to an unfamiliar and sometime frightening college environment is the first crisis encountered by students. The initial task is to begin solidifying physical and emotional independence. The varying needs for independence depend on the type of environment that was provided at home. Although experiences of deaf and hearing students are similar in some ways, it seems that many deaf students have experienced the extremes on the continuum of dependence–independence. Students in residential settings often experienced a life separate and independent from their parents. At the other extreme, deaf students may be viewed as helplessly handicapped and in need of continued protection by parents.

The impact of these dynamics on the student's level of independence can be seen in the interaction between student and parents during move-in day at college. Three typical parent–deaf student relationships can be identified that apparently influence the students' ability to successfully complete this task of breaking psychological ties and establishing independence. The first type involves students who arrive at college without their parents, and these students make sure everyone knows it. They immediately violate campus rules by organizing drinking parties in their rooms the first night. Authority is constantly challenged. The chances that they will be dismissed from college are great.

The second type of deaf student–parent relationship involves parents who seem to stifle the development of their son or daughter in many ways. This kind of parent brings their 'child' to the residence hall, sets the student in an out-of-the-way corner, proceeds to initiate all the contacts with school personnel by asking all the questions, and generally makes all the decisions. It is also this type of parent who brings a long list of questions to the resident assistant or counselor on the floor about 'What happens if . . . ?'. These patterns of overprotective and patronizing behavior are not limited to the residence hall. Communication expectations, career decision making, and selection of friends are often dictated by parents. For this type of student, the chances for attrition may be increased because of the student's inability to establish independence.

The third type of student also arrives with his/her parents. The parents help by unloading the luggage from the car and carrying it up to the room. Then, as the student gets settled in his/her room, parents help by adding a touch of home to the room. From this point on, these parents remain in the background (sometimes teary-eyed) and are eagerly available to assist when the student hollers for a helping hand.

Students from the first and second groups probably are not prepared for the psychological independence demanded by college life. The successful achievement of this and other indicators of psychological independence will have an impact on many of the remaining developmental tasks for deaf students.

Establishing Identity and Developing a Value System

Other tasks that especially have an impact on the college-age student are those of identity formation and values clarification. Challenges at this level can be especially true for deaf students, since deafness is often viewed in a different light by peers at college. Upon entering a postsecondary program, deaf students may, for the first time, be afforded the opportunity to define their own values regarding their identity as a deaf person, their communication preference, and their place in the deaf community. Deaf students often struggle with these tasks, not wanting to violate the expectations and goals set by well-meaning parents and school personnel. For example, should oral students begin to assimilate into deaf culture by learning sign language? When the majority of deaf students on campus value deafness in new and different ways, how do the students cope? Are they able to develop a sense of pride in themselves and embrace, rather than reject, the identity of a deaf person?

For students who are being mainstreamed for the first time, a robust sense of self-esteem may be needed to survive the shift from attending a school setting exclusively for deaf students to being a minority on the university campus. In addition, the task may be to overcome the projection of disability and develop an identity as a capable student. The responses are unique to each deaf college student. An oral deaf student with no previous contact with other deaf people will have needs that are different from those of students from schools with a large deaf population. With a positive collegiate experience, many students experience the growth in self-esteem and self-confidence that occurs during their time at college.

Adjusting to Life on One's Own

Without the direct interference or influence of their parents, students are left with the challenges of adjusting to life on their own (e.g. managing time, solving problems, and coping with stress). As is often the case for hearing students, the level of sophistication in dealing with these life adjustments often depends on the amount of independence and autonomy that the deaf student has been given at home. Unfortunately, if communication has been impaired in the home environment, opportunities for learning and incorporating problem-solving techniques effectively used by family members are lost. Both residential and mainstreamed students require different approaches to successfully complete the task of adjusting to college life. Many mainstreamed students experience severe isolation and loneliness during their secondary school years and have a limited circle of friends. These students, therefore, depend on parents as their primary source of support. These students may be faced with a difficult adjustment as they learn to live on their own without continuous support from their families. Students from residential programs are often used to the strict rules and structured life that characterizes these settings. In contrast, college students are expected to be responsible for their own actions, which requires students from residential schools to develop new strategies for success.

Handling Peer Relationships

Friendships developed at college can be a special thing. However, the quest to develop and maintain them can be a difficult task for many students, both deaf and hearing. Interestingly, many deaf students arrive at Gallaudet or NTID knowing at least a handful of other deaf students through a 'deaf network' consisting of friends and acquaintances from their high school programs, or through deaf athletic events or leadership programs involving deaf students from other schools.

At NTID, for example, there are more than 1,000 deaf students on a campus of 10,000 hearing students. Strong peer relationships often develop among the deaf students on campus. The same depth of relationships between deaf and hearing students occurs less often, even though students live in integrated residence halls and often attend classes together. Communication and attitudinal barriers frequently thwart the formation of comfortable and meaningful relationships between the two groups (Foster and DeCaro 1990). Even with the presence of interpreters in classes and at activities on campus, relationships remain superficial at best (Foster and Brown 1989).

In programs with a small number of mainstreamed deaf students, development of meaningful relationships may be even more difficult to attain. Students in these educational environments may experience severe isolation both socially and intellectually, or they may find their niche in a close-knit group of friends who share a common interest in social or intellectual pursuits. As noted in chapter three, failure to achieve integration within the total life of the college community may have serious implications for persistence to graduation.

Choosing and Preparing for a Career

Although college is the time for students to prepare for a career, it may also be the time when students discover that their inadequate academic preparation inhibited the realization of career goals. For deaf students, their ambitions may be even further limited because of the lack of exposure to deaf role models in a variety of professions. In addition, artificial restrictions from parents, teachers, counselors, and society in general are often imposed on students who want to go into careers that have not been traditionally pursued by deaf people such as medicine, finance, or engineering. As a result, deaf students may choose a career that does not best fit their interests or intellectual capabilities.

Preparing for Marriage and Family Life

Finally, college is the place where many students seek their lifelong mate. Since the majority of marriages by deaf people are endogamous by choice (Meadow 1975), there perhaps is an increased urgency to find a suitable spouse during their college years. For many deaf students at large postsecondary programs, the luxury of a wide selection of potential marital partners is a rare opportunity not found on campuses predominated by hearing students. For these reasons, career goals can become obscured by marriage goals.

PROMOTING STUDENT DEVELOPMENT

Regardless of the individual developmental levels, perhaps one advantage deaf students have when entering college is that, possibly for the first time, they are provided with a myriad of activities that can promote their development. A recent study of the high school experiences of deaf students found that students from mainstreamed environments participate to a much lesser degree in school activities that promote student development than do their hearing counterparts; in addition, students attending special schools often had relatively fewer opportunities since these programs were usually small in size (Holcomb 1990).

The type of postsecondary program the student attends can be an influencing factor for meeting student development needs of deaf college students. Students enrolled at Gallaudet University may have different challenges from a student attending a small local community college as the only deaf student. Similarly, deaf students at NTID find themselves trying to find a balance between a large deaf community and a predominantly hearing student population on the larger campus of Rochester Institute of Technology. Since deaf students attending small programs often do not have the luxury of full access to developmental opportunities designed specifically for them, the remainder of this chapter is devoted to a 'menu' of strategies for the design and delivery of an effective student development program that can be used in whole or in part by postsecondary programs serving varying numbers of deaf students.

STRATEGIES FOR EFFECTIVE PROMOTION OF STUDENT DEVELOPMENT

There are numerous challenges for deaf students attending a mainstreamed postsecondary program. For these students, there is perhaps no greater challenge than participating in university life outside the classroom. It is important to remember, however, that opportunities to successfully complete each task are not limited to the university setting. Students often have a separate social network outside the campus environment that can afford them similar kinds of experiences.

Many of the developmental tasks depend on successful experiences in realtionships. However, the literature has shown how difficult it can be for deaf students to develop and maintain relationships with hearing peers (Foster and Brown 1989; Foster and DeCaro 1990; Holcomb 1990). Many of the developmental tasks depend on successful experiences in relationships. To develop relationships between majority and minority group members, Amir (1969) suggested that group members should be brought together who have equal status on the characteristics most salient for the setting. In this sense, the right kind of contact in the right kind of setting is necessary to allow deaf students to be integrated fully into university life. These settings have been defined specifically by several authors as being free of communicative and attitudinal barriers (Foster and Brown 1989; Foster and DeCaro 1990; Coryell, Holcomb, and Scherer forthcoming). For this reason, it is essential that university programs be intentionally designed to provide such an environment.

Experience at NTID has demonstrated that attitudinal and communicative barriers can be removed through several avenues. These approaches, which can be applied to various settings, are briefly summarized below.

Positive Role Models

Successful deaf students as well as hearing students who have demonstrated sensitivity to deafness should be identified and promoted as role models. Use of such student mentors for newly admitted deaf students can promote growth in establishing competent relationships as well as assisting in the development of a balanced sense of autonomy in the early stages of college life. For example, these mentors can function in a variety of roles such as resident assistants on floors where deaf students reside, peer advisors, or student leaders in freshman orientation programs. An additional strategy used effectively at NTID is the Speakers Bureau, a program through which noted deaf individuals are brought to the campus to meet with students.

Education for Hearing Students

The program providing services for deaf students should design opportunities for the hearing community to learn about deafness. Those services can include sign language classes, deaf awareness experiences, and cross-cultural activities. As hearing students become more knowledgeable and sensitive about deaf culture, as well as techniques for communicating and interacting with their deaf peers, the chances increase for deaf students to become more fully integrated into the mainstream of college life. Activities such as retreats specifically focusing on deaf–hearing relationships, deafness simulations (white noise maskers), 'It's a Deaf, Deaf World', (Basile and Holcomb 1984), and sign language clubs have been organized for this purpose.

Personal Training Programs

When providing services for deaf students in a college setting, the tendency is to focus on the classroom and on those co-curricular activities that are most needed. There may be a need to provide training for deaf students in a number of areas that will directly promote achievement of the tasks defined by Chickering and Associates (1981). Programs such as assertiveness training, awareness of diversity, and sensitivity training can help deaf students who have been conditioned to assume a subordinate status among hearing people by assisting them in stepping out of this role and participating more aggressively and equally with their hearing peers. Many of these skill-building activities are incorporated in leadership retreats and workshops, debates with community leaders who are deaf, and individual counseling sessions.

Promoting Structure in Co-curricular Activities

Although interpreters expand the opportunities for deaf students, their presence does not guarantee full and equal access to information and participation. Support service personnel should encourage the design of co-curricular activities to assure maximum access for deaf students. For example, at meetings, workshops, and retreats, techniques such as seating arrangement (circular or semi-circular for maximum visibility), turn-taking (one person talking at a time), and visual feedback (positive and reinforcing facial expressions and body language) are important considerations. These techniques will allow for more complete participation by deaf students. Awareness of these needs on a campus-wide basis will also enhance sensitivity to the communication obstacles between deaf and hearing people.

Deaf students often do not have complete access to the intricacies of college culture, since much of this information is unwritten. Norms for establishing campus connections such as attending and hosting parties and participating in Greek rush are only a few examples. Extra effort must be made to ensure that this kind of information is communicated to deaf students through support groups, paraprofessionals, and the development of close contacts with hearing peers.

Networking Outside the Campus Environment

For some deaf students, the primary, and sometimes singular, purpose of attending a mainstreamed program is academic or technical skill development rather than an all-inclusive collegiate experience. For other students, repeated efforts to successfully establish relationships in a hearing environment have proven to be fruitless or unrewarding. In these cases, the developmental tasks for college-age deaf students are achieved through community networking with other deaf individuals. Universities can provide alternative support for these individuals by establishing links with community resources. The next chapter provides some detailed information about how community involvement can be achieved as part of the postsecondary experience.

These approaches are only a part of the picture. The individual needs of deaf students must be considered, and opportunities must be designed by the university to the greatest extent possible to meet those needs. A fine balance is required so as not to create a sense of dependency in the student as a result of 'spoon-feeding' practices by the university. The development of independence, rather than dependence, must be the ultimate goal.

CONCLUSION

We have spent a great deal of time describing a theoretical approach to considering the various needs of deaf students in the postsecondary environment. Perhaps a word is needed to state our feeling that this area is often neglected when establishing the need for support services in the postsecondary environment.

Even though a deaf person has access to college, he/she may remain isolated both socially and educationally from the mainstream. Such isolation, or lack of intergration into the educational community, may be an important cause of attrition among deaf persons attending college. This point especially relates to the access students have to the social life of an institution. The fact that very few programs provide support for the social aspects of college life promotes in many deaf students a feeling of isolation while attending college. Since so much socialization in our culture occurs through informal interactions such as eating, walking to class, and observing athletic events, it is not surprising that deaf students often feel socially isolated when they are not made to feel part of these activities. Given these circumstances, a deaf person may have physical access to college but remain excluded from the social mainstream of college life. In-depth interviews with students transferring to NTID from other colleges consistently indicate that limited opportunities for social interaction with peers is a major reason for withdrawing from their former college (Foster and Elliot 1986).

We do not expect to provide any magical answers for this problem, but we hope this chapter has provided some approaches to assisting deaf college students in developing as total people as defined by Chickering and Associates (1981). Programming designed to develop an understanding of the diversity in life will result in a sensitivity that will make the entire campus a better place for learning.

It is important to note that, just as opportunities may vary from one setting to another, the needs of each student are also unique. In this sense, deaf students from a variety of educational and communication backgrounds attending different kinds of postsecondary settings represent a diverse population. Each of these individuals must have the opportunity to experience positive growth in their development as a result of their collegiate careers.

REFERENCES

Amir, Y. (1969) 'Contact hypothesis in ethnic relations,' *Psychological Bulletin*, 71, 319–42.
Astin, A.W. (1977) *Four critical years. Effects of college on beliefs, attitudes, and knowledge*, San Francisco, CA: Jossey-Bass.
Banning, J. and Kaiser, L. (1974) 'An ecological perspective and model for campus design,' *Personnel and Guidance Journal*, 52, 360–75.
Basile, M.L. and Holcomb, B.R. (1984) 'It's a deaf, deaf world,' *Proceedings of the Registery of Interpreters of the Deaf Biannual Convention*.
Berdie, R.F. (1970) 'Student personnel work: Definition and redefinition,' in L.E. Fitzgerald, W.F. Johnson, and W. Morris, (eds), *College student personnel: readings and bibliographies*. Boston, MA: Houghton-Mifflin.
Butler, W.R. (1970) 'Student involvement in the decision-making process,' in L.E. Fitzgerald, W.F. Johnson, and W. Morris, (eds), *College student personnel: readings and bibliographies*. Boston, MA: Houghton-Mifflin.

Chickering, A.W., and Associates (1981) *The modern American college.* San Francisco, CA: Jossey-Bass.
Clark, R. and Trow, M. (1966) 'The organizational context,' in T.M. Newcomb and E.K. Wilson (eds), *College peer groups: Problems and prospects for research.* Chicago, IL: Aldine.
Coons, F.W. (1971) 'The developmental tasks of the college student,' in S.C. Feinstein, *Adolescent psychiatry, 1, developmental and clinical studies.*
Coryell, J., Holcomb, T., and Scherer, M. (forthcoming) 'Attitudes toward deafness: A collegiate perspective,' *American Annals of the Deaf*
Creamer, D.G. (1980) *Student development in higher education.* American College Personnel Association.
Erickson, E.H. (1950) *Childhood and society.* New York: Norton.
Erickson, E.H. (1968) *Identity: Youth and crisis.* New York: Norton.
Fitzgerald, L.E., Johnson, W.F., and Morris, W. (1970) *College student personnel: readings and bibliographies.* Boston, MA: Houghton-Mifflin.
Fley, J.A. (1970) 'Changing approaches to discipline in student personnel work,' in L.E. Fitzgerald, W.F. Johnson, and W. Morris, (eds), *College student personnel: readings and bibliographies.* Boston, MA: Houghton-Mifflin.
Foster, S. and Brown, P. (1989) 'Factors influencing the academic and social integration of hearing-impaired college students,' *Journal of Postsecondary Education and Disability,* 7, (3 and 4), 78–96.
Foster, S. and Elliot, L. (1986) *Alternatives in mainstreaming: A 'range of options' model for the postsecondary hearing-impaired student* (Technical report). Rochester, NY: Rochester Institute of Technology.
Foster, S. and DeCaro, P.M. (1990) 'Mainstreaming hearing-impaired students within a postsecondary educational setting,' Paper presented at the annual meeting of the American Educational Research Association, 16–20 April, Boston, MA.
Greenwood, J.D. (1980) 'Selected considerations for the practice of student development,' in D.G. Creamer (ed.) *Student development in higher education.* Alexandria, VA: American College Personnel Association.
Gross, K.P. (1979) 'Adult learners: Characteristics, needs and interests,' in R.E. Peterson and Associates, *Lifelong learning in America: An overview of current practices, available resources, and future prospects.* San Francisco, CA: Jossey-Bass.
Havinghurst, R.J. (1972) *Developmental tasks and education* (3rd edn). New York: McKay.
Hoetling, F.B. (1980) *Resident student development.* Columbia, SC: National Entertainment and Campus Activities Association.
Holcomb, T.K. (1990) 'Deaf students in the mainstream: A study in social assimilation,' Doctoral Dissertation. University of Rochester.
Johnson, W.F. (1970) 'Student personnel work in higher education: Philosophy and Framework,' in L.E. Fitzgerald, W.F. Johnson, and W. Morris, (eds), *College student personnel: readings and bibliographies.* Boston, MA: Houghton-Mifflin.
Kolb, D.A. (1974) *Changing human behavior: Principles of planned intervention.* New York: McGraw-Hill.
Kohlberg, L. (1963) 'Moral development and identification,' in H. Stevenson

(ed.), *Child psychology.* Chicago: University of Chicago Press.

Kuh, G.D., Whitt, E.J. and Shedd, J.D. (1987) *Student affairs work, 2001: A paradigmatic odyssey.* Alexandria, VA: American College Personnel Association.

Meadow, K. (1975) 'The deaf subculture,' *Hearing and speech action,* July–August, 16–18.

Miller, T.K. (1982) 'Student development assessment: A rationale,' in G.R. Hanson, (ed.), *Measuring student development.* San Francisco, CA: Jossey-Bass.

Miller, T.K. and Jones, J.D. (1981) 'Out-of-class activities,' in A.W. Chickering (ed.). *The Modern American College.* San Francisco, CA: Jossey-Bass.

Miller, T.K. and Prince, J.S. (1977) *The future of student affairs.* San Francisco: Jossey-Bass.

Perry, W.G., Jr. (1970) *Forms of intellectual and ethical development in the college years.* New York: Holt, Rinehart, & Winston.

Piaget, J. (1932) *The moral judgment of the child.* New York: Harcourt, Brace.

Shaffer, R.H. (1970) 'Meeting the challenges of today's students,' in L.E. Fitzgerald, W.F. Johnson and W. Morris, (eds), *College student personnel: Readings and bibliographies.* Boston, MA: Houghton-Mifflin.

Williamson, E.G. (1949) 'Establishing student freedoms and rights,' *Journal of the National Association of Student Personnel Administrators,* 2 (4), 9–13.

Winston, R.B., Jr., Bonney, W.C., Miller, T.K., and Dagley, J.C. (1988) *Promoting student development through intentionally structured groups.* San Francisco, CA: Jossey-Bass.

Personal Commentary

Willy Conley

I have been profoundly deaf since birth and, for 17 years, grew up in an environment where everyone had normal hearing and where English was my first language. Consequently, my way of communicating with people developed by speaking and lipreading. As a junior in high school, I began looking into programs at nearby colleges (I had never heard of colleges for the deaf). Here I was, planning my future – a latent, culturally-developed deaf person – bound to go through life with a strained smile, pretending to understand everything.

One day my parents and I went to Johns Hopkins Hospital in Baltimore for my annual hearing test. After my audiologist heard that I was interested in further schooling, she advised me to look into the National Technical Institute for the Deaf (NTID) at Rochester Institute of Technology (RIT). A look through the Institute's catalog convinced my parents and me to drive to upstate New York to visit the campus. Our guide was deaf, and throughout the tour he signed, gestured, used his voice and facial expressions, making explanations surprisingly easy for me to understand. Later, I learned that he used total communication, a language approach employed by the faculty and staff. I was amazed to find that NTID had an enrollment of more than 1,000 students, all with a hearing problem. The support services offered – tutors, notetakers, and interpreters – were so luxurious compared to what I was getting in public schools, which was nothing. And to discover that I would be taught by professors who understood deafness – hallelujah! For the first time in my life – with the exception of kindergarten – I actually became excited about going to school.

During the five years that I lived on campus, my identity as a deaf individual began to surface. I discovered a part of myself that was missing for 17 years: my roots in deaf culture. The natural outcome was that sign language became my second language out of need to fully understand my professors, classmates, and peers, hearing and deaf.

Never again did I have to spend long hours straining my eyes to try and capture bits of information like I did in front rows of my early school years. Public school teachers often had their backs turned to the class while writing on the blackboard and lecturing – never mind how many times they were politely asked to face the front while talking. If I was lucky, I could read a word or two off of their lips as they occasionally turned their heads sideways. When it came to class discussions I was lost, stuck with a couple of words, trying to put together a 50-piece puzzle that was missing 48 pieces.

But at NTID/RIT I was able to relax and enjoy my education. Either my instructors used sign language or I had an interpreter in front of me, allowing me to comprehend everything. A trained notetaker was nearby so I could fully concentrate on lectures and participate, unabashedly, in discussions. A tutor who knew sign language was available if information in class became too complicated. In high school it was hard to find someone in class to volunteer to take notes for me. When that rare person was found, usually I couldn't read or understand his notes. Unlike my primary and secondary school years, I finally experienced the personal reward of high marks from postsecondary studies.

Soon I became friends with many people, people who signed and people who didn't – their preferences made no difference to me. It was such a novelty to make so many friends because up until the summer of 1976 I had very few, and never so many who were understanding and unbiased about deafness. It was so overwhelming that when my second year came around, I had to slap myself to remember the primary reason for being in college. A year of study had been completed in the Applied Photography program [at NTID], and I cross-registered into the RIT School of Photographic Arts and Sciences to begin four years of study in biomedical photography. I did something that was painful – I cut back on a lot of friendships and socializing due to mounting academic pressures.

My academic routine was more manageable after two years at the School of Photography. I was offered a position as a Resident Advisor for a special interest floor with all photography majors called Photo House, located in a predominantly deaf residence hall. I was very interested in being a part of a small floor community where the residents were deaf and hearing, and used photography as the basis to develop communication and relationships.

After a year with Photo House, I accepted a new challenge: to be an Area Administrative Assistant for a predominantly hearing residence hall and resident advisor staff member. My job was to assist the area director of the hall in the supervision of 19 Resident Advisors as well as carry out the administrative duties for the housing office. Again, the interest was in encouraging deaf–hearing interaction using a higher, more visible position.

NTID supports a theater program in which students along with faculty, staff, and members of the Rochester community present well-crafted plays in sign language and voice. As my ability to understand the nuances of sign language became better, my appreciation for the theater grew. I was finally being entertained by something other than a baseball game. Another form of entertainment cropped up that I had been deprived of – captioned films. I was in heaven. I began to feel a fullness in my life – [a balance where the weight of my social life equalled the weight of academia].

I developed an urge to be a part of the theater and joined a resident troupe called SUNSHINE AND COMPANY. Part of the reason for joining was the desire to be a communicator; to convey artistic images and ideas to people just like I had seen the actors do on stage. Another part was to instill confidence in myself with my new language and new-found identity.

My entire college education was served to me like a sumptuous feast. It was all there in clear view and within reach, and I consumed it. On graduation day I was literally 20 pounds overweight, and satisfied.

In different cities around the country where I worked, I ran into deaf people, young and old, who seemed to try awfully hard to be like 'normal hearing people.' They had darting eyes and nervous smiles. When I said something, often they nodded their heads but said, 'Huh? What?' It pained me to see this because I sensed something they were not aware of was missing from their lives; a void that I used to have. I wanted to blurt out the news about deaf culture, the many clubs and organizations of the deaf, the theatres of the deaf, and the deaf sports teams and competitions. I wanted to tell them about literature and films with deaf characters and writers, show them art by deaf artists and, ultimately, introduce them to another language, rich and . . . at last, attainable.

But, sometimes I held back because of the overprotective parents who hovered closely – parents who were adamantly opposed to their child coming in contact with sign language or deaf culture for fear that their child will lose – of all things – their speech. Or, sometimes I hesitated because some deaf people were so proud of their speech and success in the hearing world that they did not need to be involved with deaf culture and sign language. It horrifies me to think where I would be today if I had not gone to a college for the deaf.

Years later, some people can't understand my drastic career change from biomedical photography to professional acting. I think there's a parallel between photographers and actors in that both are communicators of ideas and images. The biomedical photographer's job is to record medical facts on film and communicate them in a factual, visual way for doctors who need to present these facts in journals, conventions, lectures, and grand rounds. The actor's job is to absorb a playwright's text and communicate it in an accurate, artistic way to an audience. But why the career jump, my friends ask. Why not? I had passed rigorous requirements to be certified as a Registered Biological Photographer and, during a span of five years, I worked diligently for three hospitals. It was time for a change – to delve into the unknown and further explore my potential in life.

If it wasn't for my parents' unselfish support and sacrifice to get me through college, I never would have been able to do the things I have done. I am at the five-year mark working as a full-time actor and today, I am learning to write.

Willy Conley, a native of Baltimore, is enrolled in the MA Creative Writing Program at Boston University, studying playwriting. His first published story, 'A Photographic Memory,' appeared in Kaleidoscope – *an international magazine. Conley's one-act play,* Broken Spokes, *was produced off-off-Broadway by New York Deaf Theater. The full-length version of the play was produced by the American Deaf Drama Festival at the University of Texas at Dallas. Recently, his new play,* The Hearing Test, *won in the one-act category of the Sam Edwards Deaf Playwrights Competition. He still takes photographs; two were accepted by the Rosenberg Group for an October 1990 exhibition in Washington, DC.*

Chapter 8

Postsecondary education and political activism

T. Alan Hurwitz

INTRODUCTION

Political activism within the deaf community is an important vehicle in empowering deaf people and others to have a say about their own destiny. There are many ways in which an individual can contribute to the enhancement of quality of life for deaf people. One can be an activist in advocating the rights of deaf people, while another person may choose to stay in the background and offer some insights and advice as to how one can be effective in addressing certain issues and concerns of deaf persons. Others may elect to be well versed in issues and concerns of deaf people and express their opinions through printed materials. Still another person may play a role as an educator, involving students in various role-playing situations in order to teach them how to resolve societal problems and conflicts related to cross-cultural interactions among deaf and hearing individuals. The purpose of this chapter is to provide some background concerning the often overlooked role of postsecondary education in providing deaf persons with the skills and experiences necessary to play a key leadership role in their community.

This notion of self-determination by deaf persons is a relatively recent occurrence. Aristotle claimed that an individual must have perfect sensory skills in order to be functional and participate in intellectual discourse with others in a community. Because of this theory, until very recently, individuals who were deaf and unable to speak were usually shunned from the mainstream of life. It was a little over a century ago that deaf persons began to take control of their own lives. Strangely enough, this action was the result of a decision made by hearing persons about how deaf persons should communicate.

In 1880, a group of educators of deaf students congregated in Milan, Italy, and passed a resolution to ban the use of sign language in schools for the deaf. The Milan resolution was the result of more than a century of debate about how deaf children should be taught. As a result of this resolution there was a drastic decline in the employment of deaf teachers from approximately 40 per cent in the late 1800s to between 10 and 14 per cent in 1990. Ironically, prior to this conference, several deaf adults were instrumental in establishing schools for deaf people and served as principals, superintendents, and in other leadership capacities (Hurwitz 1989).

It was a direct result of the Milan conference that the National Association for the Deaf (NAD) came into existence. Throughout the 20th century the NAD has advocated for the civil rights of deaf people in education, rehabilitation, employment, social services, and other public policy issues. For instance, the NAD fought against proposed legislation to forbid deaf people from driving automobiles in several states. (This legislation was proposed five different times between the early 1940s and late 1950s.) The NAD was instrumental in the influence of other public policies such as those related to the creation of the Registry of Interpreters for the Deaf, the census of deaf people, greater awareness and understanding of aspects of deafness and deaf people, proliferation of sign language instruction for hearing people, closed captioning of television programs, expansion of telecommunication and telephone systems, and promotion of new opportunities for deaf people in a wide range of employment, including supervision, management, and administration of programs and services for deaf people.

In addition to the national organization, each of the 50 states and the District of Columbia has its own association. These state-level organizations are modeled after the NAD and make up a federation that is the governing body of the NAD. Each state association sends up to six representatives to the biennial NAD conventions to establish directives and priorities for the NAD and to elect officers of the association.

The state associations are the leading consumer advocacy organizations serving deaf people in their respective localities, and have a great need for skilled leaders. The officers and committees carry out the mandates of the membership that are established by local communities. Local organizations that are affiliated with their respective state associations are directly involved in local civic activities as these affect the lives of deaf people. Many local groups and their affiliated state associations often conduct deaf awareness activities in their communities. Some of the associations have their own home offices with staff to carry out the mandates of the board and membership.

In addition to the associations for deaf people, there are other organizations that serve the needs of the deaf community. On the national level there is a coordinating body of national organizations serving deaf and hard-of-hearing people that primarily focuses on public policy and legislative issues as these affect the quality of life of deaf and hard-of-hearing people. Currently, there are several organizations that are affiliated with this Council of Organizational Representatives (COR). In addition to the National Association of the Deaf, these organizations include: Alexander Graham Bell Association for the Deaf; American Deafness and Rehabilitation Association; American Academy of Otolaryngology; American Speech-Language-Hearing Association; Conference of Educational Administrators Serving the Deaf; Convention of American Instructors of the Deaf; Deafness Research Foundation; National Association of Cued Speech Transliterators; National Fraternal Society of the Deaf; Registry of Interpreters for the Deaf; Self Help for Hard of Hearing People, Inc.; and Telecommunications for the Deaf, Inc. The Council meets on a monthly basis in the different offices of the member organizations to review and discuss public policy and/or legislative issues, and develop plans to address them in a coordinated fashion. A legislative consultant serves as a lobbyist for the COR on a contractual basis. The Council was instrumental in influencing Congress to adopt a new law related to telecommunications for disabled people, including a national TDD relay system and a modified 911 emergency system for hearing-impaired people. The Council is involved in the policy review and development of legislative issues. This involvement has resulted in the formation of a National Commission on Education of the Deaf, and passage of the Americans with Disabilities Act, which serves as a civil rights bill for individuals with disabilities in education, employment, housing, transportation, and communications.

Whether it be at the local, state, or national level, there is a need for deaf persons to not only become aware of but to become actively involved in advocacy related to the wide variety of issues affecting the lives of deaf persons. Such advocacy is necessary not only for the enactment of legislation at all levels, but to also ensure that the deaf community is aware of the legislation, and that proper enforcement is occurring. Only through an appropriately informed deaf community can these things be accomplished. Certainly, a postsecondary program is one way to develop leadership skills necessary to provide guidance in this area.

The postsecondary environment is an important training ground for educating students to become involved in a variety of leadership activities while better informing them about political processes and social activism. A college environment is a place where deaf students have the opportunity to become involved in many different activities depending on their interests and capabilities. Student government, fraternities, sororities, academic as well as professional clubs, special interest organizations, sports, and the arts are some extracurricular areas in which student involvement can range from being officers or committee members to running meetings, developing projects, and raising funds. Since faculty and staff advisors often play an important role in advising and guiding students in developing their leadership skills, all of these extracurricular activities can have a profound impact on students' career development and mobility in the work place after they leave college. Also, these are the very leadership skills that are most needed by the worldwide deaf community.

EDUCATION

Schools play a critical part in developing students' awareness and understanding of the political process. *Formal courses* in civics or political science introduce students to the important aspects of governmental systems in their home state and on a national level – topics include the set up of congressional districts, election of senators and representatives, the process for developing legislative bills, and the separation of powers between the executive, the legislative, and the judiciary branches. Other topics cover the current issues being deliberated in the local, state, and federal governments, and the advocacy role of citizens in pursuit of these legislative bills.

However, while these courses are helpful to students, they are not sufficient to encourage students to develop their leadership skills and use them in appropriate political, civic, and community development activities. As we pointed out earlier, it is through the *extracurricular activities* in student government, sports, drama, newspaper publishing, and other special organizations where experience in leadership and participation in government is learned. These activities provide students with opportunities and challenges to learn to work together on a team and achieve common goals. Teachers play an important role in influencing and advising students to become involved and develop their leadership skills.

At the postsecondary level, one can find a selection of different opportunities for students to become involved and participate in various activities. There are fraternities and sororities, student government, discipline-based clubs, e.g. business club, engineering club, art club, computer club, and other special interest groups. Workshops on how to run an effective business meeting can be provided to students who want to develop their parliamentary procedural skills. Additional workshops can focus on topics related to fund-raising techniques, publicity and public relations, membership recruitment and development, team building, problem solving, and planning special activities in committees. These workshops are effective when combined with 'hands-on' experiential activities such as camping and backpacking, white water rafting, or an all-day outing at a beach. Guest speakers who are successful leaders can be brought into these leadership retreats to talk with students about the difficulties involved in civic and leadership activities. Deaf role models should be part of the leadership development program, so that they can interact with students and discuss the implications of leadership roles in meetings, committees, and services to the community. Role-playing activities are an effective means of educating students to learn about different aspects of leadership roles and discuss important principles of leadership.

Students should be given specific assignments to work together in teams in competition and cooperation with other teams in consultation with advisors, role models, and guest speakers. Students should also be encouraged to attend special topic seminars or community meetings, e.g. deaf culture lecture series, sign/talk show for deaf people, deaf clubs, organizational meetings in the deaf community, or even attend political meetings of other groups with an interpreter to learn about a variety of issues being deliberated by these groups. Rap sessions following each of these activities can help students to review and discuss the salient points of leadership components they might have observed. It may be helpful for students to write in their daily or weekly journals about their observations, critiques and thoughts; these journals can be reviewed on a regular basis with their advisors or assigned mentors to discuss their views, thoughts and concerns.

While most postsecondary programs provide many opportunities for students to participate in a variety of activities, care must be taken to ensure that the provision of services will permit deaf students to avail themselves of these opportunities. Thus, while most postsecondary programs for deaf students attempt to provide tutoring, notetaking, and interpreting support in the classroom, few provide any support for the extracurricular or social activities of students (Walter 1989). Yet we know from the literature on success in college that interaction in extracurricular activities is an important part of life for successful college students (Tinto 1987). Persons providing services to postsecondary-level deaf students must ensure that their students have access to the full range of activities that occur outside the classroom.

In large postsecondary programs for deaf students there are opportunities for students to join organizations or clubs specifically for deaf persons. For instance, at Rochester Institute of Technology's National Technical Institute for the Deaf (NTID) there is a student government organization for deaf students known as the NTID Student Congress (NSC). NSC is divided into four categories: Academic Affairs, Social Affairs, Athletic Affairs, and Legal Affairs. Each category is led by a student with a committee to address specific issues, concerns and needs of deaf students. They meet on a regular basis with faculty advisors. The Academic Affairs group has been instrumental in meeting with key administrators at NTID to share their concerns about academic issues, English language assessment and instruction, interpreting services, quality of teaching, and sign language skills of teaching faculty. The dean of NTID has established a Student Leadership Advisory Council consisting of student leaders from NSC and other student organizations, and meets with them on a regular basis with an agenda established jointly by the dean and student leaders.

There are other student organizations on the campus in which deaf students can become members and be actively involved. There are three deaf fraternities and two deaf sororities in addition to approximately 15 other Greek organizations for RIT students. Deaf students have the option to join deaf Greek organizations or hearing Greek organizations, depending on their interests, aims, and needs. There are also academic-based clubs, including a business club, engineering club, and art club. There are special-interest clubs for deaf students who come from different racial and ethnic backgrounds.

In the early 1980s, several students from NTID, Gallaudet University, California State University at Northridge (CSUN), and other colleges where there are deaf students recognized a need to establish a network of college students who are deaf in more than 150 college programs listed in the *College and Career Programs for Deaf Students* (Rawlings, Karchmer, and DeCaro 1988). With support of administration at NTID, Gallaudet, and CSUN, student leaders from these schools established a National Association of Hearing-Impaired College Students (NAHICS), which was eventually affiliated with the National Association of the Deaf. The organization had its own board of directors and met on a regular basis to discuss the needs of deaf college students. Workshops related to leadership development and college student issues were provided to students in NAD conventions. At this writing, this organization is inactive due to lack of support for student leaders by the NAD and sponsoring organizations. There is a general consensus among deaf college students that there is a need to re-establish such a network so that they can exchange information about programs and services.

Deaf postsecondary students have the opportunity to influence educational practices within their own institutions if they understand how change is effected. A good example of this occured at NTID as a result of the student revolt at Gallaudet University concerning hiring of a new president. After returning from Gallaudet in support of the students' cause, deaf RIT students presented four issues to be addressed by the RIT administration. These four issues related to quality of sign language of instructors, improvement of services to deaf students, addition of more teachers who are deaf, and elimination of the patronizing attitudes of people toward deaf students on the RIT campus.

The students met with the administration and presented their issues and proposed specific strategies to address these issues. As a result, the dean of NTID created opportunities for students to serve on institutional committees. The president of RIT followed up with an appointment of a deaf person to serve on RIT's Board of Trustees. The provost worked with the dean of NTID to provide orientation to deafness and deaf culture, as well as sign language instruction, to vice presidents and deans at a retreat. Additional workshops are now being developed for faculty in other colleges of RIT. All of these changes in practice were the result of the leadership and empowerment of students to clearly define and state the four issues they had identified.

While activities on campus are important for developing leadership skills for deaf students, the college environment can also promote awareness of, and involvement in, other local or national issues that affect deaf persons. In this way, the program acts as a bridge between the relatively isolated life of the campus and the activities of the community. What must be provided by the school is advisement by qualified and concerned faculty regarding the issues at hand. Because of the inherent difficulties deaf students have in effectively using the traditional media as sources of information, it is critical that faculty and staff be available to tutor and advise deaf students concerning the implications of important issues. This is a role that must be provided by any program that hopes to serve deaf students fully in a postsecondary environment. A few examples illustrate how this can help college students increase their awareness of important legislative issues.

Mario Cuomo, governor of New York, was influenced by the advocates of the Public Law 94–142, Education of All Handicapped Children Act, to redirect funds from the special schools for the deaf to local educational agencies, so that each local school district would be given full authority to determine placement for each child with a disability. Many people in the area of education of deaf people feared that this would necessitate closing or scaling down resources in special schools for deaf children. The governor's proposed budget determined that each local school district would have to pay the full costs of placing a deaf child in a school for the deaf and be reimbursed partially (about 65 per cent) by the state one year later. The deaf community, including deaf adults, parents of deaf children, teachers of the deaf, and friends of deaf people, feared the worst possible situation for deaf children, and mobilized political activities to influence local state senators and members of the assembly to oppose the Governor's proposal. Even school administrators and boards from local school districts expressed their concern that many local education agencies were programmatically and financially unprepared to deal with this issue. They endorsed the deaf community's protest.

A massive campaign of letter writing, telephone calls through the New York State Relay Service, and telegrams to the state legislature and to the governor's office was initiated by various community organizations throughout the state in close cooperation with school administrators and parent groups. Deaf students at NTID were actively involved in these efforts. More than $3,000 was raised by the deaf community in Rochester alone, and several NTID student organizations contributed. The funds were used to charter buses to Albany for a statewide rally at the Capitol and the legislative building. Many NTID students joined in the trip and participated in meetings with hundreds of legislators and their staff in their offices.

The net result was the resounding defeat of the governor's proposal, and the continuation of the schools for deaf students. It was a wonderful experience for everyone in the deaf community, including the college students. One legislator, who spoke at the recent convention of the American Deafness and Rehabilitation Association, told the audience that he had never seen such well-organized political activism with respect to any proposed legislative bill in his many years of political life. He also said that as a result of this political activity, the budget for the special programs became the highest priority of all budget items to be protected by the legislature.

An example at the national level relates to the pending federal legislative bill to mandate the Federal Communications Commission to initiate a study on the creation of a nationwide telecommunications relay service for speech and hearing-impaired individuals. This bill was at risk of not being acted on as the Congress was nearing the end of its session in 1988. The United States Senate had passed the bill, but in the House of Representatives, the bill was referred to seven different committees for their deliberations and vote before it could be acted upon the main floor of the House of Representatives. The National Office of Telecommunications for the Deaf, Inc. and the National Association of the Deaf took a number of desperate actions to lobby the seven committees to get this bill moved on to the floor for a vote before the close of the Congressional session. Gallaudet University sent more than 100 students to visit the offices of representatives and their staff. Students from NTID and some faculty members drove to Washington, DC, to join in the lobbying efforts. Again, the net result was that the bill moved expeditiously through these committees and was overwhelmingly passed.

CONCLUSIONS

As we enter the 21st century, the necessity for political awareness and adept leadership skills will become even more important to all minority groups. It will be necessary for leaders to be aware of the changing conditions worldwide that might affect attitudes toward a group or implementation of legislation supporting a specific cause.

We will no longer have the luxury to say that what happens in another country will have no effect on what happens in a small town in the American Midwest. For example, it is certain that the recent changes in eastern Europe and the Soviet Union will have long-term effects on social legislation in the western world well into the next century. Unless leaders of the deaf community are sensitive to these issues, they will have difficulty mustering the governmental support necessary to win their causes.

Postsecondary education must be looked upon for providing students not only with the technical skills to acquire jobs, but with the skills necessary to become leaders in their communities. Too often we focus on those activities in the classroom, and seldom remember to provide support for those activities outside of the classroom. It may be that these are equally as important as what transpires in the classroom, and by paying more attention to the extracurricular world we will ensure that graduates will not only enhance the quality of their lives but the lives of all deaf and hard-of-hearing people.

As a result of passage of the Americans with Disabilities Act, there is a need for leaders in the deaf community to inform their constituencies of the provisions of the legislation, and then act as a watchdog to ensure that industry and government comply with the legislation. Where will the deaf persons come from who truly understand this legislation? Who will explain its implications to the average American deaf worker? It will probably need to be the deaf college graduate who understands both the legislation and the nature of deafness.

REFERENCES

Hurwitz, T.A. (1989) *Encyclopedia on Deafness and Deaf People.*

Rawlings, B.A., Karchmer, M., and DeCaro, J. (1988) *College and Career Programs for Deaf Students.* Washington, DC: Gallaudet University and Rochester, NY: Rochester Institute of Technology.

Tinto, B. (1987) *Leaving College.* Chicago, IL: University of Chicago Press.

Walter, G.G. (1989) 'Adherence of postsecondary programs to the CEASD principles basic to the establishment and operation of postsecondary education for deaf students,' Paper presented at the International Symposium on Postsecondary Education for the Deaf, Edmonton, Alberta, Canada.

Personal Commentary

Gerald Nelson

The seeds of my leadership qualities were probably sown when I was a youngster. My parents served on numerous boards within their community; their activities exposed me to civic and community activism. During my high school days at the Minnesota School for the Deaf I was involved with the Jr. NAD and the Literacy Society. I quarterbacked on the varsity football team; I also had major roles in several school plays and variety shows. In fact, most of my classmates were involved with extracurricular activities and this seemed like an ordinary thing for all of us to do.

In the fall of 1969, I entered the National Technical Institute for the Deaf, a college of Rochester Institute of Technology, attending classes with hearing people for the first time in my life. This was a new experience for me and I remember myself being reserved and not participating in activities. I remained relatively obscure among deaf peers and focused my attention on my academic studies in engineering which were difficult at that time. During that first year, the NTID Student Government was fledgling and had trouble being recognized as a viable student organization by the RIT Student Government. I recall scoffing at that group as it never provided me with incentives to get involved.

Then, and I remember this vividly . . . at the end of my first academic year, the NTID Dean presented me with the Achievement Award which is given to a student who has shown great academic achievement during the year. Naturally, I was stunned. NTID students said 'Who?' when word about my receiving the award reached them. Ironically, this event further fueled students' perceptions of me as being 'the one with the brains.' In retrospect, this was a pivotal point, marking my entrance as a student leader at NTID.

During my second year at NTID, I became involved with issues of concern to NTID students. There were frustrations among students with the NTID administration in various areas. A notable area involved the NTID students taking part in speech therapy which was, at that time, a non-credit 'course' requirement. Students felt this was an unnecessary repeat of earlier, unpleasant experiences from their grade school years. With seemingly no resolutions to students' frustrations, I began publishing an underground paper in order to stir public interest and bring attention to these issues in the hope of creating opportunities for changes. The paper immediately gained notoriety because of its satirical and provocative articles (mostly directed to the administration), written by 'The Phantom.' When my role as writer and publisher of the paper became public, this created even more opportunities for me to get involved with student and administration-related politics.

In late 1971, my energies shifted to helping the NTID student body gain recognition as a governing group within the larger RIT Student Government. The NTID Student Government was pretty much dead, having floundered over several years. A core group of us labored to develop a new set of bylaws which were eventually approved by the RIT Student Government. This paved the way for the creation of the NTID Student Congress (NSC), which still stands today. I am particularly proud of this achievement.

Students urged me to become the first president of the NSC. I recall being reluctant to take on the responsibilities involved with this position. I jokingly asked for a petition of 160 names of NTID students (out of a body of 300). Sure enough, a petition with about 180 names appeared. I felt empowered by the students and decided to take on the challenge. The rest is history.

It was at this point when I began to understand the meaning and importance of trust. Fellow students put trust in me to provide leadership, and to make changes for the better. I learned to trust myself more, especially in letting my intuition guide me. This was the basis of my current reputation as a person who will take risks to achieve what I want. I see that the NSC continues to stand strong, so I know that I must have laid a solid foundation back then.

After graduating from RIT and landing an engineering job in Minnesota in January 1974, I immediately got involved with a local deaf group, the MinnePaul Athletic Association. Three years later, I was elected to the Board of the Minnesota

Association of the Deaf Citizens (MADC) as the youngest board member ever. By then, I felt good knowing that the MADC members saw my potential as their leader by way of empowering me as their representative on the board.

Eventually, the demand for my time and expertise increased and I became more involved with politics at the state level. By then, the value of trust was of paramount importance to me. This was also a time when I began to more fully appreciate the value of honesty. I saw cutthroat politics being played out by the state-level bureaucrats at the expense of deaf people and vowed never to do the same.

With increasing community advocacy and leadership responsibilities, I reached the point where I wanted to be in a career involving deaf people and their right to determine their own destinies. In 1981, I left the well-paid engineering profession to return to school for a master's degree in administration. Within six months after graduation, I became the executive director of a statewide advocacy and public education agency.

Looking back, I know that the development of my leadership qualities date to my family upbringing and high school days, nurtured through my college years and refined over the years through my work and involvement with the deaf community. Close friends and colleagues saw my leadership potential and qualities and persuaded me many times to assume leadership roles.

Some say my engineering background also gave me the essential organizational skills needed for leadership. Much of my management knowledge is also based on fundamental leadership qualities. I have been told of my ability to envision the possible and communicate this in the form of a 'vision' to others. I am also a person who others can depend on to do as I promised. In short, I am a strong believer in honesty and trust. Most importantly, I stick to my principles even though it may hurt me – and others – at times.

Now, you tell me what is so black and white that prepared me for involvement with politics in the deaf community. Leadership is that which is seen through the eyes of the beholder.

Gerald Nelson currently teaches business administration and management courses to undergraduate students at Gallaudet University, Washington, DC. He is also the vice president of GNB Consultants, a management and organizational development consulting firm. For eight years prior to this, he was the executive director of various nonprofit organizations serving deaf and hard-of-hearing persons.

Jerry, as many call him, graduated from the Minnesota School for the Deaf. He earned his bachelor's degree from Rochester Institute of Technology with support from the National Technical Institute for the Deaf. After eight years as an engineer, Jerry attended California State University at Northridge (CSUN) and earned, through Leadership Training Program, his master's degree in education administration and supervision. It was soon after CSUN when he began managing nonprofit organizations.

Jerry has two sons, Max, 17, and Chris, 16.

Part III

Outcomes of postsecondary educational programs for deaf students

Postsecondary educational institutions are service organizations. The consumers of the service are the students who pay their tuition and attend classes in an effort to acquire skills which they believe will enhance the quality of their personal and professional lives. In order to meet the needs of these students, institutions must design programs with the potential consumers in mind, using the kinds of demographic and descriptive information presented in Part I. They must consider the kinds of issues and strategies described in Part II as they work to create a campus environment which facilitates the academic and social development of matriculated student/consumers. Lastly, they must describe and analyze the outcomes of postsecondary education by measuring the extent to which completion of the program influences the lives of graduate/ consumers and helps them attain their goals. It is this task which is the focus of discussion in Part III.

One of the primary functions of postsecondary education is career preparation. Employment attainments of graduates should therefore be a major area of study for postsecondary institutions. What is the employment rate of graduates? How do their salaries compare with those of people without degrees? What is the career mobility of graduates? Are graduates satisfied with their current jobs and future employment opportunities? Do the employment attainments of graduates suggest gaps in the postsecondary curriculum? If so, how can these gaps best be filled? These are the kinds of questions administrators of postsecondary institutions should routinely ask about graduates.

In the final part of this book, two approaches to studying the employment experiences of deaf graduates of postsecondary educational programs are described. The first approach, presented in Chapter 9, involves quantitative research. Through analysis of survey data and administrative records provided by the US Internal Revenue Service and the US

Bureau of Labor Statistics, comparisons were made between deaf people and their hearing peers, and between deaf people who did not attend postsecondary programs and those who did. The results demonstrate clearly the positive impact for deaf people of postsecondary education on participation in the labor force, occupations, and earnings, as well as the reduction of the gap which has historically existed in the US between deaf and hearing people with comparable levels of education. This information is enormously useful for planners and administrators of postsecondary educational programs for deaf students, since the findings suggest that continued support for these programs is worthwhile. It also offers information to potential student/consumers about the extent to which a postsecondary education may help them achieve their career goals. At the same time, there are areas of the work experience which cannot be examined using quantitative research data. Qualitative methods such as open-ended interviews and participant observation are helpful for describing and analyzing the perspectives of deaf employees on various dimensions of their work experience, as well as those of their supervisors and co-workers. These methods also provide detailed accounts of day to day employment conditions and interactions. For example, analysis of interviews with deaf college graduates, presented in Chapter 10, suggests that the toughest communication barriers encountered by these workers are those associated with access to informal social networks, also known as 'office grapevines.' Information about these more subtle dimensions of the work experience, while not part of the technical curriculum, highlights areas where students and alumni may benefit from additional or related coursework. Examples include courses on communication at work, interpersonal skills, corporate culture, and management training.

In summary, the chapters included in Part III offer readers two quite different approaches to studying employment outcomes of postsecondary education for deaf graduate/consumers. Results from these studies demonstrate the significant impact of postsecondary education on access to employment, and highlight areas where barriers in the work place persist. The studies described in each chapter should not be interpreted as *the* way to study outcomes; rather, they are *examples* of ways in which quantitative and qualitative data can be used to learn about the employment outcomes of postsecondary education. Other researchers will no doubt design quite different studies, based on their graduate populations and the specific questions they wish to address. However, regardless of the populations and topics to be studied, it is recommended that both quantitative and qualitative approaches be considered in developing a comprehensive program of research in this area.

Chapter 9

Effect of college on employment and earnings

*William A. Welsh and
Janet MacLeod-Gallinger*

INTRODUCTION

Given that many individuals willingly (even eagerly) invest between two and 10 years of their lives, and very often tens of thousands of dollars to acquire the better job that usually comes with a degree, a job must be something of great consequence. It is probably fair to say that one's job is among the most important parts of the lives of most people. In fact, the last time someone asked you: 'What do you do?' or even 'What *are* you?' your instinct was very likely to respond, 'I am an engineer,' 'I work in computer programming,' 'I grind lenses,' or even, 'Well, I am out of work right now.' At least in most of Western culture, our occupation – that activity consuming roughly half of our waking hours – is tied inextricably to our concept of ourselves. Our self-image rises and falls with our occupational successes and failures. Although most of us are required to work, we do not work *only* because we must; most workers have more interest in their jobs than simply the regular paycheck. Katzell (1979) describes the results of several national surveys that indicate that 70–80 per cent of Americans would persist at work even if there were no financial need. This is not to imply that all persons are completely satisfied with their careers. Kerr (1979) notes that there is significant disaffection among those holding low-paying jobs with no chance for advancement, and adds that ' . . . throughout society, more education, more knowledge about jobs, more mobility, and more financial resources all mean that individuals are more eager and free to decline "bad" jobs and to search for "good" jobs. (p. xix)'

Occupations are certainly not the only thing in our lives; millions of people have a multitude of other pursuits. Career is one of the lowest common denominators, though. Not everyone has a spouse, children, avocation, or some other combination of people and activities that accounts for their free time activities on a daily basis; however, as of the beginning of the 1990s, approximately 109 million Americans had jobs (US Bureau of Labor Statistics, 1989), and the labor force will likely expand by 19 million during the next 10 years. (Fullerton 1989)

Why are our jobs so vital to us? Rosenthal (1989) notes that there are a variety of rewards we receive from our occupations, and that the reward structure is probably different for everyone. What is important '... is determined by many factors. These values are derived from the socioeconomic background and the environment in the geographic area in which [people] live. In addition, [importance is determined by] different interests, perceived abilities, and interests in activities other than work...'(p. 4). He goes on to say that some of the many potential rewards we receive from our jobs are the following: wages, the feeling of being part of a team, the ability to see the results of work, the opportunity to be creative, the chance to solve problems, the power to influence others, the opportunity to use skills obtained through hard work, the learning of new skills, status, security, and the receipt of recognition for a job well done.

There are social compensations, as well. Many Americans make all or most of their friends at work, and to a greater or lesser extent, plan their social lives around the extracurricular activities of their co-workers. Even beyond friendships, daily interaction with the same set of persons with common vocational interests helps to influence our avocations, interests, opinions, and values. It is clear, then, that work is a prominent part of our lives.

Occupations play a central role in the lives of deaf persons as well. They reap many if not most of the same rewards from their job that hearing people do. This chapter is about the occupational attainments of deaf people and the impact education has on those attainments. Employment of deaf people from a historical perspective is reviewed in the first section, followed by a discussion of contemporary employment conditions. Finally the effects of postsecondary education on career attainments of deaf people are discussed.

HISTORICAL EMPLOYMENT CONDITIONS

Van Cleve and Crouch (1989) write that the industrial revolution, and the accompanying shift from an agrarian to an industrial economy, was not a harbinger of good times for deaf workers. The entire American occupational structure changed dramatically. Many jobs in an agricultural economy '... could be learned without hearing, [because] individuals could depend on visual observation, long practice, and an intimate acquaintance with their teacher or coworkers' (p. 155). However, this 'learning from life' did not generally occur when a majority of workers were on the production line, where people were treated much more impersonally.

As a result, deaf people entered an extended period of time during which they had to endure severely depressed employment conditions. With few exceptions, deaf people were employed at levels significantly below those of their hearing peers. Lunde and Bigman (1959), in describing the results of their survey, noted that 'the most striking fact ... is the high proportion of the deaf who are skilled or semi-skilled manual workers .... These two groups constitute more than 70 per cent of all respondents' (p. 21). They report that only 17 per cent of all deaf workers were 'white collar' at that time, compared to 47 per cent for the American work force. Although similar statistical analyses are not available for earlier decades, it seems safe to say that any occupational mobility deaf people had made in the work place had been slow since the onset of industrialization. Boatner, Stuckless, and Moores reported similar findings:

> the occupational status of the young deaf adult of New England remains low in comparison to the general population. Seventy-one per cent of the males and 54% of the females ... are employed in unskilled or semi-skilled occupations. The unemployment rate of 17% ... is approximately four times that of the general rate of the state of Connecticut. On all bases of comparison, the salaries of young deaf adults interviewed are considerably lower than those of the hearing.
>
> (1964: 108)

Stahler (1969) and Williams and Sussman (1971) describe the principal work-related problem of deaf people as being underemployment. Schein and Delk agree, adding specifically:

> While education as a single criterion for underemployment is inadequate, it does provide a gross indication. For example, almost 43% of deaf adults who have completed 13 years or more of school (i.e., have one or more years of higher education) have principal occupations in the following categories: clerical, transit

and nontransit operatives, farm and nonfarm laborers, and service and household workers. Underemployment certainly describes many of these job placements, though not necessarily all.

(1974: 85)

In a study of salaries, Weinrich (1972) estimated the cost of deafness in terms of lost lifetime wages at more than $260,000. He believed the discrepancy was due primarily to the fact that far more hearing than deaf people attend college, and consequently, have higher earnings.

This was almost certainly an underestimate, since Weinrich assumed that deaf and hearing persons of equal educational attainment would be paid equal wages. This is probably not true. Welsh, Walter, and Riley (1989a) demonstrate that deaf people earn less than hearing people at all educational levels. Schroedel (1976) adds that vertical mobility is, and has long been, a problem for deaf people. He states that deaf persons enjoyed considerably less upward movement than their hearing peers over the period 1920–70.

Generally, the studies that have been carried out concerning the employment status of deaf people agree that deaf people, as a group, do not attain occupations, or earn equal compensation for equivalent jobs held by their hearing peers. Most of the studies (Lunde and Bigman 1959; Boatner, Stuckless, and Moores 1964; Williams and Sussman 1971; Weinrich 1972; Schein and Delk 1974) were completed before the impact of equal rights legislation and the growth in postsecondary educational opportunities could be realized. What are the current employment conditions of deaf adults?

CONTEMPORARY EMPLOYMENT CONDITIONS

The Secondary School Graduate Follow-Up Program for the Deaf annually surveys graduates of 27 secondary programs for deaf people from various parts of the United States (MacLeod-Gallinger 1981–90). Results indicate that there is still a sizable gap between the occupational attainments of deaf people and their hearing peers. Cumulative results from annual surveys to date include information about the labor force participation, employment rate, type of occupation, and earnings for more than 6,000 deaf adults from all over the United States. The statistics that follow are based upon results from survey years 1985–90, and include 3,753 respondents.

Labor Force Status

Every citizen age 16 and older can be characterized by his or her labor force status. Those who are working and those who have actively sought employment in the last four weeks are considered *in the labor force*. All others are *out of the labor force*. The *unemployment rate* is calculated by dividing the number of persons in the labor force who are unemployed but actively looking for work by the total number of persons who are in the labor force. Table 9.1 presents labor force participation and unemployment rates of deaf respondents and persons nationally by age groups.

The labor force participation of the deaf respondents is lower relative to persons nationally for all age groups. However, advancing age reduces the discrepancies. The figures in Table 9.1 are not broken down by gender, but other analyses show that deaf females demonstrate slightly higher participation rates relative to hearing females, while deaf males have participated at rates approximately equal to their hearing counterparts. Looking solely at persons over the age of 20, 77 per cent of both deaf and hearing males were in the labor force while 63 per cent of deaf females and 58 per cent of hearing females were in the labor force. The higher participation rate of deaf females may be accounted for by the facts that deaf people marry somewhat later in life (Schein and Delk 1974), and fewer of the deaf respondents in the survey had left the labor force to become homemakers than was the case for their hearing peers.

Despite relatively high participation rates, deaf adults are less often successful in their job-seeking efforts as compared to hearing persons. This is evidenced by their overall higher unemployment rates. It is especially the case for deaf persons under age 35. Fewer than one-third of deaf adults in this age group who want to work can find a job. Generally, the gap between the unemployment rates of deaf and hearing people decreases with age; however, even in the 35-44 age group, the rate for deaf people is almost twice that of their hearing peers. The employment picture for the latter part of the 1980s is not much better than it has been historically. The overall unemployment rate for the respondents age 20 and older averages about 20 per cent. This is equivalent to what was reported by Boatner, Stuckless, and Moores in 1964.

Table 9.1 Labor force participation and unemployment rates of deaf and a national population of workers by age level

Age	Participation		Unemployment	
	Deaf %	National %	Deaf %	National %
16–19 Years	37	50	56	16
20–24 Years	64	76	41	9
25–34 Years	77	84	19	6
35–44 Years	79	85	8	4

Source: Employment & Earnings Feb. 1990 (March 1990 issue)

Occupation

A comprehensive occupational classification was developed by the US Bureau of the Census (1982). Both the Bureau of Labor Statistics and the Follow-up Program use this system to report persons' occupations. The system groups all into six major categories as follows:

Managerial and Professional (e.g. accountants, engineers, teachers, biologists, artists);
Technical, Sales and Administrative Support (e.g.,computer programmers and operators, health technicians, retail sales, bookkeepers, secretaries);
Service (private household workers, custodians, child care workers, cooks);
Farming, Forestry, and Fishing;
Precision Production, Craft and Repair (tool and die makers, machinists, engravers); and
Operators, Fabricators, and Laborers (assemblers, truck drivers, laborers).

Although the federal government has not officially used the term white- or blue-collar workers, most of those traditionally thought of as 'white-collar' workers are employed in the Managerial and Professional, and the Technical, Sales and Administrative Support occupational categories, while the remainder are considered 'blue-collar' workers.

Table 9.2 contains the percentages of workers employed in each occupational category. Since occupational distributions differ for all workers by gender in nearly every subgroup the percentages are broken down by males and females.

Significant differences exist between the occupational distributions of deaf and hearing persons. Deaf people are still greatly underrepresented in the Managerial and Professional occupations, i.e., those that require the highest education levels and pay the highest salaries. They are also over-represented among Service and Operators, Fabricators, and Laborers, which require the least education and pay the lowest wages. In terms of occupational distribution, there have been some changes since the Lunde and Bigman (1959) and Schein and Delk (1974) studies. Among those occupations classified as unskilled or semi-skilled, there has been some movement from the Operative occupations to the Service occupations. There has also been a shift from the semiskilled Precision Production, Craft and Repair occupations to Technical, Sales or Administrative Support. For deaf females this movement has translated primarily to clerical jobs, while among males it has more often meant a move toward technical jobs. These changes reflect shifts in the economy over time, i.e., an increase in the number of service jobs, and a decline in the manufacturing sector in the United States during the past quarter of a century, as well as an increase in technical and administrative support occupations. Nevertheless, deaf workers still dominate the less skilled areas of employment and are half as likely to hold Managerial and Professional Specialty positions as their hearing peers.

Table 9.2 Occupational groupings of deaf adults and the national population of workers ages 25–44

Occupation	Males		Females		Total	
	Deaf %	National %	Deaf %	National %	Deaf %	National %
Managerial/Professional	10	26	16	27	12	26
Tech/Sales/Admin. Support	26	20	49	45	36	32
Service	15	10	14	17	14	13
Farming/Forestry/Fishing	2	4	2	1	2	2
Precision Prod/Crafts	13	20	2	2	8	12
Operators/Fabricators	35	21	17	9	28	15

Source: US Bureau of the Census (1982)

Earnings

A significant discrepancy between the wages and salaries of hearing and deaf people has historically been found. Weinrich's (1972) analysis was the first systematic examination documenting the differences, but there was an earnings gap that had existed long before that. In their follow-up of a deaf sample of the Census, Barnartt and Christiansen (1985) discovered that the gap between deaf and hearing persons' incomes had widened between 1972 and 1977, most especially for deaf women. What is the case currently?

Data displayed in Table 9.3 represent salaries that have been converted to 1990 dollars using the Consumer Price Index – all urban consumers, US city average. The earnings gap between the deaf sample and persons nationally persists for each successive age group. There appears to be no systematic relationship between age and the size of the wage discrepancy.

Deaf males on the whole earn proportionately much less than males nationally – 77 per cent of their earnings. The disparity between deaf and hearing females is less great – 88 per cent of women nationally. But women earn less than males generally, and deaf females earn the lowest wages of all.

Lower relative earnings of deaf workers occur *for both genders and within every occupational grouping*. Data appear conclusive that the gap in earnings between deaf and hearing people has not been closed.

Table 9.3 Median weekly earnings ($) of deaf adults and the national population of full-time workers by age and gender

Age	Females		Males		Total	
	Deaf	National	Deaf	National	Deaf	National
16–19 Years	179	197	160	220	165	208
20–24 Years	230	272	255	297	244	286
25–34 Years	292	350	369	454	334	407
35–44 Years	399	384	465	558	438	481

Source: National data from US Dept. of Labor, Bureau of Labor Statistics, First Quarter 1990. NEWS: UDSL 90-197 (April, 1990).

Summary

The data are hardly encouraging. Deaf adults age 20 and older participate in the labor force about as often as their hearing peers;

but, they are unemployed as much as three times as often among the younger age groups and at least twice as often among those with more time in the work force. They are underrepresented in Managerial and Professional occupations, and consequently overrepresented in occupations that require less training, afford less status, and pay less money. Even worse, within the *same occupational classifications* they earn significantly less money.

These results are not appreciably different from results reported in 1959 by Lunde and Bigman; in 1964 by Boatner, Stuckless, and Moores; in 1974 by Schein and Delk; and in other studies. As a group, deaf people have not experienced noticeably improved employment conditions in at least 30 years, and quite possibly not since the turn of the century. Can we regard all efforts to reduce the gap between deaf and hearing people as failures? What about education? What has been accomplished in the schools?

POSTSECONDARY EDUCATION AND CAREER ATTAINMENTS

A discussion of education prompts the fundamental question, 'Why do people seek an education, in particular a postsecondary education?' College graduates are rewarded in many ways for their investment. Bowen (1977) notes that the graduates' emotional and moral development is facilitated, they become better, more productive citizens, their family life and leisure time are enhanced, and they are actually healthier.

It may be a cliché to say that there are as many reasons for attending college as there are people who attend. However, many, if not most, do so, at least partly, in the hope of a better job. Data from the US Bureau of Labor Statistics (1988) show that their hopes are not unreasonable; education exercises a dominant influence over career. College graduates are more likely to be in the labor force, less likely to be unemployed, and much more likely to be in the managerial or professional occupations that are thought of by most people as having greater prestige, status, and desirability (Duncan 1961; Stevens and Cho 1985).

It involves no great leap of faith to say that those who worked for improved educational opportunities for deaf people expected that this would result in improved career opportunities. Have their efforts been equally successful in this area? What have these programs accomplished? Have graduates shown any sign of closing the gap between their attainments and those of hearing workers? The following sections contain data on the effect of postsecondary education on the labor force status, occupation, and earnings of deaf people.

Labor Force Status

The authors examined the effects of postsecondary education in terms of three levels of attainment: those with only high school degrees; graduates with sub-baccalaureate (diplomas, certificates, and associate) and baccalaureate or higher degrees. Table 9.4 displays information on labor force status and unemployment rate.

Generally speaking, the more education deaf adults receive, the greater their labor force participation and the lower their unemployment. It is dramatically clear at the baccalaureate level. Yet, the situation among sub-baccalaureate degree earners suggests that this holds true for deaf males only, since females with one- to three-year degrees exhibit similar unemployment rates as those who do not have postsecondary degrees. Although all the reasons for this occurence are not clear, we can speculate that some of these women are in fact discouraged workers; that is, they are not seeking employment, because the jobs they can find are either very low paying, or not commensurate with training. One factor may be that many of them earn degrees in programs that are not competitive in the job market. This exception noted, in most instances increased education does positively affect the labor force status of young deaf adults.

Table 9.4 Labor force status of deaf high school and college graduates ages 25–44

Education level	Participation			Unemployment		
	Male %	Female %	Total %	Male %	Female %	Total %
High School only	86	63	75	17	22	19
Sub-baccalaureate	91	72	82	7	25	15
Baccalaureate and above	100	88	93	3	3	3

Occupation

How does obtaining a degree effect the type of jobs deaf persons have? The relationship between college degree and occupational grouping is shown in Table 9.5. The more education deaf adults receive, the more likely they are to be employed in one of the Managerial or Professional Specialty occupations. A deaf graduate with a sub-baccalaureate degree is more than three times as likely to be employed in one of these occupations as one without a college degree. Even more compelling is the effect of earning bachelor's and master's level degrees. Deaf adults with four-year and higher degrees are 10 times more likely to be employed in Managerial and Professional Specialty occupations than sub-baccalaureate degree holders. Moreover, these rates are equivalent to rates for a national sample of US workers.

As degree level increases, percentages employed in lower skill areas decrease. Given that this is true, the question becomes one of how to increase the percentages of deaf persons pursuing and completing higher level degrees. Among respondents of the Follow-up sample, each year approximately 16 per cent complete degree programs, but only 3 per cent of the total are at the bachelor's level or higher.

Table 9.5 Occupations of deaf high school and college graduates ages 25–44

Occupation	High School N	High School %	Sub-Bachelor N	Sub-Bachelor %	Bachelor and above N	Bachelor and above %
Managerial/Professional	13	2	12	6	89	64
Technical/Sales/Administrative Support	216	36	86	46	30	22
Service	112	19	17	9	5	4
Farming/Forestry/Fishing	12	2	2	1	2	1
Precision Products/Craft/Repair	43	7	30	16	4	3
Operators/Fabricators/Laborers	205	34	42	22	8	6

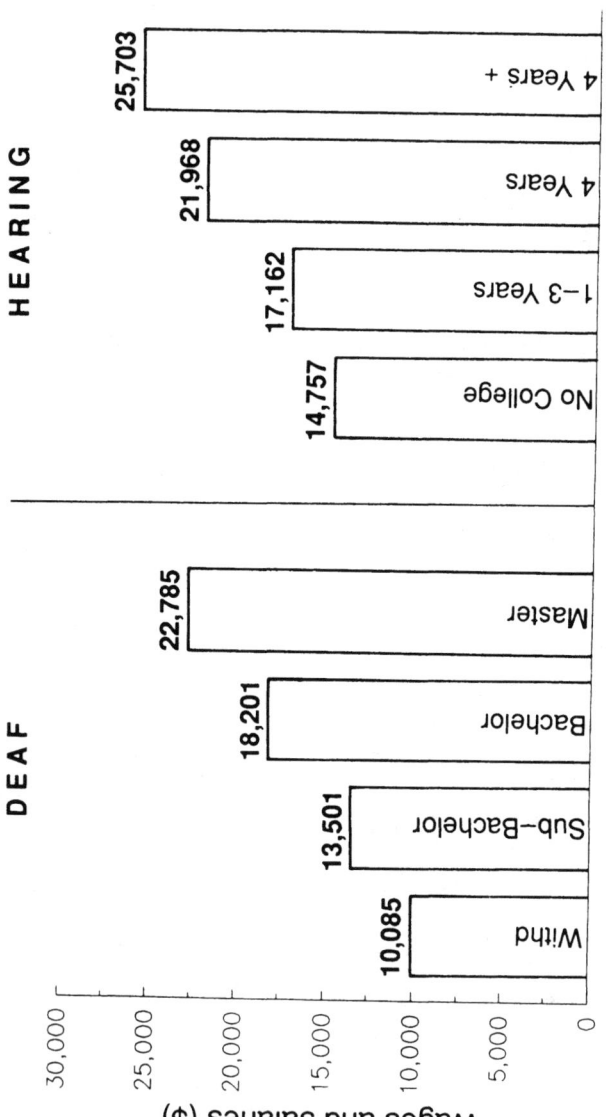

Figure 9.1 Mean 1985 wages and salaries of deaf and hearing college graduates

Source: US Bureau of Labor Statistics (1988)

Earnings

What about earnings? Earnings are not all things to all people, but more money does allow us to buy more education, to have more leisure time, and to pursue avocations that we might not otherwise be able to pursue. Welsh, Walter, and Riley (1989) examined the earnings of alumni of five postsecondary programs for deaf persons from various parts of the country. Their 1985 earnings were reported by the US Internal Revenue Service. Data on hearing persons were obtained from the US Bureau of Labor Statistics. Results of the analysis are shown in Figure 9.1.

Two inescapable conclusions can be reached from these data. First, it can be deduced that earnings of deaf people increase dramatically as the degree levels they attain get higher; and, second, the discrepancy between deaf and hearing people (Figure 9.2) decreases the higher the degree. This could be the result of less salary discrimination for persons employed in the professional occupations as compared to those persons employed in the semi- or unskilled occupations.

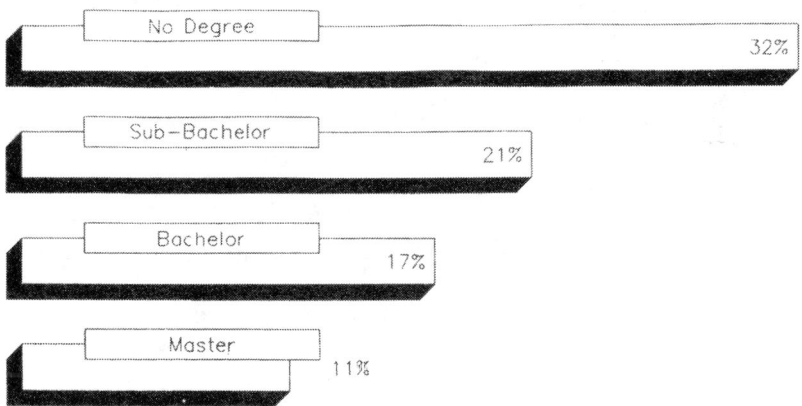

Figure 9.2 Percentage differences in earnings between deaf and hearing workers
Source: US Bureau of Labor Statistics (1988)

EDUCATIONAL OPPORTUNITIES; DEAF AND HEARING PEOPLE

The preceding sections of this chapter may appear to conflict. On the one hand, we are saying that conditions of deaf people have not improved appreciably over a long period of time. On the other, we indicate just how much a college degree helps. The resolution to this apparently incongruous information may lie in an examination of the difference in educational opportunity for deaf and hearing people.

Table 9.6 shows the education level of the US population aged 25–44 in 1988.

Table 9.6 Postsecondary attainment of hearing persons ages 25–44, 1988

Total	Number (%of Total) 1–3 Years of College	4 or more Years of College
77,167,000 (100)	15,992,000 (20.7)	29,105,000 (24.8)

Source: US Bureau of Labor Statistics (1988)

Some 45.5 per cent of hearing workers have had significant college experience, *at least* one year. We cannot say with certainty precisely how many completed their degrees. However, given that a majority of attrition occurs *before* one year of college is completed (Tinto 1987), and that it is also probably true that most of those with four or more years of college have at least a bachelor degree, it appears *very conservative* to estimate that about 33 per cent of the population attains some formal certification (Beal and Noel 1980).

There is no complete set of data on the deaf population of the United States with which to make comparative statements. However, given what is known about reading achievement in deaf secondary school leavers (see Chapter 1), the chances are overwhelming that at least 90 per cent of deaf high school graduates will not attain any postsecondary certification. If this estimate is correct, the chances for a hearing person are about 3.7 times as great as for a deaf person to attain some formal certification. Additionally, their chances for a bachelor's degree or higher appear to be almost 10 times as great.

DISCUSSION

The data presented here *uniformly* support the value of acquiring a postsecondary education. Deaf people who earn degrees are in the labor force more often, unemployed much less often, get higher level jobs, and earn significantly more money. Not only is some postsecondary education an improvement over a high school degree, it is clear that more college is better than less. Bachelor's degree recipients fare better than sub-bachelor's graduates in all ways measured in this study, and, in terms of salary, master's degree recipients fared best of all. At the same time, *overall* conditions of deaf people have improved very little. What are we to conclude from these findings?

It appears that we have, to some extent at least, put the cart before the horse. If we continue to increase the number of opportunities for deaf people to attain a postsecondary education without increasing their academic preparedness, what can we expect to accomplish? After all, availability does not ensure access. Overall, the basic academic skills of young deaf adults have not improved significantly during the last quarter of a century.

What needs to be done, then? What can we do to improve the education and ultimately, employment opportunities of deaf people? It appears obvious that first, the systems we use to teach deaf children to read need to be improved. Reading levels are often insufficient to gain entrance to postsecondary education. This of course, has long been the challenge in teaching deaf persons, and not one that these authors are prepared to address.

What else is indicated in the way of educational change? There are additional compelling reasons to re-examine educational programs offered to deaf people. Chapter 1 discusses the changes that will most likely occur in the work force at the beginning of the next century, and the impact these changes will have on deaf persons. Assuming current projections for the future work force are accurate, if present employment patterns observed among deaf adults are not altered they will only further the discrepancies documented in this chapter. Both *un*employment and *under*employment are serious concerns among deaf adults, and economic trends suggest that both conditions will persist unless deaf people acquire higher achievement levels, and thereby greater access to college education and opportunities for technical and professional employment. Although more young deaf adults are entering a more diverse range of educational programs, they are still highly concentrated in programs that lead to occupations predicted to have little or negative growth in the near future.

In order to effect change, the basic academic skills of deaf students must be improved so that, ultimately, a larger portion of deaf individuals will be able to enter and graduate from postsecondary educational programs. Moreover, institutions providing support services to deaf students must be expanded to include more academic rather than vocational programs. We cannot afford to keep deaf persons occupationally segregated, particularly when the outlook for employment in jobs for which most of them still receive training is beginning to narrow. And this is especially the case for young deaf women.

We can, however, state that curricula for deaf students at elementary, secondary, and postsecondary levels need to be linked by common goals, and they must be kept updated. Career education efforts need to be bolstered as well. Part of this education must be to broaden options for programs of study that are presented to both male and female deaf students. There is still much evidence that young deaf adults are channeled into too narrow a range of programs.

Educational institutions must be kept in tune with the changing demands of our economy. There is a need to establish and maintain programs that connect businesses to educational institutions. Deaf students need models and mentors as much or more than their hearing peers, yet have less often had the benefit of them. Not only does more learning occur from such direct exposure, but motivation and realistic goal setting are fostered by these contacts.

It has been suggested that if deaf learners need more time to complete programs, then this should be considered as an option. We know that deaf high school students graduate one to two years later than their hearing peers, and that they often require more time to earn postsecondary degrees. We are talking about extended time for better preparation, not merely extra time or 'timing out.' Again, any options considered must take into account the overall goals of elementary through postsecondary educational systems.

Finally, we need to recognize that there are other problems, which are related generally to communication barriers, that need to be dealt with. They will not be easily solved (any more than the issue of reading ability will be) but they must be addressed to ensure that deaf people are able to succeed educationally and occupationally.

REFERENCES

Barnartt, S. B. and Christiansen, J. B. (1985) 'The socioeconomic status of deaf workers: A minority group perspective,' *Social Science Journal*, 32, 19–32.

Beal, P.E. and Noel, L. (1980) *What works in student retention*. Colorado Springs, CO: American College Testing Program.

Boatner, E.B., Stuckless, E.R., and Moores, D.F. (1964) *Occupational status of the young deaf adult of New England*. Washington, DC: Vocational Rehabilitation Administration, Department of Health, Education and Welfare.

Bowen, H.R. (1977) *Investment in learning*. San Francisco, CA: Josey-Bass.

Duncan, O.D. (1961) 'A Socioeconomic Index for All Occupations,' in A.J. Reiss, Jr., et al. (eds), *Occupation and social status*, 115–24. New York: The Free Press.

Fullerton, H.N. (1989) 'New labor force projections, spanning 1988 to 2000,' *Monthly Labor Review*, 112, 11. Washington, DC: US Department of Labor, 3–12.

Katzell, R.A. (1979) 'Changing Attitudes toward Work,' in C. Kerr and J.M. Rosow (eds), *Work in America: The decade ahead*. New York: Van Nostrand Reinhold.

Kerr, C. (1979) 'Introduction: Industrialism with a human face,' in C. Kerr and J.M. Rosow (eds), *Work in America: The decade Ahead*. New York: Van Nostrand Reinhold.

Lunde, R.S. and Bigman, S.K. (1959) *Occupational conditions among the deaf: A report of a national survey*. Washington, DC: Gallaudet College.

MacLeod-Gallinger, J.E. (1981–90) *Secondary School Graduate Follow-up Program for the Deaf* (Technical reports). Rochester, NY: Rochester Institute of Technology.

Rosenthal, N.H. (1989) 'More than wages at issue in job quality debate,' *Monthly Labor Review*, 112, 12. Washington, DC: US Department of Labor, 4–8.

Schein, J.D. and Delk, M.T. (1974) *The deaf population of the United States*. Silver Spring, MD: National Association of the Deaf.

Schroedel, J.G. (1976) 'Variables related to the attainment of occupational status among deaf adults,' New York: New York University, Unpublished Doctoral Dissertation.

Stahler, A. (1969) 'Underemployment,' in R.L. Jones and K. Stevenson (eds), *The deaf man and the world*. Council of Organizations Serving the Deaf, National Forum II, 33–40.

Stevens, G. and Cho, J.H. (1985) 'Socioeconomic indexes and the new 1980 census occupational classification scheme,' *Social Science Research*, 14: 142–68.

Tinto, V. (1987) *Leaving college*. Chicago, IL: University of Chicago Press.

US Bureau of the Census (1982) *Classified and alphabetic indices of industries and occupations* (Final edition). Washington, DC: United States Government Printing Office.

US Bureau of Labor Statistics (1988) *Educational attainments of workers*. (March).

US Bureau of Labor Statistics (1989) *Monthly Labor Review*, 112, 12. Washington, DC: US Department of Labor, 70.

Van Cleve, J.V. and Crouch, B.A. (1989) *A place of their own*. Washington, DC: Gallaudet University Press.

Weinrich, J.E. (1972) 'Direct economic costs of deafness in the United States,' *American Annals of the Deaf*, 117 (August), 446–54.

Welsh, W.A. and Walter, G.G. (1988) 'The effect of postsecondary education on the occupational attainments of deaf adults,' *Journal of the American Deafness and Rehabilitation Association*, 22, 1, 14–22.

Welsh, W.A., Walter, G.G., and Riley, D. (1989a) 'Providing deaf people with the opportunity for a degree: Benefits to individual and society,' *Journal of the American Deafness and Rehabilitation Association*, 23, 1, 7–13.

Welsh, W.A., Walter, G.G., and Riley, D. (1989b) *Earnings of deaf college alumni in the United States*. Rochester, NY: Office of Postsecondary Career Studies and Institutional Research, National Technical Institute for the Deaf at Rochester Institute of Technology.

Williams, B.R. and Sussman, A.E. (1971) 'Social and psychological problems of deaf people,' in A.E. Sussman and G.L. Stewart (eds), *Counseling with deaf people*. New York: Deafness Research and Training Center, New York University.

Personal Commentary

Robert Menchel

It is difficult to begin to describe my employment career. I am from a generation that was looked upon as being very limited in what careers there were for a person who was deaf. In order to understand the success as well as the barriers of my career, one must understand the system that was in place 20 or 30 years ago. Looking back today I do not really blame any of the people that played a negative role in my life. I understand that was the way the system was in those days and the way society looked at those of us who might be a little different.

To begin, I, like any other teenager, had dreams of the future. Even when younger I was not much different from any other child. I believe that almost all children look at themselves when they grow up and dream about becoming a policeman, a fireman, a doctor, or maybe following in their father's footsteps (if he is a shoe salesman you can take that literally). Anyway, by the time I was in high school I had dreams of going to college the same as my hearing friends. I never thought of my deafness as a barrier to a college education and a good future. I dreamed of becoming an architect and my hero at that time was Frank

Lloyd Wright. However, reality and dreams often do not go together. Being the only deaf student in the high school posed problems for the teachers and the administration. The main problem was they did not know what to do with me since they never had a deaf student in the school before, so they put me in a homeroom class with visually impaired students because they felt that there was not much difference between a blind student and a deaf one. With the innocence of one who did not know better, I went through high school taking a course in American history here, an art course there, a general business math course now and then, and a drafting class which I loved. It is amusing to remember how much I enjoyed drafting; I was in my element then. The teacher gave me free rein to draw what I wanted and I began to design houses and buildings. You would have thought with a talent like that this young man would be encouraged to go to college and become an architect, but since I was deaf they told me to become a draftsman.

Upon graduating from high school with a general diploma, (which in those days was not acceptable for college entrance), I had no choice in the matter of where I could go for a college education. The door to college was tightly closed. However, by good fortune, New York State had just begun a new educational venture, and was setting up what was to become the Community College System. These schools would take anyone who applied who had graduated from high school, and so I found myself in the first class at Hudson Valley Community College. For lack of a better thing to do, and because I thought that drafting was to be my destiny, I enrolled in the Mechanical Technology program. Upon graduation I was unable to obtain employment, even after several months of looking and interviews. It seemed that in that period of time, 1955, the idea of a deaf professional was still something that society was not accustomed to accepting.

Rather than accept this as a setback in my career, I decided to obtain a bachelor's degree in Mechanical Engineering. I felt that with that degree I was sure to obtain a good job. I did not give much thought to how difficult it was going to be to get into college and how difficult it would be to get through an engineering college if I was accepted. I just decided to do it and applied to several engineering colleges. The difficulties that I had in getting into college at this time are another story in themselves. I will not go into detail but just say that there were a lot of barriers in my path to obtaining my bachelor degree. Nevertheless, with determination and a strong will, I overcame many of them and obtained a BS in Physics from Clarkson College of Technology. I felt at this time (1961), that things would be different for me in obtaining employment in my chosen field. This was a period of high employment for those who had an engineering or science degree and many of my classmates had two, three, or more job offers. I felt that now I was on equal footing with my classmates and should be judged by the fact that I had completed the same requirements and was graduating in the upper half of my class, with a degree in one of the tough sciences, physics. I had more that 63 interviews with some of the leading companies in America. From all of these interviews I obtained not one single job offer. It was a very discouraging period in my life because I felt that after all this work and the struggle to obtain this education, the doors to a professional life were still closed to me. All I knew was that I had been rejected by companies that were offering jobs to my classmates, the same classmates that I had helped with some courses, the same classmates that had lower grades than I did, the same classmates that had shared their college life with me. The one difference was that they heard and I did not. I could sense during an interview that the interviewer was not comfortable with me and wanted to get the interview over as fast as possible. They could not see me as a physicist, only as a deaf person, and the concept that a deaf person could have completed the requirements for this degree and graduated was not in their frame of reference; they just could not accept the fact. They could not seem to see how I would be able to perform the work. They came from a normal hearing world where the idea of a deaf person in this environment was something they could not handle. Reflecting on these times, I do not blame these people. It was the sense of the time, it was the framework that society had built and there was not much one could do but accept the fact that this was the way things were and keep trying.

I had to swallow my pride and accept a position with the US Air Force Research Laboratory in Bedford, Massachusetts, which I obtained through the help of a friend who was an officer in the Air Force. At a time when there was high employment for any graduate with a degree in science or engineering, and companies were paying high salaries to get these graduates, I started my career in 1961 with a great salary of $75 a week. There was not much that I could do but I was determined to do the best job that I could and prove to these people that I was capable of working in this field, my deafness notwithstanding. I was assigned to the development of one of the first computerized weather systems in existence at that time and performed a good job in developing and implementing the system. After two years I began to look around for a better opportunity and a better paying job. Through my wife's uncle, who held a high position at AVCO Corporation, I was hired to work on the Apollo heat shield for the moon project. This was a most exciting time to be involved in the forefront of mankind's journey into space. I was assigned to the development of new non-destructive testing methods for determining the ability of the heat shield to stand up to the rigor of re-entry that it would be subject to. In this role I had the responsibility for determining if the space shield met the standards that had been set for it, and had to develop a new test instrument to measure the amount of moisture in the shield. This instrument, for which I was granted a patent, determined the limits of moisture allowed in the shield after milling, because if the amount was exceeded, the shield would either crack during re-entry or not be able to protect the astronauts.

I was quite happy in this work and enjoyed it very much. One day I was called to my supervisor's office. He told me that NASA was very pleased with my work and wanted to incorporate the results that I had obtained into the final project report. In the next breath he told me I was laid off. So, there I was, praise on one hand and termination on the other. Other people were also being laid off due to the ending of the contract with NASA. At this time my wife was expecting our second child. We had just bought a new house a few months before and had started to furnish it. At this time my wife was in

Albany visiting her parents and I asked a friend to call for me. There I was, out of work and needing to find a new job fast. The next day I noticed an advertisement in the paper stating that Xerox Corporation was seeking people and was interviewing in the Boston area. I asked a friend to call for me; when he did the interviewer asked him why he was calling for me. When he explained I was deaf he said I should come in anyway. Well, I went in and had a good interview. They offered me a job, but it was not until several months later that I found out the supervisor who had hired me had a mentally retarded daughter, and had more understanding of my needs.

I spent 13 years at Xerox until one day I decided that there was more in life than a good pay check and benefits. I wanted to do more with my life than spend it in the laboratory, so I applied for a Social Service leave in 1977 to work with handicapped children under the sponsorship of the American Association for the Advancement of Science. I was to be a role model for handicapped children across the United States. This was a step that changed my life because at the end of that year on leave I had visited more than 200 programs for handicapped children in 22 states and in Europe. I had spoken to more than 5,000 parents, teachers, counselors, and, of course, the children themselves. I encouraged many not to limit themselves and had found a new career for myself working with people. Upon my return to Xerox they did not know what to do with me, so after much delay they asked if I would like to go on loan to the National Technical Institute for the Deaf (NTID) for two years. Of course there was a risk of losing my job at Xerox, but I decided to take the chance and that is what lead to my becoming a member of the NTID staff.

Looking back on my employment history I ask myself, 'What was it like?' 'What can a deaf person expect in the working world?' 'Have things changed or are things much the same as they were 10 or 20 years ago?' These questions have to be asked and answered in light of my own experience. Between 1960 and 1982 sufficient changes occurred to make this an era of changes in social and economic conditions that brought many handicapped people into the mainstream of American life. This humanitarian revolution brought many hearing-impaired citizens out of the closet of isolation and into the active arena of competition for training, jobs, and recognition. Yet, at the same time during my own working experience, there were not many changes in the employment picture for deaf people. They still faced the attitudes of personnel people who did not understand their ability and potential. The opportunities for promotion and upward mobility were either nonexistent or few and far between.

Yet at the same time over the years I have seen improvement in the employment picture for deaf people. There are many deaf people in occupations that were undreamed of before. We see them in engineering, science, medicine, business, construction, computer systems, sales, law, education, and just about any field that you can name. Part of this change happened because of the changing attitude of society, and partly due to the change in the employment picture wrought by the impact of postsecondary education, as well as the impact of technology, which removed many of the barriers that were in the marketplace.

What was it that permitted me to overcome some of the barriers that society placed in my path? What was the factor that led to success? Those are hard questions to answer. Speaking for myself, I feel that part of the answer is within the individual, the drive to succeed, motivation, and supportive parents. The latter is very important in the role of a deaf person's success in life. I was fortunate to have parents who were supportive and encouraging. Although they had a very hard time accepting my deafness, nevertheless they believed in me and encouraged me to get the best education that I could. When institutes of higher education were unwilling to give me the chance to prove that I could do it, my parents fought for my rights to an education. This encouragement and support is very important in my life and is a determining factor in the lives of many other successful deaf people. Another factor is the understanding that in order to be successful in today's society you need the best education that you can get. Therefore, I knew that I had to get an education if I wanted to enjoy a life equivalent to that of my hearing peers. My own drive and determination and a lot of hard work is what made this possible for me. It should be remembered that I come from a generation that did not have the good fortune of having the support services that exist today.

Although faced with a barrier to equal employment I did not give up. It is important for people to realize that they will not get the first job they apply for; it takes time, patience, and an understanding that you are competing with a lot of other people for the same job. One must keep on trying and in due course an opportunity will open up. It is also important that one realize that the first job is only the first step in a long career. To be successful in the work place one must keep up with what is going on around him or her and the changes that are happening in business and industry. It is not enough to get a degree and then feel that your learning days are over now; it is just a job. I had to learn to keep up with technology, I had to learn how to deal with people and how to overcome some of the barriers that were in the business world. For example, there is always the problem of using the telephone. Today, with TDD's and computers, this problem is relatively easy to solve, but it is not enough just to approach your supervisor and ask for a TDD. You have to justify it and show how having a TDD or some other communication device will be a benefit to your employer and how it will help you in the workplace.

Finally, you need good communication skills. I cannot stress enough the need for good skills in writing and reading. Without the ability to express your ideas in a manner that others can understand, your career will be very limited in scope and in the opportunity for advancement. Business today, no matter what field, depends on communication to provide information to other people and to enable one to perform one's own job. Without good communication skills, be they spoken, written or signed, one will not make it in today's complex world.

In conclusion, I have seen many changes over the years. When I became deaf at the age of 7 my parents were afraid that my life would be limited to selling newspapers on the street or having some other kind of very low level job with no future. We had no idea of what deaf people did to earn a living, or what was required to enter any of those fields. We could dream of becoming a doctor but knew it was impossible because of the need to wear masks; how could we read lips? We had no idea of what it took to become a doctor; college was closed to us. Outside of Gallaudet there were no other institutes of higher education for deaf people. Over the years things changed, more and more deaf people began to break down the education barriers. Slowly but surely deaf people have entered fields that had been closed to them and in so doing they opened the doors to others.

Institutes of higher education for the deaf were established, laws were passed that removed barriers, attitudes of society changed, deaf people went out into the working world and proved they could do the job. We have come a long way. Many barriers have been removed, yet the job is not finished. As each of us moves out into the world of work we have a responsibility to do the best job we can, and prove to employers that we can do the job because only through this proof will we open opportunities for other deaf people to follow us and have the rewards of a good job and a good life.

Mr. Menchel is presently employed as an Assistant Professor of Mathematics and Physics at the Rochester Institute of Technology, National Technical Institute for the Deaf in Rochester, New York. Mr. Menchel holds an AAS Degree in Mechanical Technology from Hudson Valley Community College, Troy, New York, a BS in Physics from Clarkson University, Potsdam, New York, and an MBA from Rochester Institute of Technology. Prior to his present position Mr. Menchel worked in business and industry for twenty years in the private and government sector. He has considerable experience in the field of employment of the deaf, having held a position as an employer developer and placement advisor at RIT/NTID for eight years.

Chapter 10

Accommodation of deaf college graduates in the work place

Susan B. Foster

INTRODUCTION

As noted in Chapter 9, research has shown that deaf college graduates generally earn more than deaf people without postsecondary certification. However, wages are only one of many important aspects of job quality; other factors to be considered include working conditions, job satisfaction, and job security. In his discussion of 'non-wage characteristics of jobs,' Rosenthal (1989) notes that individual characteristics, skills, and circumstances influence one's perception of working conditions; what is important to one person may be incidental to another. A working parent may appreciate a flexible work schedule; employees who don't have children at home may prefer regular hours. Similarly, some people enjoy outdoor work, while others are more comfortable in an office environment. Research designed to study these areas must therefore be able to take into account the varying perspectives of workers and the ways in which their individual circumstances shape their interpretation and understanding of the work environment.

The preponderance of research on the employment conditions of deaf people has focused on broad demographics, including participation in the work force, occupational status, and earnings (see, for example, Boatner, Stuckless, and Moores 1964; Lunde and Bigman 1959; MacLeod-Gallinger 1985-90; Schein and Delk 1974; Welsh and Walter 1988). There has been less research on the day-to-day employment experiences of deaf people. One of the most extensive efforts to collect detailed descriptive data of this sort was conducted by Crammatte (1968). Through in-depth interviews with 87 deaf professionals, Crammatte explored many issues central to the quality of the work experience, including communication, job tailoring, and attitudes of and about adult deaf persons.

The research presented in this chapter is in the same general tradition as Crammatte (1964). The focus is on nonwage job characteristics and day-to-day employment experiences as seen from the perspective of deaf workers. Through in-depth interviews with deaf college graduates, some of the challenges deaf people face in interactions with hearing co-workers are examined. In particular, issues surrounding communication in the work place are described.

The chapter is divided into two sections. In the first part, the interview study is described and findings presented. The chapter continues with a discussion of the impact of communication barriers on the employment and careers of deaf college graduates, and suggestions regarding the role of postsecondary education in facilitating accommodation of deaf people within the work place.

THE INTERVIEW STUDY[1]

In 1986, a study was undertaken to learn about the employment experiences of deaf students who had graduated from Rochester Institute of Technology (RIT). In the following pages, the methods used to collect and analyze data are described, and central findings related to communication presented.

Methodology

Qualitative research methods were used to collect and analyze data. Qualitative research is grounded in the phenomenological perspective of human behavior, and relatedly, symbolic interactionist theory. Symbolic interactionism was developed through the work of Robert Park (1915), W.I. Thomas (1951), and George Herbert Mead (1934, 1938), among others. More recently, the theory has been expanded by Herbert Blumer (1969) and Howard Becker (1970). At the root of symbolic interactionism is the idea that human behavior is a product of how people interpret their world. Research conducted through this theoretical approach requires the use of methods designed to get at people's interpretations of events. These methods are known as 'qualitative methods,' and include open-ended, in-depth interviews and field observations (Bogdan and Biklen 1982; Bogdan and Taylor 1975; Spradley 1979).

The design of the study involved the collection of detailed

descriptive information through interviews with 25 deaf college graduates. The names of 50 potential participants were selected at random from a list of approximately 160 deaf graduates of Rochester Institute of Technology. A letter was sent to each of these graduates in which the study was described and an invitation to participate extended. The letters were followed by a phone call from the researcher (using a TDD – a telecommunication device for the deaf) in which the interview project was explained, questions answered, and the invitation to participate restated. Interviews were scheduled with the first 25 people who agreed to participate.

Description of the People Interviewed

Fifteen men and 10 women were interviewed, ranging in age from 23 to 46. All have a severe to profound hearing loss. Degrees received from RIT are: certificate (1), diploma (6), associate (9), bachelor's (8), and master's (1). Two participants went on to receive bachelor's degrees, and one a master's degree from other colleges after completing their degrees at RIT.

Only four people had remained in the same job since graduation. Nine had been in two jobs since graduation, six had three jobs, three had four jobs, and one had held five jobs since graduation. At the time of the interviews, 20 participants were employed. Three were out of the labor force. Two were unemployed. The employed participants were working in a variety of jobs, including histologist, social worker, civil draftsman, mail handler, and payroll clerk. Of the 20 participants who were employed, 14 were working in positions related to their college major; the others had made career changes, either voluntarily or because they were unsuccessful in securing or maintaining employment within their original field of expertise.

Findings

Graduates had much to share on the topic of communication in the work place. Their comments suggest that communication with co-workers is frequently challenging and often frustrating. In the following pages, the findings are presented within five topic areas:

(1) communication barriers and strategies,
(2) functional versus personal/social communication,
(3) responsibility versus dependency,

(4) misunderstandings, and
(5) impact of communication barriers on career advancement.

Communication Barriers and Strategies

Graduates described barriers to communication at work and strategies they use in dealing with these barriers. Their comments are organized below within the categories of telephone, meetings, and one-to-one communication.

Two of the 25 graduates use the telephone at work with an amplification device; the others use a TDD or have a hearing person make the call for them. No one mentioned the local telephone relay service. One person said his company provides a TDD for deaf employees; however, he added that since few departments have TDDs, he can only call home or accept calls from other people with TDDs.

Graduates noticed their hearing co-workers on the phone during the day, and frequently felt left out because they could not make casual phone calls. Some believe that deaf employees work harder than hearing employees because the latter are always talking:

> You have to work harder to impress the company, you have to work faster to prove that the deaf can do it. Not like hearing people – they all talk and listen . . . all the time. Deaf people can't hear, right? They concentrate on their work!

Hearing people were frequently unaware of the protocol involved in placing a phone call for a deaf co-worker. As a result, graduates often found themselves in the position of having to instruct co-workers in the rules for placing or receiving a call for a deaf person. One person described her frustration with a hearing co-worker in this situation as follows:

> It was difficult. I have to ask a person to make phone calls, and those people don't know how to make phone calls [for deaf people] . . . . When I tell this person what I want and she relays the message and then she [hangs up] . . . I say 'Wait a minute! I have a question after you tell me what this person said!' They didn't know. So I warn 'em. 'Don't hang up!' It's my phone call, not theirs. It was hard. But I learn to be patient with them, because they volunteer. It was hard to get somebody to help you.

Some graduates disliked having to depend on hearing people to make phone calls for them. Occasionally, they sensed that co-workers disliked or resented being asked to assist with calls, which made them even more reluctant to ask for help. One person said the stress resulting from her dependency on a hearing colleague for assistance on the phone contributed heavily to her decision to leave the job, and subsequently, her field of work.

Graduates often found *meetings* difficult. Although most had requested an interpreter for meetings at one time or another, only five said they routinely had an interpreter or were in situations where the hearing people knew enough sign language to communicate directly with them. A few graduates said they had interpreters occasionally. One person said an interpreter was provided after he complained, but only for a few meetings.

Most people agreed that they missed important information at meetings. However, some found meetings more accessible than others. Generally, the degree to which they successfully participated in meetings depended on factors that were not directly within the control of the deaf person, including the number of people at the meeting, the lighting and seating arrangements, and the willingness of hearing participants to repeat information as needed, take turns, and speak slowly and clearly.

Graduates used a variety of strategies to manage communication at meetings. Most often, they got information from one or two key people, usually after the meeting was over, as in the following example:

> *Interviewer:* Did you ever miss important information that the hearing people got [at meetings]?
> *Graduate:* Well, sometimes yeah . . . . But John always left me notes . . . they were just short and brief because he was a union steward . . . so I didn't have any worries. So I say 'Hey, what happened?' And he would tell me a little bit about it, and that was fine. Yeah, John would be a good informer.

Others requested that the information presented at the meeting be given to them in writing or that the rules for discussion be modified to facilitate their participation:

> I came up with a good idea. I spoke to my boss and asked her what she thinks, [and] she agreed. I . . . asked her to show me her agenda, what she's gonna talk about [at the meeting] . . . . It worked . . . and she said that she's willing to stop the meeting if [I] want to know [something that was said]. And I said, 'Sure.' And I tested it, and people didn't mind.

While these strategies helped, graduates still felt they often missed important information at meetings. Even when they received an agenda, they were usually unable to participate in group discussions. Minutes, while providing a summary of the points covered at a meeting, rarely capture the details (some of which may be quite relevant) or tone (which may shed light on the outcome) of the discussion. Equally important, graduates felt left out of the conversation and camaraderie that often occurs at meetings, as illustrated by the following quotation:

> She [my supervisor] would talk with me after the meeting. We get together a few minutes. She said a lot at the meeting and in the office we talked about 10 minutes! And then I say, 'We had a meeting for one hour, and now you talk to me for 10 minutes! This is it? Ten minutes! I want to know what people said, what people were laughing about!'

As described earlier, graduates sometimes requested accommodations at meetings. Often these requests were ignored, or if met, inadequate to allow their full and informed participation. When this happened, a few graduates persisted in their request and some were successful. For example:

> They [meetings] were a big problem, because when I first went there they never bothered to call me for any meetings, and then I asked the employer, 'What are they talking about' [And he said] 'Oh, nothing important.' I'd say 'Why are you leaving me out? I have a right to know what's happening.' And I walked up to the supervisor and said, 'I would appreciate that you'd [notify] me by doing some writing as to what you're talking about.' So they did that. And I didn't want to hear any excuses any more because no matter what they're talking about, it's still important to me.

More often they would avoid meetings or attend without participating. Sometimes the frustration would build over time, resulting in a blow-up, as in the following instance:

> They have meetings and it's really difficult on me sometimes. And I'm forced to be there, and like, all the time fighting over it, saying 'I need an interpreter – it's a waste of my time to go to the meeting.' But they'll say, 'Well you have to read my lips,' and all that. Then . . . about a month ago, they were supposed to have a meeting. . . . And I told my supervisor, 'Look, I won't go to the

meeting! Would you want to go to a foreign speaking meeting yourself?' And he left me alone after that. You know, he realized, what's the use . . . .

Graduates used a combination of *one-to-one* communication modes on the job, including lipreading, speaking, writing, sign language, fingerspelling, and gestures. The decision to use one or more strategies varied according to the individual and situation.

Graduates said their success as one-to-one communicators frequently depended on conditions beyond their control. For example, the characteristics of the hearing person could drastically affect the success of the communication. Hearing co-workers who demonstrated patience, a willingness to communicate, and some knowledge of the communication needs of deaf people were the easiest to work with. Sometimes, familiarity with the daily work routine was an aid in communication; just knowing what was supposed to happen next facilitated discussion. Similarly, working with the same people over time often improved communication because of increased familiarity with individual communication styles.

Many of the graduates employed a range of special strategies designed to encourage or facilitate one-to-one communication with co-workers, clients, and supervisors. Some used humor to 'break the ice' with hearing co-workers. For example, one person said that when people exaggerate the way they talk to him he tries to joke them out of it: 'I normally tease them and say, "You got a mouth problem or something? [That's my way of telling them] Be yourself . . . " But I always make sure I use the sense of humor.'

Almost everyone said they had to teach their hearing co-workers basic rules for communication with a deaf person, including speaking slowly and clearly, being willing to repeat or write the message if necessary, and facing the deaf person when speaking. Some people taught hearing co-workers sign language and/or fingerspelling. Several graduates had one or two key co-workers with whom they could communicate fairly well; they came to rely on these people to keep them informed or mediate between them and the other employees.

A few found that confrontation was sometimes necessary for communication to succeed. In the following example, a man describes his response to a situation in which his requests for written communication by hearing co-workers were repeatedly ignored:

One time I was real demanding. I said 'Start writing it down.' And they kept nodding, and I said, 'Hey, write it down.' So they reluctantly did it and they started to write, and I'd write back and forth, and then we'd be able to understand.

Functional v. Personal/Social Communication

Communication at work can be defined as (1) functional, that is, having to do with the day-to-day operations of the job, or (2) personal/social, that is, having to do with informal communication networks, such as 'the grapevine,' which develop in work settings. Most graduates felt they were able to communicate functionally in that they learned their jobs and performed them adequately on a day-to-day basis. However, they were rarely able to develop communication networks with their co-workers that allowed them to participate fully in social interaction. This frequently left them feeling isolated and out of touch, as illustrated in the following quotation:

> They [co-workers] like to talk. I couldn't hear their talking. I'd love to hear what they're talking about . . . . It's sad because I can't hear what they're saying, to share the fun, the jokes.

Another described her longing for what she called 'real conversation,' and the loneliness she felt when her efforts to join the group were rejected:

> *Interviewer:* At lunch and break time, do you sit with the hearing [people]?
> *Graduate:* Yeah, but they don't bother talking to me – not much. I guess it's because they're too busy talking with [other hearing] people to bother talking to me.
> *Interviewer:* So what do you do?
> *Graduate:* Well, I just try to ask questions or whatever. Sometimes I feel funny, you know. Like last week, I wanted to ask a girl a question, but I thought to myself, here they're carrying on a conversation and I don't understand and I'm asking the girl a question. What if what I was going to ask would be way off from what they were talking about?
> *Interviewer:* So what did you do? Did you ask it anyway?
> *Graduate:* Yeah, yeah, I tried to.
> *Interviewer:* Did she respond?

Graduate: Oh, yeah. But they're not interested in me. They're not, no. They're not interested in being friends . . . . Forget it. They only would talk to me for business things, you know, say 'We have a meeting,' or just small [things], nothing really like a conversation. Or they might say 'How're you doing?' But they don't go into real conversation at all. It is lonely there . . . .

In some instances, the rejection was more subtle. For example, one person said that he was invited by hearing co-workers to go for drinks after work but that nobody made an effort to include him in the conversation. In another instance, the co-workers' invitation to the deaf person to go with them to a bar was double-edged, since their choice of location betrayed their lack of awareness of her communication needs:

Sometimes they say, 'Let's go to a bar,' and I get so frustrated. You know, I don't go to the bars. I get frustrated. Why that place? It's so dark! I can't see! What good is my being there if I can't understand [the conversation]?

Sometimes important information was circulated through the grapevine. In these instances, the deaf employees found themselves in the difficult and often upsetting situation of being the 'last one to know.' The following story is illustrative:

Graduate: It's not fair . . . there are some things that everyone knows except me . . . and I wouldn't even know anything. That's why some of the people are ahead of me in some ways, because they know about the change or whatever, and I don't know anything about it. When I ask about it, they say, 'We done away with that a long time ago,' and I'll say, 'Well, why didn't you tell me?'
Interviewer: What is it that you're talking about – a machine or something?
Graduate: Well, it's some command you use on the machine, but they don't use it any more . . . . Or like, they know about a meeting, or even a shutdown. They would know about it a long time before I even know about it . . . like before that one week . . . everyone knew that they had a shutdown . . . . But one girl, she's more open with me. She's a very nice girl, and she told me that there would be a shutdown. And I said 'I didn't know that.' You know, it was a good thing, because if she didn't say anything, I wouldn't know about it.

Responsibility v. Dependency

Graduates often found themselves in a 'Catch-22' regarding communication in the work place. On the one hand, many said the responsibility for communication rests with the deaf employee, since they are expected to teach hearing co-workers about communication strategies, set the ground rules for accommodations, break the ice during awkward moments, and request clarification when necessary. Assuming this responsibility requires almost endless patience, endurance, and effort, as well as a healthy dose of assertiveness. Some examples:

> *Graduate:* It can be war out there, especially for a person who can't talk or hear. You are not going to find a company that everybody is deaf. A lot of hearing don't have the patience or want to spend the time.
> *Interviewer:* So what can a deaf person do in those situations?
> *Graduate:* Communicate, talk, ask for help, use a paper and pencil. Maybe sit down with the boss, even though it may take longer to communicate . . . tell him your feelings, [ask him] 'What do you want to do?' They don't know unless you say something. They are not going to come to you.
>
> If you haven't got patience, it's not going to work . . . . I mean, you're not going to work and find everything easy, are you? You think when you go to work the hearing people will learn sign language? No, they don't learn nothing about deaf people. Nothing. We have to educate them. [It] take[s] time and patience to educate them.

On the other hand, there is always a sense of dependency on hearing co-workers, since most communication strategies require their sustained cooperation and good will. This led some people to adopt a position of acceptance and even resignation regarding communication with hearing people:

> *Graduate:* My first job . . . I didn't know how to speak English very much. I go in cafeteria [and] everybody was talking to me. I don't understand it very much, but to say, 'Huh, what?' about a hundred times, I rather shut up and say, 'Yeah, yeah.' [Nodding head yes.]
> *Interviewer:* Oh, so you nod?

Graduate: Yeah, well, what can you do? It's not that deaf people can improve. The hearing people can. They can go to school and learn sign language. We cannot make anything better. Is that why they call it 'handicap'?

[Advice to young deaf adults starting first job . . . he or she should] learn to accept what is going around him or her in regards with attitudes that he can maybe see from the hearing workers . . . like, if they are not enthusiastic and talking with you or to be with you, just accept it. Like I said earlier, you have to learn to accept the hearing people.

Regardless of who is responsible, communication with hearing coworkers is almost always a stressful experience for the deaf employee. For those who have developed effective communication strategies, there is still the effort of total visual concentration and vigilance. For those who are experiencing communication difficulties, there is concern about whether the message was given or received correctly. For some people, the cost is simply too great:

Many deaf people are frustrated just with the communication alone. The communication breakdown, I mean. Sometimes you can't understand [what the hearing people are saying]. You never get an interpreter. You don't feel comfortable. [I decided] that's not where I belong, no . . . that's why I quit. Because I felt frustrated. I let myself put up with that when I really can't get through, so I decided to quit before it got worse and worse. Maybe it's not a good idea to quit, but to save myself – it was better to quit than to be miserable.

Misunderstandings

Differences in communication modes used by deaf and hearing people sometimes lead to misunderstandings in the work place. For example, hearing people can frequently work while chatting, while the deaf person must usually stop what he or she is doing in order to communicate. One problem experienced by several graduates was that they were not permitted to pause in their work or leave their work stations, even briefly, in order to communicate with coworkers. They felt their supervisors did not support their habit of pausing for conversation because they did not understand their need for a visual break from the work or their need to socialize with others. An example:

> I have problems at work . . . most of the time I concentrate on my work . . . but once in a while I feel like saying something, you know, get into a conversation . . . and the supervisor would come up . . . and he'd say, 'Stop talking, get to work . . . .' I've seen them sit back and talk . . . . Maybe they feel like I need to be in my [work] place . . . but I need a break, too . . . . I need a break from my area. [But] they [hearing people] talk on and on while they work.

Another misunderstanding stems from the need felt by many of the graduates to keep up with office chitchat. They said they would sometimes watch their hearing co-workers in an effort to follow conversations or ask a co-worker to tell them about a personal phone call, noting that most hearing people interpreted this as pushy, nosy, or just plain rude. However, from the deaf person's perspective, they were just trying to become part of the group. The following quotations are illustrative:

> [Talking about coffee breaks] . . . I can't keep up with the other people, when they're talking with the group. I read the paper. I drink my coffee. When I don't have my paper, I watch other people, how they talk. And they look at me, they look strange at me. I don't know what they think of when they look at me. I feel funny . . . left out . . . . You wonder what they're talking about . . . . Sometimes I ask. Sometimes they say, 'No, you don't have to know.' You know, some people are nice, some people are not.

> If you are talking with [hearing] friends, you would say, 'Hey, what did you say?'. . . . They say 'That is none of your business.' I don't mean to be nosy. I was just wondering what they were saying, that is all. Hearing people do have the advantage of overhearing. They don't have to ask. [Asking] puts them off. Like the phone. [I might want to know] who was that on the phone. I don't do that to hearing people. [But] in the back of my head, I am curious. It doesn't mean that I am nosy. I just [wonder, was it] a mother, a friend, just let me know who it was. I don't mean I want to know what you talked about but just who. [Was it] your husband? Fine! Your children? Fine! O.K.

Impact of Communication Differences On Employment Opportunities And Career Advancement

Most of the graduates believe they have been turned down for jobs at one time or another because they are deaf. For example, some said they were not hired for a particular job because they were unable to make or accept telephone calls without modifications or assistance, while others noted that their jobs had to be redefined in order to assign phone responsibilities to a hearing co-worker. A few were more general in their explanations, as in the following quotation:

> They've got the power – they're hearing. You know, like from my experience, I sit down and interview with them all – and sure enough, I know that, hey, they look at me as a deaf person and they'll put my application in the file, and that's the end of it. You know, they say, 'Well, you can't do this because you're deaf,' and they don't want to be sued, so they'll just say, 'Hey, we'll see if there are any openings, and we'll go through the process,' and they'll just put the stuff in the trash can anyhow. You know, so you don't get them for discrimination and stuff. You don't have anything to prove . . . you can't tell 'em, you know, 'Why not me?' . . . . They're the ones that decide anyhow, so I'm stuck.

Most of the graduates either were not interested in or felt they would not have an opportunity for promotion at work. Eleven said their company (or, more specifically, their supervisor) was unlikely to promote them; another 10 graduates expressed fear and anxiety over promotion. Often, their explanations had to do with communication. For example, some graduates felt they would not be promoted because management jobs require frequent use of the telephone or communication during meetings and one to one. Others worried about making mistakes because of communication breakdowns. The following quotations are illustrative:

> *Interviewer:* In the future . . . would you apply to be a manager?
> *Graduate:* No, thanks! There's a lot of pressure . . . no, medical technologist would be enough for me . . . . The supervisor uses the phone so much. Thirty or 40 times a day, she's on the phone. The doctor, pathologist [call], she has to respond. No. And a lot of paper work. She has to go to a lot of meetings [in different places, traveling] . . . . If it was only a lab and a health center, fine . . . I could handle that. I could interact with the people. But

going to all those different places and trying to interact, that would be too difficult.

Graduate: My project manager is trying to boost me up.
Interviewer: Really, promotion?
Graduate: Yes. I'm trying to hold it down.
Interviewer: Why?
Graduate: The load of responsibilities . . . more work, more depth, more engineering level. I am qualified, yes, but you can develop a high stress to it. It's a lot of pressure and I don't like pressure.
Interviewer: Pressure from what?
Graduate: Communication between one person to another person, become a middle man . . . suppose I misunderstood them . . . it would be totally my fault because I'm vulnerable when it comes to hearing impaired.

Being an outsider to the office grapevine and other informal communication networks was also perceived as a barrier to promotion. In the following example, a woman explains why she is unwilling to consider a management position:

I don't have that ability as the management . . . . I don't want to . . . be a manager or anything [because] I don't want responsibility. I don't want any problems with communication with hearing people. If I become a boss, it's gonna be a problem. I think it's better if you're hearing and you hear what's going on before you fall off the top. I don't know. I'm afraid of losing power . . . . If you want to get up to the top, you have to stay in power, defend yourself from falling off. You have to hear what's going on or you have some trusty persons by your side. Hearing people can hear what's going on. I'm deaf. I can't hear. Even somebody talking behind my back, I can't hear. And so the chance is you can be beat out easily.

Underlying all these explanations is the assumption that the employer can or will not make the necessary accommodations to enable the deaf employee to become a full participant in communication in the work place. While graduates felt that deaf employees can do a lot to enhance communication, they were also quite clear that they cannot do everything.

DISCUSSION

The findings from this study suggest that communication between hearing and deaf people in the work place is often difficult, due to differences in communication modes and languages. However, these differences can be managed or compensated for with appropriate accommodations. For example, TDDs, amplifiers, relay services, or electronic mail can be used for communication traditionally conducted by voice telephone. Participation at meetings can be enhanced by the use of written agendas and minutes, interpreters, seating and lighting arrangements, and turn-taking strategies that enable deaf participants to follow the discussion. One-to-one conversation is facilitated when everyone is aware of the communication needs of the deaf employee and motivated to make the interaction a success. In short, there are measures that can be taken to significantly improve communication between hearing and deaf people in the work place; *differences become barriers when these steps are not taken.*

Graduates used many strategies to adjust for communication differences in the work place, including humor, teaching others about deafness, explaining rules for communication, and requesting support services and devices. However, these strategies were only successful to the degree that hearing co-workers, supervisors, and clients were willing to meet them halfway — to respond to the humor, provide the requested services, and modify communication habits in order to include everyone. As a result, graduates sometimes walked a tightrope in that they were expected to assume responsibility for making the interaction successful while acknowledging their dependence on the good will of hearing people (as the majority and dominant linguistic group). This asks a lot of the deaf employee, including the ability to be assertive one minute and passive the next, as well as a command of a wide range of strategies and awareness of when to apply each.

Both 'functional' and 'personal/social' communication present challenges to interaction between hearing and deaf people that may impede the career development and specifically the upward mobility of deaf employees. However, it is generally easier to effect changes in functional communication, since these types of interactions are more structured and under the control of supervisors. For example, information can be made available to employers about working with a deaf person through a range of formats, including brochures, workshops, videotapes, and discussion sessions. The deaf employee can explain his or her communication needs to supervisors and co-workers. Physical modifications can be made in the work environment. Free sign classes can be offered on site, and hearing employees encouraged to attend.

It is more difficult to improve personal/social communication, since these kinds of conversations are unplanned and take place in unstructured settings where the dynamics of interaction cannot easily be predicted or controlled (for example, in the coffee room or cafeteria, by the elevator, at the water fountain, in the rest room, and so forth). Moreover, these interactions depend much more heavily on the good will of hearing people; people cannot be forced to spend their free time together or include someone in the office grapevine. Depending on his or her personality and social skills, the deaf employee may find it difficult to enter social groups, use humor to break the ice, or identify and cultivate relationships with key hearing co-workers who can become mentors and facilitate access to informal communication networks.

Implications for Postsecondary Programs Serving Deaf Students

The people interviewed for this study are all college graduates. Yet, it would seem from their experiences that a college degree does not ensure participation in communication in the work place. Given that communication is generally essential to success on the job, and that deaf employees are likely to encounter communication differences in interaction with hearing co-workers that can become barriers if they are not properly managed, the question arises as to whether postsecondary educational institutions can or should play a role in preparing deaf students to access communication at work.

Certainly an argument can be made against adopting such a role. For example, it can be said that much of what it takes to be a skilled communicator has to do with personality, including the ability to assert oneself, break the ice during strained interactions, and stand up for one's rights when necessary. Some might say that these are not skills that can be taught; rather, they are acquired over a lifetime, through interactions with friends, family, and classmates. It might also be argued that postsecondary institutions have enough to do teaching technical skills; interpersonal skills such as those required for communication are outside the scope of what can reasonably be considered a college curriculum.

On the other hand, many communication barriers can be traced to ignorance on the part of participants, including lack of awareness of what is required or available as well as failure to understand how communication differences isolate the deaf employee. In these situations, *information* may be very helpful. Similarly, a person may be outgoing and assertive, but unaware of how to approach a group or identify potential mentors; *social skills and strategies* are essential to success in these instances. The very nature of their structure and mission ensures that postsecondary educational institutions routinely provide students with many opportunities for social and emotional growth; targeting the development of particular interpersonal skills may not be all that difficult or inappropriate. In fact, Chapters 7 and 8 focused specifically on ways in which postsecondary educational institutions should and can facilitate the *total* growth of students, including personal, social, and political development.

Given this, what might colleges do to promote in their deaf students the development of skills that will enable them to become effective and full participants in the culture and community of the places they choose to work? The following is a partial list of ideas.

First, deaf postsecondary students can be offered courses on communication in the work place. Specific topics should include general information about types of communication encountered in the work place (for example, functional and personal/social) and the role of each in job satisfaction and career development. Additionally, students need specific strategies for managing communication differences.

Second, cooperative work experiences can be incorporated into the educational curricula for deaf students. This will give students an opportunity to practice their communication and related interpersonal (as well as technical) skills on the job and then return to the postsecondary environment to build on strengths and work on weaknesses.

Third, deaf students in mainstream postsecondary programs face communication differences (and quite probably barriers) on a daily basis. Counseling and seminars that build on these experiences by treating them as a kind of 'practicum' for employment may be helpful. In particular, students should be encouraged to pilot strategies for managing communication with hearing teachers, students, and staff with the goal of evaluating their success and developing a repertoire for use on the job.

Fourth, career development and work placement programs at

postsecondary educational institutions can develop information for potential employers of deaf graduates; dissemination strategies might include written materials (brochures, books, and flyers), workshops, videotapes, and visits from deaf alumni. Information should be included that describes what employers can expect as well as what can be done to minimize communication differences and ensure the deaf employee access to communication. Perhaps, and what is most important, specific information should be included to facilitate accommodation; for example, it is not enough to suggest that TDDs can be used by deaf people to access the telephone – information about the types of devices available, their features and cost, and where to call to order one are also needed.

Last, postsecondary institutions need to become models for other institutions, including employers and service organizations. If they cannot make their environment accessible to deaf students, they cannot expect others to do so. Certainly they face many of the same challenges. Modifications in classrooms and other structured settings are much easier to effect than are those in social areas of campus life (Foster and Holcomb 1990; Foster and Brown 1989; Brown and Foster 1991). At the least, such institutions must make 'functional' communication accessible to deaf students. Regarding personal/social communication, they must be guided by the highest possible standards. Only by becoming experts can these institutions gain the knowledge and credibility necessary for teaching others how to create truly accessible environments.

NOTE

1 This portion of the chapter is taken, with permission from the publisher, from an earlier article entitled 'Employment Experiences of Deaf College Graduates: An Interview Study' (*Journal of Rehabilitation of the Deaf*, 21, (1), July, 1987, 1–15).

REFERENCES

Becker, H. (1970) *Sociological work: method and substance*. Chicago, IL: Aldine.
Blumer, H. (1969) *Symbolic interactionism: perspective and method*. Englewood Cliffs, NJ: Prentice-Hall.
Boatner, E.B., Stuckless, E.R., and Moores, D.F. (1964) *Occupational status of the young deaf adult of New England*. Washington, DC: Vocational Rehabilitation Administration, Department of Health, Education and Welfare.
Bogdan, B. and Biklen, S. (1982) *Qualitative research for education: an introduction to theory and methods*. Boston, MA: Allyn and Bacon.

Bogdan, B. and Taylor, S. (1975) *Introduction to qualitative research methods: a phenomenological approach to the social sciences*. New York: Wiley.

Brown, P. and Foster, S. 'Integrating hearing and deaf students on a college campus: successes, and barriers as perceived by hearing students,' *The American Annals of the Deaf*, 136, 1, 21–7.

Crammatte, A.B. (1968) *Deaf persons in professional employment*. Springfield, IL: Charles C. Thomas.

Foster, S. (1987) 'Employment experiences of deaf college graduates: an interview study,' *Journal of Rehabilitation of the Deaf*, 21, 1, 1–15.

Foster, S. and Brown, P. (1989) 'Factors influencing the academic and social integration of hearing-impaired college students,' *Journal of Postsecondary Education and Disability*, 7, 3–4, 78–96.

Foster, S. and Holcomb, T. (1990) Hearing-impaired students: a student-teacher-class partnership,' in Neville Jones (ed.), *Special Educational Needs Review, Volume 3*, London: Falmer Press 152–171.

Lunde, R.S. and Bigman, S.K. (1959) *Occupational conditions among the deaf: A report of a national survey*. Washington, DC: Gallaudet College.

MacLeod-Gallinger, J.E. (1985–90) *Secondary school graduate follow-up program for the deaf* (Technical reports). Rochester, NY: Rochester Institute of Technology.

Mead, G. H. (1934) *Mind, self, and society*. Chicago, IL: University of Chicago Press.

Mead, G. H. (1938) *The Philosophy of the act*. Chicago, IL: University of Chicago Press.

Park, R. (1915) *Principles of human behavior*. Chicago, IL: The Zalaz Corporation.

Rosenthal, N. H. (1989) 'The Quality of jobs: more than wages at issue in job quality debate,' *Monthly Labor Review*, 112, 12, 4–8.

Schein, J.D. and Delk, M.T. (1974) *The deaf population of the United States*. Silver Spring, MD: National Association of the Deaf.

Spradley, J. (1979) *The Ethnographic interview*. New York: Holt, Rinehart & Winston.

Thomas, W. I. (1951) *Social behavior and personality*. New York: Social Science Research Council.

Welsh, W.A. and Walter, G.G. (1988) 'The effect of postsecondary education on the occupational attainments of deaf adults,' *Journal of the American Deafness and Rehabilitation Association* 22, (1), 14–22.

Personal Commentary

Jean Cordano

I can still remember my first day at work as staff medical technologist on 19 September 1959. I felt somewhat at a loss, first, because of the size of the laboratory and second, because of the limited number of laboratory procedures. The pea-sized laboratory contrasted with the huge laboratories at the

University (of Wisconsin) Hospitals where I interned. The procedures were few and manual, whereas the procedures at the University Hospitals were numerous and mostly semi-automated. The laboratory was staffed with a part-time ASCP (American Society of Clinical Pathologists) registered medical technologist and a full-time medical technician. There was a visiting pathologist (a professor at Marquette University School of Medicine [now Medical College of Wisconsin]), who came out once a week to take care of surgical tissue procedures and answer physicians' questions regarding diagnosis and treatment. No one needed to work a full eight hours, and we had to take turns covering emergency calls.

I remember at the job interview the administrator asked me about patient contact. I said 'If I could get along in a hospital of 900 beds, why not at this hospital of 90 beds?' My point was well taken. She also asked me how I would respond to the phone. I suggested that a signal light be installed in the laboratory to let me know that I had received a call; then, I would go to the switchboard to pick up the message. To respond to a call from home, I suggested that the hospital call me twice with a one-minute interval. On the second call, I would pick up the phone and relay a message that I was coming. It worked and I stayed on at the lab. Communication between the lab technicians and the physicians was not much of a problem because all the physicians' orders came in writing and test results had to go back in writing.

In three years, I became chief technologist. I must say I had a big dream for the lab, but I first had to win the confidence and support of the pathologist. I took up the leadership, adding new procedures and refining old ones, and managing daily activities of the laboratory. It took three years before I was given a free hand to manage the technical aspects of our lab work. At that time we still had a hard time finding ASCP registered medical technologists, so I had to accept high school students with science background. I trained them using the 'show and tell' technique along with written procedures. Eventually they picked up signs from me for everyday expressions.

In the mid 1960s, our laboratory experienced an exploded growth due to the introduction of automated instrumentation and sophisticated procedures. This brought quite a number of registered medical technologists to our laboratory. I usually started communicating with them by using paper and pencil and then I would teach sign language during lunch and breaks. I think the fact that I was their supervisor motivated them to learn sign language. They picked up signs fairly easily, but had more difficulty with sign reading and fingerspelling. While a few people needed some prodding, many members of my staff found signing enjoyable and attended an adult education course in sign language at the nearby vocational-technical school. In time, most of them became quite fluent. Thanks to them, communication within the laboratory, especially in groups, was more relaxing, informative, and productive.

The hardest time I had with communication was when someone did not like to write. There are three kinds of hearing co-workers when it comes to writing; those who are willing to write, those who do not like to write but will reluctantly do so, and those who will not write at all. Those in the last category would ask someone in the laboratory who could sign to help them communicate with me. Naturally, I resented them at first, because I thought it was their job to communicate with me directly. But on second thought I decided that I had only two choices – to be bitter or to be contented with that. I chose the latter. I recall an experience with one person who was unwilling to write to me. As it turned out, I was glad that I did not press her on this because she later explained that she did not choose to write because she felt that I was a better writer and thus had an advantage over her. As I listened to her explanation, I realized that, strange as it seemed, this was her problem – not mine. I suspect that other people were afraid to write anything down in case the paper would be kept and eventually used against them.

Also, it was not easy to talk with co-workers who communicated through writing but were reluctant to do so. At first I was abrupt with them, being afraid that I was taking up so much of their time. That was a mistake. For example, I remember one time when I went to a nursing station to find out more information on a patient. I did not begin with niceties such as 'Hello – how are you? or 'Excuse me – are you busy?'

As a result, the nurse felt like I was interrupting her work and reacted accordingly. As a result of this and other similar experiences, I reached the conclusion that it pays to break the ice first when communicating in writing, as in other forms of communication.

It took almost no effort to communicate with the patients. When the patients first saw me with the blood collection tray, they would have their arm ready for me. Once in a while I would detect some fear in their eyes when I told them that I could not hear, but by smiling and using body language I just reassured them that I knew what I was doing. Often they smiled back and said I did not cause any pain. I had only one patient who, at his wife's request, refused to let me draw him. It was she who worried about my deafness. When I asked the wife to leave the room, the patient did not mind me drawing him at all. I used the same trick with parents of sick children. I became friends with patients who frequently came to the laboratory. I missed the contact with patients when I became the director, and often they asked to say hello to me.

In the chapter, the graduates said that communication differences can sometimes be a barrier to promotion. As a deaf person who became manager of her department, I feel like I can address this topic from a rather interesting perspective. As you can see from my story, I grew with the laboratory. From a small lab with only two workers in 1959, we grew to 23 workers in 1989. As the lab manager, it was my responsibility to manage and guide this growth. I approached this task with the goals of the hospital and my communication and management style in mind. For example, when I had enough high caliber technologists, I created a laboratory structure consisting of six sections managed by technologists appointed as section chiefs; that way I could delegate appropriate responsibility and decision-making to them. When I added the second shift and then the third shift, scheduling became time consuming and required much phone work. In order to ensure adequate 24-hour coverage and monitor daily activities in the laboratory, I created an assistant chief technologist position. As it turned out, the assistant chief technologist and I worked together for more than 15 years and happened to have the same perspective on many things. That, of course, made my work easier. Furthermore, she would let me know about certain problems that were 'brewing' in the lab before they got out of control, especially those which should be referred to me for solution. The medical decisions were left to the pathologist, now full time, who was the go-between for the laboratory and the medical staff. Of course, the higher I moved upward, the less contact I had with my workers below the section chief level. While I missed the contact with workers, this system enabled me to concentrate on administrative work.

I must say that in general my task as a manager was no different than the task which hearing laboratory managers face. I did practically everything that a manager was entitled to do. At the same time, as a deaf person who has managed hearing employees, I have my own feelings about what works best, as well as special strategies. For example, when it came to hiring, I would first do the interviews in a general way and then have the section chiefs explain in detail what would be expected of the applicant if they were hired. Then I would make my decision on the basis of my interview and the feedback from the section chiefs. I made sure that my workers understood the departmental objectives and then allowed my section chiefs to manage them in their own way, as long as it was cost-effective.

One of the most important things for me as a manager was to make workers feel they are part of the team and instill good feeling about their work. Communication at lab meetings became strained as the size of the laboratory work force became larger and fewer people knew sign language. My strategy for making sure everyone was comfortable and communicating well as a team was to allow the chief technologist to conduct the meeting. I would make statements as needed and then stay to answer questions. Sometimes a staff member would interpret for me; other times I would read the minutes.

I liked the way the hospital was managed. I was allowed to develop my own departmental objectives which, of course, had to be within the guidelines or strategies set up by the administration and hospital board. Thanks to the quality assurance program required by the hospital accreditation commission, every problem and subsequent solution had to be documented in writing; I could keep myself abreast through reviewing these materials and asking questions if I had any. The chief technologist and I were required to submit a progress report every two weeks and then meet in person with our assistant administrator, who gave us many helpful suggestions for solving some problems that had to be dealt with on higher levels (for example, hiring a new technical staff person, securing funds to purchase a new instrument).

For the last 10 years of my employment (I retired in 1989), the hospital administrators favored the participatory type of management. To me as well as other departmental directors, this meant more intra-departmental and hospital-wide communication. The managers had to attend weekly management council meetings; be involved in committee meetings to develop, implement, and monitor programs; attend seminars to polish up on management techniques, and so forth. I handled these meetings in a variety of ways. For example, at the council meeting the chief technologist, who is also on the team, took notes for me and spoke for me when I asked, as well as for herself. However, I found out that much of the meeting time was devoted to reading aloud new policies and procedures just as if the presenter wanted to be sure that everyone heard and understood. At times well-written minutes were more useful than attending the meeting. I was always provided with an interpreter for management seminars. However, I also found out that even with an interpreter, I would still be behind the subject; for example, when I asked a question, they were already on a new subject. Sometimes I tape recorded these seminars and would have my clerk type it up.

Perhaps the reader is wondering why I did not have an interpreter for the council or committee meetings. It could have easily been done if the hospital had an on-site interpreter. However, we did not have this set-up. Interpreters are not easily available in our town, and have to come from Chicago, two and a half hours away. Our state agency requires 48 hours notification for an interpreter and limits last-minute requests to emergencies only. Also, today many interpreters demand that they take turns interpreting every 15 minutes. Because of these constraints, I felt that requesting interpreters for council and committee meetings would not be practical and also that the cost would be prohibitive.

Of course, expectations and career objectives change as any worker matures. For example, I recall that as a young employee, it was a time for searching and exploring careers. I went through several different jobs within 10 years – linotype operator, teacher, poultry disease laboratory technician, and TV assembler. Once I found a career to my liking, I spent a lot of dedication and hard work toward achieving my goals. I must say I was fortunate to be able to move upward when not all could do this. Otherwise I might have had to reevaluate my career objectives, and consequently make a job change. When I got older, it was a time of accepting what I had and then making strong commitments toward job, family, and retirement.

The level of education greatly affects the person's work experience. For example, technical education played a big role in my career. First, I had to meet the rigid academic requirements of a medical technologist. Then I had to take the ASCP registry examination. When I passed it, I became (to the best of my knowledge) the second deaf person ever registered by the ASCP. Being registered, I was looked upon as a knowledgeable person. This field was, and still is, challenging, rapidly growing and rapidly changing; I had to keep abreast or fall out. I kept up in many different ways, including attending evening classes (mostly to get better understanding of the capabilities of the computer), reading all journals I could find, listening to sales talks (I did get many useful ideas from them), and attending outside seminars (mostly to get acquainted with new federal or state regulations and how they would be implemented).

I also think that colleges can do much to prepare deaf students for communication in the work place. For example, colleges can teach students to anticipate the kinds of communication barriers they may encounter; get them to know the hearing person or persons they need to communicate with; and find out not how they can communicate with the hearing, but rather how the hearing can communicate with them.

Jean Cordano lost her hearing when she was 4 years old from meningitis. She graduated from the North Dakota School for the Deaf in 1946. She then attended Gallaudet University from which she received a BS degree in chemistry and mathematics in 1951. Between 1951 and 1958 she held an assortment of jobs. In 1959, she completed the fourth-year medical technology courses at the University of Wisconsin-Madison and at the same time her internship at the University Hospitals. Upon passing the examination provided by the American Society of Clinical Pathologists in 1960, she became a registered medical technologist. Immediately after her graduation and until her retirement in 1989, she worked as a medical technologist, starting as a staff technologist and ending up as the administrative director of the Clinical Laboratory at Lakeland Hospital, a 127-bed facility located in Elkhorn, WI. She is married and has three daughters and two granddaughters.

Concluding remarks

Robert Panara

Deaf Students in Postsecondary Education, edited by Susan B. Foster and Gerard G. Walter, represents a highwater mark for contributions of its kind. Ever since deaf students began attending community colleges and regular four-year institutions of higher learning in significant numbers, many professional articles, monographs, and books have been published on the subject. However, none of these embrace the full scope of research and the latest perspectives such as is accomplished by this book.

Actually, it is an anthology of readings which covers three major areas, namely: the demographics of postsecondary education for deaf persons; the environment of postsecondary education for deaf persons; and the outcomes of postsecondary education for deaf persons. Within each major area, there are individual chapters which focus on special issues, problems and achievements manifested over the years. In most instances, the authors pinpoint specific needs and offer recommendations for improvement in accommodating deaf persons attending postsecondary educational programs. Specific areas addressed within chapters include providing financial assistance and equal opportunities for learning, eliminating barriers of communication, improving the quality of social life and participation in extracurricular activities, developing leadership qualities, and encouraging involvement in political activism. Finally, there is a succinct study, backed by pertinent statistics, showing the effect of a two or four-year college program on employment and earnings following graduation.

The contributing authors are highly respected professionals in their chosen disciplines, most of whom have the experience of being involved in the study of this subject from its earliest beginnings. It is further evident in their objective and balanced analyses as well as in the comprehensiveness and depth of references cited.

An added highlight of this anthology is the exclusive feature of a 'Personal Commentary' after each chapter which provides special insight into 'the deaf experience'. They are written by mature, professional deaf persons who look back to the time of their individual onset of deafness and the experience of 'growing up deaf' while going to school. These school years include a wide variety of academic, social, and domestic experiences – both within a mainstreamed setting and in a special or residential school program for the deaf. Some personal commentaries go beyond graduation from college and vividly describe 'the deaf experience' when applying for a job and inside the work place itself. All of these 'Personal Commentaries' share a common theme – that of coping with prejudice and ignorance; of overcoming communication barriers; of survival tactics through sheer persistence and study; of learning 'to make friends and influence people;' of assimilation into deaf life and culture and thereby developing self-esteem and assertiveness; and, above all, the untold value of obtaining higher degrees through postsecondary educational programs of study.

Given that 'mainstreaming is here to stay,' as is the popular consensus, and that deaf students have greater opportunities to pursue the full and rich range of career programs offered by two and four-year colleges for the hearing, I nevertheless have some reservations about the success rate of most students in future years. Here, I am taking into account the *typical* classroom or lecture hall situation in which the deaf student is *wholly* dependent upon an interpreter. Granted, the student also has additional support service personnel such as notetakers and tutors. Still, only the student with advanced reading and writing skills that are on a par with their hearing peers will make any real progress in the average postsecondary education program.

From my own experience of being 'on both sides of the fence' – as a deaf student and as a deaf teacher – I see a great need for qualified and experienced teachers of the deaf to be added to the 'mainstreamed' work force in sufficient numbers so as to make a pronounced impact. This includes both hearing and deaf teachers who have bonafide master's and Ph.D. degrees in their chosen discipline as well as longtime actual teaching experience, and who can communicate fluently and directly with deaf students, and thereby *control the climate and the pace* of the teaching/learning process.

Furthermore, if accommodations are made to provide equal opportunities for qualified deaf role models to teach integrated classes, the picture could change greatly. I can visualize an improved retention rate and greater numbers of deaf students 'making it' through both secondary and postsecondary mainstreamed school programs. In support of this so-called 'blanket statement', I will take the cue from my fellow deaf contributors and offer my own 'Personal Commentary' for illustrative purposes. This will focus chiefly on my experience for one year as a Visiting Professor at California State University, Northridge (CSUN). It also draws on my career of teaching deaf students at the college level for almost 40 years; having previously taught for four years in a residential school (the New York School for the Deaf ['Fanwood'] at White Plains, NY); at the college level, 18 years were spent at Gallaudet University where I taught deaf students only; and 20 years at NTID/RIT where I taught deaf students only and integrated classes of deaf and hearing.

As a member of the English Department at CSUN (1975–76), I taught a wide range of courses – 'Freshman English' and 'Advanced Writing' to classes with all deaf students, and 'Western World Literature', 'Introduction to Theater' and 'Speaker's Bureau' in classes composed of deaf and hearing students with the latter in the majority. Additionally, I was given full freedom to develop a curriculum and offer two new courses, 'Deaf Studies in Literature' and 'Creative Interpretation of Literature in Sign', for integrated classes.

In the classes with all deaf students, I could provide *direct services* through the medium of total communication. This mode of teaching without an interpreter helped enhance the listening/communication skills of deaf students by providing opportunities for *full participation* in question–answer sessions, class discussions and reports, and teacher–student dialogues. Communication was *total* in the classroom because I spoke and understood their language, which could be any combination of Signed English and ASL, or ASL and PSE. Consequently, there was much improvement in the quality and depth of their written reports, personal essays, and documented papers because the deaf students had more opportunity to express their thoughts and ideas in class, exchange information with peers, and compare individual experiences.

In classroom situations involving deaf and hearing students, I utilized my skills in simultaneous communication, which meant I would communicate directly with the deaf students in class while also making myself understood to hearing students. Here, however,

I made full use of the support service personnel provided by CSUN. An interpreter was always nearby to 'field questions' put to me by hearing students and relay them to both me and the deaf students via simultaneous communication in either the expressive or receptive mode. The same procedure was used during discussions voiced by hearing students.

Conversely, when deaf students raised their hand to pose a question in sign language, or else participate in dialogue or present a class report, the interpreter was there to provide voice-over for the hearing students. Moreover, there was a notetaker assiduously at work who later provided copies of class notes for all deaf students.

The sum result of this approach to the teaching/ learning process was that communication was *total* – total in the sense that every possible mode was used, including AV devices such as the overhead projector, captioned slides and videotapes, and my own lecture notes which were distributed to both deaf and hearing students. Add to that much writing on the blackboard to stress key terms and phrases, proper names and titles of works, etc., and it should be clear what I mean by 'controlling the pace' of the teaching/learning process. Both deaf and hearing students seemed to benefit from this teaching approach. Hearing students commented that they understood the lesson or lecture even better, that it was more visual, gave them more time to absorb the main points or analysis of the literary work, and that it was 'the come-alive classroom!'

Deaf students also appreciated the 'total communication' approach, often comparing my class favorably with others in which the instructor relied wholly on the interpreter to convey the lecture. Translated: the instructor's pace in the other classes was too fast to follow, much less have any kind of active participation in the way of question–answer, class discussions, and the meaningful give and take of dialogue.

To quote Marshall McLuhan, 'the medium is the message' – and deaf students obviously took pride in having one of their own people teach integrated classes, using the medium of *total communication*. If they 'put out' more, with 110 per cent effort, I believe it was because they didn't want to let me down! In this, too, was the spinoff value of having 'role models' in mainstreamed classes – and, as I stressed previously, this applies to secondary education as well.

Similarly, the course in 'Deaf Studies' gave the hearing student a better awareness of deafness and deaf people. They derived new insights in analyzing the image and function of deaf characters in the literary work, including 'the deaf experience', and they could appreciate how these characterizations sometimes serve as symbols to parallel the condition of *Everyman* – a face in 'the lonely crowd' and a victim of 'the communication breakdown' in modern society.

Finally, the course helped the deaf student discover his or her 'Roots' in tracing the achievement of notable deaf Americans, of their contributions to the economic, social, and cultural growth of America, as well as to that of the deaf community. It thus forged yet another link, not only in 'the great chain of being,' but also *of belonging* and of becoming a leader of the future.

I hope that the chapters in this text will provide readers a means to develop a sensitivity to the needs of deaf persons who seek to pursue higher education. Only through such a sensitivity on the part of faculty, staff, and students at an institution, can true mainstreaming hope to be achieved. This should be a goal of anyone hoping to develop a program to support deaf students in college.

Index

All entries refer to deaf students unless otherwise specified

academic achievement skills *see* persistence; reading; writing
academic integration 46; and withdrawal 55, 57, 58
access 139–40; to activities 159, 173; on campus 136; to postsecondary education 15, 25, 27, 32, 35; *see also* community colleges; postsecondary education
achievement and motivation 83
advisors 100, 104–5; characteristics of 104–5
advocacy 168, 169, 170; self 108, 111
agency-orientated learning 74, 75
AHSSPPE 25
Albertini, J. 73, 76, 77, 87n
Allen, T. 6, 8, 32, 124
Amara, R. 18
American Association for the Advancement of Science 81, 83, 206
American Council on Education 149
American Deafness and Rehabilitation Association 176
American Sign Language *see* ASL
Americans with Disabilities Act (1990) 17, 170, 177
Amir, Y. 158
Anderson, T.H. 102

Aristotle 168
Armbruster, B.B. 102
ASL 101, 120, 140n, 238; and hearing students 138, 139; poetry 121; *see also* sign language
assertiveness training 159
assimilation 119, 120, 126, 136; educational models 122–3; and mainstreaming 121, 124, 125
Association for Handicapped Student Service Programs 25
Astin, A.W. 147
attrition rate *see* postsecondary education; secondary education; withdrawal
audiological services 71
Austin, G. 124
Avery, J.C. 101

backgrounds of students 84, 127–8, 161; case study 129–30; and learning 72; and successful programs 66
Bakan, D. 74, 75, 76
Bakhtin, M.M. 68, 69
Banning, J. 147
Barnartt, S.B. 192
barriers: attitudinal 155, 158; communication 81, 96, 155, 158, 200; and employment 211, 212; financial 81; stereotyping 81 to learning 83;
Basile, M.L. 159

Index

Beal, P.E. 198
Bean, J.P. 44, 49
Becker, H. 211
Beecher, J. 102
Belenky, M.F. 71, 74, 75, 79, 87n, 119
Bellugi, U. 120
Bender, R.E. 121
Berdie, R.F. 149, 151
Bigman, S.K. 187, 188, 191, 193, 210
Biklen, S. 211
bilingualism 69, 125, 126
blacks: drop out rate 16; reading skills 13, 14; secondary qualifications 6, 7
Blatt, B. 123
Blumer, H. 211
Boatner, E.B. 187, 188, 189, 193, 210
Bogdan, B. 211
Bonney, W.C. 147, 149
Bowen, H.R. 193
Brill, R.G. 27
Bronfenbrenner, U. 126, 127
Brooks, Dianne (personal commentary) 60–4
Brown, J.S. 72
Brown, J.W. 81
Brown, P. 156, 158, 227
Bushnaq, S.M. 29, 31
Butler, W.R. 149
Butler-Nalin, P. 6

Caccamise, F. 76
California State University at Northridge 28, 173–4, 238–9
Callaghan, Thomas L. (personal commentary) 114–17
campus 128; culture and organization 128–9; everyday life 118; experiences 130; learning 133–5
Canada 43
career/careers: attainments 193–7; development 226; education 200; preparation 156; promotion 213, 221–3, 231
Carrier, Carol A. 102

case study *see* 'Nancy and Jack'; personal commentaries
CEASD 32, 33, 34
change, deaf student as agent 80–3
Chickering, A.W. 147, 149–50, 151, 159, 161
Cho, J.H. 193
choice 136, 139
Christiansen, J.B. 192
civil rights 169, 170
Clark, R. 147
Clarke School for the Deaf 114, 115
Clinchy, B.M. 71, 74, 79, 119
co-curricular activities: access to 159. *see also* extracurricular activities
Cohen, O.P. 13–14
collaborative learning 86
Collins, A. 72
communally orientated learning 74, 75
communication: and advisors 105; barriers 81, 96, 155, 158, 200; and career advancement 221–3, 231; and employment 211, 212; functional 212, 217–18, 224, 226, 227; with hearing students 136–7; informal 215, 217–18, 223, 225; needs 85; in personal commentary 40, 41; personal/social 212, 217–18, 224–5, 226, 227; problems 36, 37; strategies 216; total 26, 163–4, 238, 239; and withdrawal 50–1, 57, 58; work place 220–7, 229–30, 234, 237
community colleges 24, 25, 27; access 27; and persistence 55, 56; in personal commentary 203
computers 109
Conley, Willy (personal commentary) 163–7
Coons, F.W. 151
Cordano, Jean (personal commentary) 228–35
Coryell, Judith 147–63
Council of Organizational Representatives 170
counseling 35, 100, 105–6; career

56; and persistence 56, 57; and work preparation 226
Crammatte, A.B. 210–11
Crawford, K. 227
Creamer, D.G. 147
crisis and support 151–2, 153
Crouch, B.A. 186–7
culture, deaf 82, 93, 94, 121, 125, 140n, 240; and identity 164; and interaction with hearing 139; orientation to 174; and parents 166; promotion of knowledge 158; studies of 120
cultures and learning 71–2
Cuomo, Mario 175
curriculum requirements 17, 200

Dagel, D. 47, 50, 54, 56
Dagley, J.C. 147, 149
Davis, C.A. 81
deaf/deafness: conceptions of 119–20; as deficiency 119–20, 124; defined 18n, 140n; as different ability 120, 125; as disability 137; education for hearing students 158–9; educational models 122–6; interaction with hearing students 118–40; medical model 121; organizations for 170; societal response 120–2; studies 239–40; *see also* culture; employment; population; postsecondary education; programs; workplace
DeCaro, J. 174
DeCaro, Patricia Mudgett 118–42, 156, 158
Delgado, G.L. 15
Delgado College, New Orleans 29
Delk, M.T. 187–8, 189, 191, 193, 210
demography *see* population
dependency 212; and telephone calls 222; in work place 219–20, 222, 224
Deutsch, A. 123
development, student *see* student development

development/developmental: courses 107; theories 147
dialogue 79–80, 81
direct instruction 111
Dowaliby, F. 47, 50, 54, 56
Drucker, P. 16
Dubois, N.F. 102
Duguid, P. 72
Duncan, O.D. 193

earnings 43–4; differentials 196–7; and education level 196–7, 199; effect of postsecondary education 185–200
education: for hearing students 158–9; history of educational models 118–26; and occupation 195; opportunities 198, 199, *see also* postsecondary; secondary; withdrawal
Education, Department of, statistics 4, 5, 6
Education for All Handicapped Children Act (1975) 124, 175
Education of the Deaf, National Commission on 170
Education of the Handicapped Act (1973) 25
Elbow, P. 73
Eliot, T.S. 78
Elliot, L. 50, 52, 54, 58, 161
Ellison, R. 86
employment: contemporary conditions 188–93; effect of postsecondary education 185–200; experiences 210–11; history of 186–8; and in-service training 18; interview study 211–23; labor force status 189–90; non-wage characteristics 210, 211; in personal commentary 202–9, 228–35; satisfaction 210, 226; underemployment 187–8, 199; *see also* labor force; occupation; work place
empowerment of students 98, 111, 112, 139–40, 174; and integrated settings 135, 136; and

mainstreaming 121–2, 125; and political activism 168
England 91
epistemological development 69, 70–1
Erickson, E.H. 147, 151
experience, deaf 76; and learning 70, 71
extracurricular activities: access to 173; isolation in 91; and political activism 171–2; and social integration 52–3

Farrugia, D. 124
female *see* women
feminist inquiry and learning 69, 74–8; collaboration 76–7; connected thinking 75–6; and learning orientations 74–5
financial assistance, federal 17, 25, 27–9
Fischgrund, J.E. 13–14
Fitzgerald, L.E. 148
Fley, J.A. 148, 149
Foster, Susan B. 85, 118–42, 156, 158, 161, 210–28; on withdrawal 50, 52, 54, 58–9
Franklin, E.L. 51, 55
Freire, P. 73, 79
Freud, S. 75
friends 53–4, 155–6; and persistence 58
Froehlinger, V.J. 124
Fullerton, H.N. 186
Furth, H. 119

Gagnard, R. 29
Gallaudet University 13, 14, 26, 61; admission requirements 13; deaf president 79–80, 120, 174; numbers at 32–3; peer relationships 155; in personal commentary 93–4, 144–5; social integration 52; and student development 150, 151, 157, 158; student organizations 173–4
Gannon, J.R. 119, 120, 123
gender studies 74
Gilligan, C. 74, 75

Goldberger, N.R. 71, 74, 79, 119
Goldmann, W.R. 103
Greek organizations 148, 159, 173
Green, R.R. 123–4
Gross, K.P. 147
group discussions 84, 85; at work 215
group interaction 41
Grumet, M. 74

Harnisch, D.J. 6
Harris, D. 77, 87n
Havinghurst, R.J. 147
hearing students: education for 158–9; interaction with deaf students 118–40
Henderson, J. 108
Hispanics 20–3; drop out rate 16; reading skills 13, 14; secondary qualifications 6, 7
Hodges, M. 84
Hoetling, F.B. 148
Holcomb, B.P. 159
Holcomb, Thomas 85, 147–63
housing 35
Humphries, T. 77, 120, 140n
Hurley, E.A. 85, 110
Hurwitz, T.Alan 101, 168–77
Husserl, E. 70

identity, establishment of 154
incidental learning 152, 225
independence 160; emotional 153–4
inequalities 137; *see also* earnings; employment
information 15–16; access to 72, 81, 94; for employers 226, 227; for hearing 239–40; reducing barriers 225
Innes, C. 52
instructional process *see* teachers/teaching
integration *see* academic integration; social integration
interaction between deaf and hearing students 118–40, 155, 157–8, 161; campus organization 128–9; case study 128, 129–35, 136; ecological model 126–35;

importance of knowlege 138, 139; individual characteristics 127–8; program for deaf on hearing campus 135–40; stereotyping 137, 138; and student development 160
interpersonal skills 225, 228
interpreting 15, 58, 65, 100–2, 112, 237; availability of 34, 35; and communication 116, 117; at CSUN 28; definition 101; lag 36, 85; National Registry of 169; need for manager 101–2; at NTID 164; at work 214, 215
isolation 156, 160, 161

'Jack' case study *see* Nancy and Jack
Jackson, B.F. 77
Jacobs, L. 106
job satisfaction *see under* occupation
Johnson, W.F. 148, 149
Johnston, W.B. 16, 24
Jones, J.D. 147, 148, 149
Jordan, Dr I. King 82–3

Kaiser, L. 147
Kaplan, F. 123
Karchmer, M. 174
Katzell, R.A. 185
Kerr, C. 185
King, S.J. 25
Klima, E.S. 120
Kluwin, T.N. 122, 124
knowledge and stereotyping 137, 138
Kohlberg, L. 147
Kolb, D.A. 147
Kuh, G.D. 151
Kyle, J.G. 120, 121

labor force: education and participation 194, 199; educational requirements 16; participation 184, 188, 190, 192; projected 186; shortage 17; statistics 190, 192, 193, 194, 195, 196, 197, 198; status 189–90, 194
Lane, H. 119
Lang, Harry G. 52, 67–89

Langford, J.B. 6
Lauritsen, R. 29
Layne, C.A. 85, 110
leadership skills 28; need for 176–7; in personal commentary 178, 180
Leadership Training Program 28
learning 41, 67–87; agency-orientated 74, 75; barriers to 83; and bilingualism 69; collaborative 76–7, 82, 83, 86; communally orientated 74, 75; connected thinking 75–6; courses in 107; and cultures 71–2; and experience 76; feminist inquiry 69, 74–8; finding voice 77–8; incidental 152, 225; models of 69–70; and phenomenology 70, 72; process orientation 72–4; reflective and phenomenological orientations 69–74; and relativism 71, 72; self-directed 86; social and political consciousness 69, 78–83; and teachers 72
Lee, G.E. 56
legislation 17, 24, 98, 124; enforcement of 170; and political activism 177; and pressure groups 169, 170; removing barriers 209. *see also individual acts*
Lenning, O. 55
Lewis, J.P. 103
Lichtenstein, S.J. 6
Liscio, M.A. 25
Longitudinal Transition Study, National 7, 8
loop system 109
Lunde, R.S. 187, 188, 191, 193, 210
Luria, A.R. 77

Macdonald, J. and S.C. 74, 76
MacLeod-Gallinger, Janet 185–202, 210
mainstreaming 237, 239–40; arguments for 123–4; and persistence 51, 53; in personal commentary 90, 142–3; resources 96–113; strategies 110

male learning 74, 75
Massachusetts, University of 114–16
mathematics 36, 58, 76; problem solving 73–4
Matson, F. 69
McLuhan, Marshall 239
Mead, G.H. 211
Meadow, K. 156
Meath-Lang, Bonnie 67–89
meetings at work 214–16, 222, 224, 232, 233
Menchel, Robert (personal commentary) 202–9
mentor *see* advisors
Mertens, D. 124
Metzner, B.F. 44
Milan resolution 169
Miller, T.K. 147, 148, 149
minorities: achievement levels 6, 7, 12–14, 16; growth of population 12–14; in postsecondary education 10–12; struggle 80; and time control by whites 137
misunderstandings at work 213, 220–1
Moores, D.F. 119, 122, 124, 187, 193, 210
motivation 200; and achievement 83; and withdrawal 54, 56
Mullins, Jane (personal commentary) 89–95
Myklebyst, H.R. 120, 121

NAHICS 174
'Nancy and Jack' case study 128, 129–35; campus experiences 130, 134–5, 136, 139; everyday campus learning 133; pre-college experience 129–30; residence life 130–3
Nash, Kenneth 3–20
National Association for the Deaf 169
National Association of Hearing-Impaired College Students 174
National Technical Institute for the Deaf 27–8; admission requirements 13; convocation on attitudes 81–2; peer relationships 155; persistence factors 47, 49, 50, 51, 54, 56, 59, 161; in personal commentary 145–6, 163–5, 178–9; political activism 173–4, 175–6, 178–9; process writing 73; RTGD 108; social integration 52, 53; Speakers Bureau 158; and student development 150, 151, 157; student organizations 173–4; support services 164; use of simulators 85–6
Nelson, Gerald (personal commentary) 178–81
Noel, L. 198
normalization 121, 123, 125, 136
Norris, W. 148
notetaking 15, 36, 58, 102–4, 116; availability 35; and computers 109; and contact with instructor 109; at CSUN 28; at NTID 164; in personal commentary 40; quality control 104; and resource model 100; self-generated 102–3; and tape recorders 115–16; training for 34, 103–4; and tutoring 107, 112
NTID *see* National Technical Institute for the Deaf

occupation: and education level 195; mobility 187, 188; need for degree 16; satisfaction 185, 186; and self-image 185; types of 188, 190–1, 192, 195; *see also* employment; unemployment
Omi, M. 119
Opton, K. 110
oralists 144
organizations, student 173
Osborn, T. 8, 124
Osguthorpe, R.T. 103

Padden, C. 77, 120, 140n
Pagano, J. 75
Panara, J.E. 103
Panara, Robert 236–40
parents 207; and deaf culture 166;

patronizing by 153; student relationship 153–4
Park, R. 211
Pascarella, E.R. 44, 46
patronizing 81–3, 174; by parents 153; support services as 97
peer groups 108, 155–6
Pendergrass, R.A. 84
Perry, W.G. 70–1, 72, 147
persistence 43–60, 238; and admission screening 55; basic skill development 55; effect on total enrollment 45; in personal commentary 63; programming to increase 55–7; rates 2, 44; reasons for withdrawal 47–54; and secondary education 47, 49; and social integration 156; theoretical model 44–6; *see also* withdrawal from college
personal and social development 41, 66, 124, 149, 159, 226; *see also* social integration
personal commentaries 237; Dianne Brooks 60–4; Gerald Nelson 178–81; Jane Mullins 89–95; Jean Cordano 228–35; Miguel Sanchez 20–3; Paul Taylor 39–42; Robert Menchel 202–9; Solange C. Sevigny-Skyer 142–6; Thomas L. Callaghan 114–17; Willy Conley 163–7
personal and social development 41, 66, 124, 149, 159, 226; *see also* social integration
Peterson, R. 25
Peyton, J.K. 76
phenomenology 70, 72, 211
Piaget, J. 77, 147
Pinar, W.F. 74
planning, involvement of student in 96
pluralism 119, 120, 122, 125, 126, 137, 140
political activism 17, 168–77; encouragement of 66; methods of training 172–3; need for 176–7; in personal commentary 178–9; postsecondary education as training ground 171; and schools for deaf 175–6
population of deaf students 3–18; decline of 4–5, 9–10; exit status of secondary leavers 5–7; future 9–18; projected 3; size 4, 5
postsecondary education: access 15, 25, 32, 35; barriers to entry 6–7, 8–9, 12; basic principles 30; and career attainments 193–7; deaf relative to hearing students 29–30, 31; growth in 35; numbers in 7, 9–10, 25; opportunities for 26–9, 198, 199; race/ethnic numbers 10–12; requirements for teachers 84–6; and secondary school performance 7, 8; services provided 30–5; *see also* community colleges; population; programs; withdrawal
power *see* empowerment
Preblud, S.R. 10
Prince, J.S. 148
problem solving 84, 106; courses in 107; and incidental learning 152; and learning 72, 73
programs for deaf students: access 34; basic principles 33, 140; characteristics of 24–37; definition 32–3; enrollment numbers 14; goals of 36–7; growth in 15, 16; on hearing campus 135–40; level of education 33–4; need for evaluation 66; outcomes 183–227; possible future 18; requirements 1–2, 65–6, 183, 184; resource needs 66; services provided 30–5; *see also* support services
Pullen, G. 120, 121

qualitative research 184, 211
questioning 84
Quigley, S.P. 30

Rawlings, B.A. 6, 15, 25, 30, 32, 43, 174

reading skills 36, 84, 107, 200, 237; and educational opportunities 198, 199; levels of 32; of minorities 13, 14; and persistence 55, 56, 58; in personal commentary 90
Reagan, T. 119, 120, 125
Real Time Graphics Display 108
Redden, M.R. 81
Redding, R. 13–14
Reed, L. 76
reflection and learning 69–74
regional programs 29
Rehabilitation Act (1973) 27
relativism and learning 71, 72
remedial programs 35
residence life, case study 130–3
resources 1; barriers 81; benefits 110; guiding principles 97–100; ideal versus real 98–9; impact of 109–11; in-classroom 100–4; in mainstream classroom 96–113; model of provision 100–9; need for planning 85; outside classroom 104–7; quality control 112; requirements 98–100, 112; social activities as 107, 108; and student involvement 111, 112; technological advances 108–9; versus support 97; *see also* counseling; interpreting; notetaking; tutoring
Riley, D. 43, 44, 45, 188, 197
Rochester Institute of Technology 27–8, 116–17; research at 128–9; study of graduates 211–23; *see also* National Technical Institute for the Deaf
Rogers, Carl 95
Rohland, P. 71, 87n
role models 139, 156, 158, 238, 239; and political activism 172
Rosenthal, N.H. 186, 210
Rowe, M. 137
RTGD 108

Sanchez, Miguel (case study) 20–3
Saur, Rosemary E. 85, 96–112
Schein, J.D. 29, 31, 187–8, 189, 191, 193, 210
Scherer, M.J. 47, 48, 50, 54, 56
Schildroth, A.N. 6
Schoenfeld, A.H. 73
schools for deaf 175–6
Schroedel, J.G. 188
Seattle Community College 29
secondary education: achievement 8, 16; drop out rate 6, 8, 9, 16; exit status of students 5–6; and persistence in college 47, 49; support services 8
segregation 123, 124
self-determination 149, 168
self-image and occupation 185
Sevigny-Skyer, Solange C. (personal commentary) 142–6
sexism 74
Shaffer, R.H. 148, 149
Shaver, D. 8
Shedd, J.D. 151
Shuy, R.W. 76
sign language: classes 224; clubs 159; and hearing 224, 229–30; misunderstanding of 138; signed English 101, 111, 238; *see also* ASL
simulators, deafness 85–6, 159
situated cognition 72, 73
social integration 36, 46; activities; as resource 107, 108; and extracurricular activities 52–3; and persistence 156; social programs 35; social skills 225; and withdrawal 51–4, 55, 57, 58, 160
Spady, W. 44
special classes 35
Spradley, J. 211
staffing: for programs 30; for support services 34–5
Stahler, A. 187
Staton, J. 76
stereotyping 81, 137, 138
Stevens, G. 193
Stinson, Michael 43–60
Stoke, W.C. Jr 120
Stone, J. 73–4, 76
Stuckless, E.R. 15, 30, 33, 101,

108, 187, 193, 210
Student Congress 173, 179
student development 147–61;
breaking psychological ties
153–4; career preparation 156;
developmental tasks 151–6, 157,
158; establishing identity and
values 154; historical perspectives
148–51; life adjustments 155;
models of 149, 150; networking
outside college campus 160; peer
relationships 155–6; personal
training programs 159; preparing
for marriage 156; promotion of
157; strategies for 157–60
Student Leadership Advisory
Council 173
students *see* education; persistence;
population; postsecondary
education; secondary education;
withdrawal
study skills 106, 107
support services 15, 25, 35–6; and
crisis 151–2; dependency on 117;
NTID 28; objection to term 97;
in personal commentary 40;
staffing 34–5; types of 35; and
withdrawal 43, 57
Sussman, A.E. 187, 188
symbolic interactionism 211

tape recorders 112, 115–16, 233
Tarule, J.M. 119
Taylor, Paul (personal
commentary) 39–42
Taylor, S. 211
TDD system 170, 212, 213, 224,
227
teachers/teaching 17, 85; affecting
withdrawal 50–1; and
collaborative learning 76–7, 82,
83; deaf 174; deficiencies in 120;
and gender studies 74; and
learning 72; need for skilled 237;
pace of 237, 239; patronizing
81–2; in personal commentary
40; requirements for 84–6; and
resources 109–10; role in
leadership skills 172; and sign

111; and stereotyping 81;
training programs 28
technical training 27–8, 29
Technical and Vocational Institute,
St Paul 29
technological advances 24; and
deafness 121; as enhancing
services 108–9
telecommunications relay service
176; *see also* TDD system
telephone calls 227; and
dependency 213–14, 222; *see also*
TDD system
Tennessee, University of 29, 30
Terenzini, P. 44, 46
theater 165–6
Thomas, W.I. 211
Tiffany, M. 138
Tinto, V. 52, 53, 173; on
institutional commitment 37, 54;
persistence model 44, 46, 47; on
withdrawal 43, 49, 198
Todorov, T. 68
total communication 26, 163–4,
238, 239
transgredience 68
transliterating 101
Traxler, S. 29
Trow, M. 147
Turk, Frank 151
tutoring 15, 26, 35, 100; and
instructor 109; and notetaking
107; skills required 106–7

Uguroglu, M.E. 83
unemployment 189–90, 193, 199;
and education level 194

value system, establishment of 154
Van Cleve, J.V. 186–7
Vocational Education Act (1968) 15
Vocational Rehabilitation Act
1973) 98
Vocational Rehabilitation Office 15
voice 77–8, 79; definitions of 78;
and writing 77
Vygotsky, L. 73, 76, 77

wages *see* earnings

Wagner, M. 7, 8
Walberg, H.J. 83
Walter, Gerard G. 9, 17, 173, 188, 197, 210; characteristics of programs 24–39; on persistence 43–60
Weinrich, J.E. 188, 192
Weis, L. 137, 139
Wells, D.O. 29
Welsh, William A. 43, 44, 45, 185–202, 210
Welty, Eudora 78
Whitson, J.A. 68
Whitt, E.J. 151
Williams, B.R. 187, 188
Williamson, E.G. 149
Wilson, J.J. 103
Winant, H. 119
Winston, R.B. Jr 147, 149
withdrawal from college 2, 16, 43; academic factors 49–51; background factors 47–9, 55; and career development 56; and commitment to college 54, 55, 57–8; and communication needs 50–1, 57, 58; early intervention 56; and motivation 54, 56; reasons for 44, 47–54, 160; social factors 51–4; and social integration 55, 57, 58; and sponsored activities 52–3; and support programs 43, 57; and teaching 50–1; *see also* persistence
Wolfensberger, W. 123
women: earnings 192; labor force status 189, 194; learning orientation 74, 75; silent 79; struggle for voice 80
Wood, D.J. 120
Woolf, Virginia 78
work *see* earnings; employment; labor force; unemployment
work place: communication 211, 212, 217–18, 220–7, 234, 237; graduates in 210–27; meetings 214–16, 222, 224, 232, 233; misunderstandings 220–1; social situations 218; strategies 216, 226
writing skills 26, 76, 84, 237; in personal commentary 90, 91
Wulfsberg, R. 25